The Many Drafts of D. H. Lawrence

Historicizing Modernism

Series Editors
Matthew Feldman, Professorial Fellow, Norwegian Study Centre, University of York; and Erik Tonning, Professor of British Literature and Culture, University of Bergen, Norway

Assistant Editor: David Tucker, Associate Lecturer, Goldsmiths College, University of London, UK

Editorial Board
Professor Chris Ackerley, Department of English, University of Otago, New Zealand; Professor Ron Bush, St. John's College, University of Oxford, UK; Professor Finn Fordham, Department of English, Royal Holloway, UK; Professor Steven Matthews, Department of English, University of Reading, UK; Dr Mark Nixon, Department of English, University of Reading, UK; Professor Shane Weller, Reader in Comparative Literature, University of Kent, UK; and Professor Janet Wilson, University of Northampton, UK.

Historicizing Modernism challenges traditional literary interpretations by taking an empirical approach to modernist writing: a direct response to new documentary sources made available over the last decade.

Informed by archival research, and working beyond the usual European/American avant-garde 1900–45 parameters, this series reassesses established readings of modernist writers by developing fresh views of intellectual contexts and working methods.

Series Titles
Arun Kolatkar and Literary Modernism in India, Laetitia Zecchini
British Literature and Classical Music, David Deutsch
Broadcasting in the Modernist Era, Matthew Feldman, Henry Mead and Erik Tonning
Charles Henri Ford, Alexander Howard
Chicago and the Making of American Modernism, Michelle E. Moore
Ezra Pound's Adams Cantos, David Ten Eyck
Ezra Pound's Eriugena, Mark Byron
Great War Modernisms and The New Age *Magazine*, Paul Jackson
James Joyce and Absolute Music, Michelle Witen

James Joyce and Catholicism, Chrissie van Mierlo
John Kasper and Ezra Pound, Alec Marsh
Katherine Mansfield and Literary Modernism, edited by Janet Wilson, Gerri Kimber and Susan Reid
Late Modernism and the English Intelligencer, Alex Latter
The Life and Work of Thomas MacGreevy, Susan Schreibman
Literary Impressionism, Rebecca Bowler
Modern Manuscripts, Dirk Van Hulle
Modernism at the Microphone, Melissa Dinsman
Modernist Lives, Claire Battershill
The Politics of 1930s British Literature, Natasha Periyan
Reading Mina Loy's Autobiographies, Sandeep Parmar
Reframing Yeats, Charles Ivan Armstrong
Samuel Beckett and Arnold Geulincx, David Tucker
Samuel Beckett and the Bible, Iain Bailey
Samuel Beckett and Cinema, Anthony Paraskeva
Samuel Beckett's 'More Pricks than Kicks', John Pilling
Samuel Beckett's German Diaries 1936–1937, Mark Nixon
T. E. Hulme and the Ideological Politics of Early Modernism, Henry Mead
Virginia Woolf's Late Cultural Criticism, Alice Wood
Christian Modernism in an Age of Totalitarianism, Jonas Kurlberg
Samuel Beckett and Experimental Psychology, Joshua Powell
Samuel Beckett in Confinement, James Little
Katherine Mansfield: New Directions, edited by Aimée Gasston, Gerri Kimber and Janet Wilson
Modernist Wastes, Caroline Knighton

Upcoming Titles
Samuel Beckett and Science, Chris Ackerley

The Many Drafts of D. H. Lawrence

Creative Flux, Genetic Dialogism, and the Dilemma of Endings

Elliott Morsia

BLOOMSBURY ACADEMIC
LONDON • NEW YORK • OXFORD • NEW DELHI • SYDNEY

BLOOMSBURY ACADEMIC
Bloomsbury Publishing Plc
50 Bedford Square, London, WC1B 3DP, UK
1385 Broadway, New York, NY 10018, USA
29 Earlsfort Terrace, Dublin 2, Ireland

BLOOMSBURY, BLOOMSBURY ACADEMIC and the Diana logo are trademarks of Bloomsbury Publishing Plc

First published in Great Britain 2021
This paperback edition published in 2022

Copyright © Elliott Morsia, 2021

Elliott Morsia has asserted his right under the Copyright, Designs and Patents Act, 1988, to be identified as Authors of this work.

For legal purposes the Acknowledgements on p. xv constitute an extension of this copyright page.

Cover design: Jade Barnett, Eleanor Rose

All rights reserved. No part of this publication may be reproduced or transmitted in any form or by any means, electronic or mechanical, including photocopying, recording, or any information storage or retrieval system, without prior permission in writing from the publishers.

The third party copyrighted material displayed in the pages of this book are done so on the basis of fair use for the purposes of teaching, criticism, scholarship or research in accordance with international copyright laws, and is not intended to infringe upon the ownership rights of the original owners. Please contact the publisher if you own any of the work contained within the book as some copyright was difficult to trace though every attempt was made to try and clear these for use.

Bloomsbury Publishing Plc does not have any control over, or responsibility for, any third-party websites referred to or in this book. All internet addresses given in this book were correct at the time of going to press. The author and publisher regret any inconvenience caused if addresses have changed or sites have ceased to exist, but can accept no responsibility for any such changes.

A catalogue record for this book is available from the British Library.

A catalog record for this book is available from the Library of Congress.

ISBN: HB: 978-1-3501-3968-8
PB: 978-1-3501-8543-2
ePDF: 978-1-3501-3969-5
eBook: 978-1-3501-3970-1

Series: Historicizing Modernism

Typeset by Deanta Global Publishing Services, Chennai, India

To find out more about our authors and books, visit www.bloomsbury.com and sign up for our newsletters.

For Fiona and Djuna.

I shall write it as long as I like to start with, then write it smaller. I must always write my books twice.

D. H. Lawrence (1913: i. p. X)

And turn for the support and the confirmation not to the perfected past, that which is set in perfection as monuments of human passage. But turn to the unresolved, the rejected.

(1923: 2003, p. 384)

It is far, far better to read one book six times, at intervals, than to read six several books.

(1931: 1980, p. 60)

Contents

List of illustrations	xii
Editorial preface to *Historicizing Modernism*	xiv
Acknowledgements	xv
List of abbreviations	xvi
List of manuscripts	xvii
Note on the text	xviii
Introduction	1

Part One Critical frameworks

1	Anglo-American traditions, genetic criticism and recent developments	13
	Introduction	13
	Anglo-American critical traditions	14
	Genetic criticism	26
	Recent developments	30

Part Two 'Odour of Chrysanthemums' (1909–14)

2	Setting the scene	43
	A 'mature' text?	43
	Compositional history and alternative versions	47
	Networks and emotions in the 'immature' early sections	48
	Economic cuts	52
	'Culmination' and the problem of endings	55

Part Three *Women in Love* (1913–21)

3	Re-evaluating the compositional history	63
	Pre-genesis: Lawrentian preparations for writing	63
	Rewriting: Multiple drafts	68
	The outbreak of war	70
	Return to 'The Sisters': *Women in Love* and the travails of typing	74
	Coda	78

4	Early fragments and multiple drafts	84
	Genesis I (1913-14): Plotlines, rough drafts and 'real being' as process	84
	The Sisters I: 'he would empty every drop of blood out of his veins, to warm her'	90
	The Sisters II: 'Do you love me?'	92
	The Wedding Ring: 'It was a shell now'	94
	Genesis II: 'Prologue'	100
	Genesis II: 'The Wedding'; mapping 'A ghostly replica of the real'	104
5	Genetic dialogism in the notebooks	123
	Introducing the early 'notebooks'	123
	Adjectives, viewpoints, enchantment	126
	Recoiling from the past: 'Memory was a dirty trick'	130
	The sublime aesthetic object: 'There, in the infolded navel of it all, was her consummation'	134
	The rewritten dialogues: 'One must turn one's face away from the old'	136
6	Genetic dialogism in the typescripts	141
	Introducing the typescripts	141
	Process or product	142
	Rewriting dialogues/dialogic rewriting: 'Sisters' and 'Shortlands'	144
	Cuts: 'As if too much was said'	149
	Smashing the mirror: 'Class-Room' and 'Moony'	155
	'Exeunt'	160

Part Four *The Plumed Serpent* (1923–6)

7	Criticism, composition and writing depression	165
	Introducing *The Plumed Serpent*	165
	Protocols and preparations	169
	Writing and revision	170
	(1) MSI	171
	Chapter One: 'Now we're seeing the real thing.'	171
	Chapter Three: '"What $^{\text{is it that}}$ oppresses, or depresses you?" asked the general.'	174
	(2) MSI to MSII: Focalization and expansion	178
	(3) MSII: Light revision	182
	(4) TSII: Overview and recap	182
	Coda	183

8	Writing an ending	187
	The dilemma of writing an ending	187
	'Here!': Four versions	189
	Version one: Life by the lake	190
	Version two: 'Tell them it is all a joke, and their symbols are pretty play-things, and they are all great-god Peter-Pans.'	194
	Versions three and four: 'It was as if she had two selves'	200
	Endings: 'You won't let me go!'	205
Conclusion		211
Epilogue		219
Bibliography		221
Index		232

Illustrations

Figures

1	The first page of the earliest extant manuscript of *Women in Love* (March–June 1913)	109
2	The first page of the second earliest extant manuscript of *Women in Love* (August 1913–January 1914)	110
3	The first page of the third earliest extant manuscript of *Women in Love* (February–May 1914), later interpolated into the manuscript of *The Rainbow*	111
4	The first page of the fourth earliest extant manuscript of *Women in Love* (April 1916)	112
5	The front cover of one of the four notebooks containing the fifth earliest extant manuscript of *Women in Love* (April–June 1916)	113
6	Page 252 of notebook 7, from the set of notebooks referenced earlier	114
7	Pages 323–4 of notebook 9, from the set of notebooks referenced earlier	115
8	The first page of the first typescript of *Women in Love* (July–November 1916)	116
9	The final page of the first typescript of *Women in Love*, referenced earlier	117
10	Chapter II page of the second typescript of *Women in Love* (March 1917–September 1919)	118
11	Page 57 of the second typescript of *Women in Love*, referenced earlier	119
12	The final page of the first manuscript of *The Plumed Serpent* (May–June 1923)	120
13	The final page of the second manuscript of *The Plumed Serpent* (November 1924–July 1925)	121
14	The final page of the complete typescript of *The Plumed Serpent* (November 1924–July 1925)	122

Tables

1	Extant manuscripts for *Women in Love*	62
2	Extant manuscripts for *The Plumed Serpent*	164
3	Four rewriting phases for *The Plumed Serpent*	170
4	Four different versions of the final chapter of *The Plumed Serpent*	189
5	Three scenes added to the final chapter of *The Plumed Serpent*	195

Editorial preface to *Historicizing Modernism*

This book series is devoted to the analysis of late nineteenth- to twentieth-century literary modernism within its historical contexts. *Historicizing Modernism* therefore stresses empirical accuracy and the value of primary sources (such as letters, diaries, notes, drafts, marginalia or other archival materials) in developing monographs and edited collections on modernist literature. This may take a number of forms, such as manuscript study and genetic criticism, documenting interrelated historical contexts and ideas, and exploring biographical information. To date, no book series has fully laid claim to this interdisciplinary, source-based territory for modern literature. While the series addresses itself to a range of key authors, it also highlights the importance of non-canonical writers with a view to establishing broader intellectual genealogies of modernism. Furthermore, while the series is weighted towards the English-speaking world, studies of non-Anglophone modernists whose writings are open to fresh historical exploration are also included.

A key aim of the series is to reach beyond the familiar rhetoric of intellectual and artistic 'autonomy' employed by many modernists and their critical commentators. Such rhetorical moves can and should themselves be historically situated and reintegrated into the complex continuum of individual literary practices. It is our intent that the series' emphasis upon the contested self-definitions of modernist writers, thinkers, and critics may, in turn, prompt various reconsiderations of the boundaries delimiting the concept 'modernism' itself. Indeed, the concept of 'historicizing' is itself debated across its volumes, and the series by no means discourages more theoretically informed approaches. On the contrary, the editors hope that the historical specificity encouraged by *Historicizing Modernism* may inspire a range of fundamental critiques along the way.

Matthew Feldman
Erik Tonning

Acknowledgements

It would be remiss of a book on genetic criticism to not divulge its own origins. The book grew out of a PhD on the same subject, which was funded by the Arts and Humanities Research Council, supervised by Finn Fordham and hosted by Royal Holloway, University of London, to all of whom I am grateful; likewise my examiners. The PhD in turn developed out of a 'genetic' MA dissertation on Lawrence's short story 'The Shades of Spring', which was supervised by Suzanne Hobson and later revised and published by the *Journal of D. H. Lawrence* (*JDHL*) studies, both of whom I am grateful to. I have also included a chapter on 'Odour of Chrysanthemums', which is developed from an article originally published by the *Journal of the Short Story in English*, whom I also thank. I am grateful to *everyone* who has offered support; without it, the book wouldn't exist.

I would like to thank Katy Loffman for permission on behalf of the D. H. Lawrence estate to include lengthy extracts from Lawrence's unpublished manuscripts. Likewise the Harry Ransom Centre for permission to include reproductions of the manuscripts themselves, and to all the staff at the HRC.

Thanks to Maurice, Andy, Dianne and Paul, Matt, Ben and Phil for sponsoring the reproduced images in this book. Finally, thanks to Fiona (for many things).

Abbreviations

i.:	The Letters of D. H. Lawrence Vol. 1 (Cambridge edition)
ii.:	The Letters of D. H. Lawrence Vol. 2 (Cambridge edition)
iii.:	The Letters of D. H. Lawrence Vol. 3 (Cambridge edition)
iv.:	The Letters of D. H. Lawrence Vol. 4 (Cambridge edition)
v.:	The Letters of D. H. Lawrence Vol. 5 (Cambridge edition)
viii.:	The Letters of D. H. Lawrence Vol. 8 (Cambridge edition)
FWL:	The First 'Women in Love' (Cambridge edition)
MSI:	Manuscript 1 *(The Plumed Serpent)*
MSII:	Manuscript 2 *(The Plumed Serpent)*
N1-10:	Notebooks 1-10 *(Women in Love)*
PO:	*The Prussian Officer and Other Stories*
PS:	*The Plumed Serpent* (Cambridge edition)
Q:	*Quetzalcoatl* (Cambridge edition)
SI:	'The Sisters I' *(Women in Love)*
SII:	'The Sisters II' *(Women in Love)*
SIII:	'The Sisters III' *(Women in Love)*
TSI:	Typescript 1 *(Women in Love)*
TSII:	Typescript 2 *(Women in Love)*
TSII:	Typescript *(The Plumed Serpent)*
VG:	*The Vicar's Garden and Other Stories* (Cambridge edition)
WL:	*Women in Love* (Cambridge edition)
WR:	'The Wedding Ring' *(The Rainbow)*

Manuscripts

All original materials referred to in Chapter 2 can be found online at the following University of Nottingham website: http://odour.nottingham.ac.uk/read.asp and in the Cambridge editions of *The Prussian Officer and Other Stories* and *The Vicar's Garden and Other Stories* (see Bibliography for full references). Those referred to in Chapters 3–8 are held in the D. H. Lawrence Collection at the Harry Ransom Humanities Research Centre, University of Texas (full listings below).

D. H. Lawrence, 'The Plumed Serpent: Quetzalcoatl, Holograph in notebooks, 818pp', box 13, folder 8, and box 14, folders 1–3

D. H. Lawrence, 'The Plumed Serpent: Quetzalcoatl, Holograph and typescript with author edits, 746pp', box 14, folders 4–5, and box 15, folders 1–2

D. H. Lawrence, 'The Rainbow, Holograph and typescript with extensive revisions, March 1915, 707pp', boxes 17–19

D. H. Lawrence, 'Women in Love, Holograph fragments, pp. 291–296; 373–380', D. H. Lawrence Collection, box 23, folder 5

D. H. Lawrence, 'Women in Love, Chapter 1, "Prologue"; Chapter II "The Wedding," holograph, 55pp', D. H. Lawrence Collection, box 23, folder 6

D. H. Lawrence, 'Women in Love, Chapters 23–31, holograph notebooks, 439pp', D.H. Lawrence Collection, box 23, folders 11–20

D. H. Lawrence, 'Women in Love, Typescript with extensive author revisions, 665pp', D. H. Lawrence Collection, boxes 25–27

D. H. Lawrence, Women in Love, Version 2, holograph and typescript with extensive author revisions, 786pp', D. H. Lawrence Collection, boxes 28–30

Note on the text

All manuscript transcriptions are my own. I have used strikethroughs to indicate deletions (~~deletion~~), bold font to indicate insertions (**insertion**) and superscript to indicate text written superscript (^{superscript}). Editorial interpolations (when a reading is unclear) are placed in square brackets [editorial interpolation].

Introduction

To begin with the basics, D. H. Lawrence (1885–1930), a short-lived, early twentieth-century English author, is one of *the* great writers in history. This point, as well as the following observations, are probably under-appreciated, but, in terms of *critical acclaim*, *diversity* and *extent*, Lawrence's literary output is virtually unparalleled. He is the author of at least one broadly acclaimed work across almost the entire spectrum of writing categories, including novels, short stories, poems, plays, travel writing, non-fiction books (including textbooks, literary criticism, history and psychology), biographical and autobiographical memoirs, essays, articles, reviews and letters. To pick up on just the last category, Lawrence's many, many recipients felt obliged to preserve enough of his letters to fill seven long volumes, and this excludes the hundreds of letters written to his mother, which were destroyed by Lawrence himself after her death. In terms of sheer volume, Lawrence also produced multiple *versions* of many of the individual works within these categories (as I will go on to show in this book), that is, probably the majority of long and short fiction works, of which there are dozens, as well as a good proportion of the poems, of which ten collections were published in Lawrence's lifetime alone. In addition, and of equal importance, Lawrence is one of the first truly *working-class* authors whose works are widely recognized as classics, while he remains part of an extremely small group in that respect.

There is a connection between these facts (his class and his prodigiousness). Lawrence's father, Arthur John Lawrence (1846–1924), was a barely literate coalminer born in the village of Brinsley in Nottinghamshire, the setting for 'Odour of Chrysanthemums'. Brinsley sits near the border of Derbyshire, not far from Robin Hood's Sherwood Forest. As depicted in Lawrence's semi-autobiographical novel *Sons and Lovers*, Arthur Lawrence worked in Brinsley Colliery his entire life, often leaving home before sunrise and returning after sunset, and relying on brute force and basic tools (pickaxes, hammers, chisels, shovels and pans) to earn a rudimentary living until his retirement in 1909. Due to the Lawrences' limited means, Lawrence's mother, Lydia Beardsall (1851–1910), a former pupil teacher, also performed manual labour (in a lace factory), which perhaps contributed to her wizened appearance and relatively early death. While Lydia Lawrence's determination that her children would lead more comfortable lives – Lydia ensured that the Lawrence household included a good library of books, for example – helps explain Lawrence's own trajectory as a pupil teacher, teacher and then fully fledged writer, Arthur Lawrence's simple work ethic provides the clearest context for Lawrence's prodigious output, especially when combined with his apparently suspicious and guilt-inducing view of his son's ability to earn a far superior living by *merely* writing ('I think to this day, he looks upon me as a sort of cleverish swindler, who gets money for nothing: a sort of Ernest Hooley' (2005, p. 76)).

Throughout his wildly itinerant life, Lawrence liked to wake up around dawn, and, besides writing for several hours in the early part of the day – often while ill, and sometimes gravely so – he also did most of the manual and domestic work around the house (his wife, Frieda, was former Baroness von Richthofen) and frequently went out on walking excursions to explore the surrounding country. The couple also relied directly on Lawrence's writing to support their income. Frieda's first husband, Ernest Weekley, had cut her completely out of his and their three children's lives. Lawrence openly acknowledged writing more short stories and (later) journalistic essays and articles as they provided a more immediate and profitable form of income, compared to long fiction: whereas Lawrence initially earned around £100 for *each* of his novels, which took several years to write, in his mid and later career he could earn around £10–£50 for a single piece of short writing, which he could produce in just a few days or weeks. To put these sums into context, James Joyce – whom F. R. Leavis famously places alongside Lawrence as 'pre-eminently the testing, the crucial authors' (1955, p. 10) of the period, and who focused most of his writerly output on three long works of fiction (*A Portrait of the Artist as a Young Man* (1916), *Ulysses* (1922) and *Finnegans Wake* (1939)) – received in excess of £20,000 from his literary patroness Harriet Shaw Weaver alone.[1]

Beginning in his lifetime and continuing to the present day, Lawrence has had a strange reception history, marked by extreme highs and lows of critical acclaim and cultural disgust. Lawrence's death in 1930, at just forty-four years of age, in some ways marked the end of the golden artistic epoch known as 'Modernism'. Lawrence's own prodigious output terminated with his death, of course, along with his indestructibly hopeful attitude towards society's potential for positive change, and his own attempts to express a positive vision around which that might cohere (he wrote most of *The Rainbow*, perhaps his most hopeful novel, during the First World War). The 1930s were also marked by the continued rise of fascism and economic depression, and were rounded off by the outbreak of the Second World War. In the immediate years after his death, major writers including Aldous Huxley, E. M. Forster and Philip Larkin used sincere superlatives to describe Lawrence ('a prodigious power of rendering the immediately experienced otherness in terms of literary art'; 'the greatest imaginative novelist of our generation'; 'in many things the greatest writer of all time'), while at Cambridge University and in the journal *Scrutiny* (1932–53), the critics F. R. and Q. D. Leavis helped establish a lasting legacy for Lawrence as a major English novelist, which was capped by the publication of *D. H. Lawrence: Novelist* in 1955.[2] Yet, at the same time, Lawrence developed a reputation as a dangerous pornographer for his unashamed portrayals of intimate, emotional and sexual life: both *The Rainbow* and *Lady Chatterley's Lover* were banned in his lifetime (with copies destroyed), as were his late paintings.

Outright censorship of Lawrence collapsed following the iconic trial of *Lady Chatterley's Lover* in 1960 (*R v. Penguin Books Ltd*), and Lawrence became a more widely popular figure during the counterculture movement of the 1960s: at the end of that decade, playing the character George Hanson in the landmark film *Easy Rider* (1969), Jack Nicholson drank a toast 'To ol' D. H. Lawrence'.[3] However, Lawrence's popularization as an icon of sexual liberation set him up for a fall, and, the following year, American feminist critic Kate Millett, who marked her book's publication by appearing on the front cover of *Time* magazine, included a caustic attack on Lawrence in *Sexual Politics* (1970), which placed him alongside two very different, non-contemporary American novelists (Henry Miller and Norman Mailer) and condemned all three writers in one fell swoop for representing sex in a patriarchal manner.[4]

Millett's book was stationed at a crossroads in the history of Anglo-American literary criticism, marking the rise of ideological criticism and the politicization of university departments. According to A. S. Byatt,

> literary criticism, and the teaching of literature, became a belief system, and indeed a societal structure almost independent of books and what was or is in them. A kind of moral fervor, accompanied by a glorying in their own power, led critics to cleanse the canon, to hunt out the little snakes of sexism, racism, cultural assumptions about superiority, aestheticism, and destroy them. (2002)[5]

Lawrence became a more alienated figure in the subsequent decades, with another line of assault targeting his so-called organicism. In *Criticism and Ideology* (1976), English critic Terry Eagleton suggested that Lawrence was 'full-bloodedly "organicist" in both his social and aesthetic assumptions', claiming his work dramatized 'a contradiction within the Romantic humanist tradition itself, between its corporate and individualist components' and even going so far as to suggest that 'in this sense Lawrence was a major precursor of fascism' (pp. 157–61). That such a claim could be made by a major critic seems astonishing: aside from his obvious contempt for any highly organized form of writing, thinking or living, Lawrence provided a formal and contemporary critique of fascism in his textbook on *Movements in European History* ('another kind of bullying [. . .] a mere worshipping of force'; pp. 262–6). However, these outright judgements were generally supported by a very minimal and selective analysis of Lawrence's actual writings.[6] A further bone of contention is the misleading way in which some critics identified Lawrence's own writing with the popular critical account of his work established after his death by Leavis. To give a somewhat infamous example, in her book *Sex in the Head*, Linda Ruth Williams refers to a 'Lawrence-Leavis pact', describes Lawrence as the 'co-author of the Leavisite rule-book' (1993, p. 16) and casts Lawrence as a 'cine-phobe' throughout.[7] As Nigel Morris has already pointed out, such critics 'have usually been happy to accept unquestioningly the orthodoxy established by Leavis that Lawrence was unequivocally antagonistic towards popular forms of art and entertainment, and this has led inevitably to a somewhat stale and simplistic recycling of Leavisite views' (1996, p. 591).

The fundamental problem with superficial criticism of Lawrence is, as Janice H. Harris perfectly summed up shortly after Millet's book, that 'one can make Lawrence say just about anything', hence 'taking from him brief quotations, brief examples, is almost always misleading' (1974, p. 524).[8] Although 'Leavisism' and other traditional critical approaches to Lawrence have their limitations – and I provide a critique of traditional manuscript studies in the following chapter – Lawrence's marginalization by critics adopting a highly theoretical approach with minimal textual analysis (from the 1970s to 1990s) was relatively short-lived, unsurprisingly so, given the large regions of his writing that are glossed over by both positive and negative labels, from parochial humanist to sexual liberator, to patriarchal repressor. Geoff Dyer's comic suggestion in *Out of Sheer Rage* (1997) that he was successfully able to 'deconstruct' the Longman critical reader on Lawrence (edited by Widdowson, 1992) by setting it on fire (pp. 100–3) serves as a marker for Lawrence's return from the margins of cultural discourse.

In recent decades, a 'New Lawrence' has emerged, with critics including Michael Bell, Amit Chaudhuri, Howard J. Booth, Jeff Wallace, Susan Reid,

Catherine Brown, and others, opening new paths of enquiry by reassessing Lawrence's connections to modernist and contemporary culture (in the philosophical traditional alone: from Nietzsche, Bergson and Heidegger to Adorno, Derrida and beyond).[9] Aside from the comprehensive new Cambridge Edition of D. H. Lawrence, which I discuss in detail in the next chapter of this book, Penguin has also continued to release new editions of Lawrence, with no shortage of writers and other luminaries stepping up to pen the introductions, including the likes of Anthony Burgess, Geoff Dyer, Howard Jacobson and Doris Lessing.[10] The last few years have also seen a rise in stage adaptations of Lawrence – with recent productions including 'Husbands and Sons' (a combined adaptation of 'A Collier's Friday Night', 'The Widowing of Mrs Holroyd' and 'The Daughter-in-Law'; dir. Ben Power and Marianne Elliott, 2015), *Lady Chatterley's Lover* (dir. Phillip Breen, 2016) and 'The Daughter-in-Law' (dir. Jack Gamble, 2018), the latter being reviewed in *The Guardian* as possibly 'the best British working-class drama' (29 May, 2018) – while James Moran (2015) has produced a new study of Lawrence as 'dramatic modernist and theatrical innovator', which includes contributions from playwrights and a screenwriter.

Turning to the aims of the present book, while Lawrence's reputation has bobbed up and down on the varying tides of culture and criticism, one fundamental thing which has arguably remained the same since his very first book publication in 1911 (his first novel, *The White Peacock*) is the underlying way in which we read and classify his writings. The recently completed Cambridge Edition of Lawrence signals the way forward by introducing alternative *versions* of his works, but, rather than alter the underlying way in which Lawrence's works are presented and read, the edition's primary editorial aim is to remove corruption and inaccuracy (as stated in the General editors' preface, located at the front of every volume). Unlike traditional Anglo-American criticism, which concerns itself with single fixed textual products, a genetic approach, as in the present book, focuses on the underlying writing processes and considers multiple different versions (including drafts). Rather than extrapolate an overarching and inherently generalized narrative from one iteration of a work, multiplicity and provisionality are at the core of 'genetic criticism'. Despite recent developments then, the present book is the first to offer a fundamentally new way of approaching Lawrence's writing.

Most of the praise or invective aimed at Lawrence over the years has taken a naïve approach to textuality and has looked for a fixed message behind the writing. While the 'New Lawrence' of recent years has emerged from a more balanced approach, which takes into account the valid changes and contradictions that emerge across Lawrence's oeuvre – a development which is connected to the much more comprehensive Cambridge Edition of Lawrence – there has not been a sea change in our approach to reading and classifying the works themselves. Instead, I suggest there is no such singular *thing* as 'Odour of Chrysanthemums', *Women in Love* or *The Plumed Serpent*. These titles, themselves the products of revisions and editorial pressures, refer to a wider array of writing than has traditionally been identified, and different chunks of which suggest different overall messages. This book's aim then is not to resolve Lawrence's work into a single, fixed product or message, but to unravel and reveal the dynamic processes of writing which drive and determine those particular instances.

In one of the very first dedicated studies of Lawrence's oeuvre, modestly subtitled 'An Unprofessional Study', Anaïs Nin pointed the way when she made the following, fundamental observation: 'Lawrence has no system, unless his constant shifting of values can be called a system: *a system of mobility*. To him any stability is merely an obstacle to creative livingness' (1932, p. 14). Lawrence was consistently and passionately averse to fixed or institutionalized forms of thinking; this underpins the unique and almost maniacally itinerant nature of his life and writing. However, while this mobility enables his writing to cross boundaries of genre, of high and low culture, of class, nation and religion, it also leaves him unusually open to appropriation by readers or critics who *do* have fixed ideas. Ultimately, Lawrence is not a writer with a fixed viewpoint. His writings stage multiple different viewpoints and explore the dialogues (both antagonistic and reciprocal) between them. A key principle in this book is therefore *dialogism*, but I will discuss the specific importance of this principle in relation to Lawrence and genetics in the next chapter. For now, picking up on Nin's point that 'stability is merely an obstacle to creative livingness' for Lawrence, I believe we can at least identify a key thematic dynamic which stretches across and binds his writings together (certainly the major works discussed in this book, the choice of which I discuss later). In the most simplistic terms, this theme is the opposition between *flux* and *stasis*, the former being associated with life, the latter with death.

In 'Odour of Chrysanthemums', Elizabeth Bates and her children await the return of the husband and father, Walter, whose prolonged absence leads to an ever-increasing tension at home, as the thread of life is suspended. In *Women in Love*, the central opposition between flux and stasis becomes a self-consciously debated topic between the characters themselves; their very sense of self also becomes respectively jeopardized as they identify with static images or memories which are themselves frozen in the past, and they either passively embrace or actively strive to overcome this predicament, with the central and iconic chapter 'Moony' (in which Birkin throws stones at a reflected image of the moon in a pool of water) dramatizing this conflict. In *The Plumed Serpent* (as in *The White Peacock*), rather than referencing the novel's cult-like religious movement, to which Kate is a spectator, the titular figure may be seen as a symbol for the central female protagonist herself, who struggles with depression during her travels in Mexico and strives to break free from her own past and anterior relations in Europe: Quetzalcoatl ascends the volcano as a bird (a peacock) but descends as a mythical snake-bird hybrid, apparently capturing the conflict between freedom (flight/sky/futurity) and restraint (gravity/earth/return).

While it may be possible to base these readings on a single version of each work (why therefore bother with genetic criticism?), it is also possible to offer a range of other, potentially contradictory readings on that basis. By contrast, a genetic approach not only allows us to trace the development and mutation of this key theme (and others) – the conflict between flux and stasis – across the various drafts and versions of a work, it also enables us to understand the role of this conflict within the process of writing, as the flux of writing is forced to resolve itself into the static written product. I believe this explains Lawrence's consistent, almost obsessive revision of *endings*, which is why my reading of each work develops into a study of the following crucial dilemma for Lawrence: *how to write an ending.*

Before concluding this introduction, as the choice of texts greatly influences the result of any reading, I want to give a brief rationale for the works chosen in this book. As this book represents the first dedicated genetic study of Lawrence (and genetic criticism relies on details), in order to provide sincere genetic readings I first of all wanted to select a *small* number of works. As mentioned, and as other readers and critics can better avow, Lawrence was also a great writer of poems, plays, letters, travel books and many other types of literature. However, on balance, Lawrence probably dedicated the greatest amount of time and energy to *fiction*, and to long fiction in particular. My choice therefore reflects this, and, as I wanted to provide a *representative* study of Lawrence, I also wanted to choose a small number of works which would allow us to track Lawrence across different stages of his writing career and get to the 'heart' of his writing, potentially reflecting both the highs and the lows. In summary then, the three chosen works track the majority of Lawrence's writing life, from 1909 to 1926; 'Odour of Chrysanthemums' is one of Lawrence's breakthrough works, it was accepted for publication in a major journal when Lawrence was a young man and written and set in England; *Women in Love* is one of Lawrence's most influential works (I place it alongside *Ulysses* as the two great stand-alone novels of the twentieth century), it occupies the central phase in his career and was written and set in both England and Europe; *The Plumed Serpent* is one of Lawrence's most heavily criticized works, it occupies the mid to late stage of his career and was written and set in a non-European land.

In the final chapter of this book, I discuss the final chapter of *The Plumed Serpent*, one of the most heavily rewritten sections in Lawrence's entire oeuvre, which yet contains a sequence of largely unrevised and quotidian yet lyrical miniature scenes of life beside a lake, as observed by the novel's protagonist. The shortest of these scenes is a single line, which describes a peon (or day labourer) at work as follows:

> A man was stripping ~~reeds~~ **palm-stalks**, squatting in silence in his white cotton pants, under a tree, his black head bent forward. (MSI 466)

This man's absorption in simple though subtly skilled labour resonates with a fundamental belief of Lawrence's, which is the self-rewarding nature of work, something which almost amounts to a *theology* of process. Lawrence touches on this subject in a book review written shortly before his death in 1930, which is possibly the last piece of work he completed:

> 'To please God'" in this sense only means happily doing one's best at the job in hand, and being livingly absorbed in an activity which makes one in touch with – with the heart in all things; call it God. It is a state which any man or woman achieves when busy and concentrated on a job which calls forth real skill and attention, or devotion. (1974, p. 395)

A thing which Lawrence essentially dedicated his life to, a thing which is traditionally associated with the 'working' rather than the 'leisure' classes, but which any person is capable of doing and sharing, the riddle that is work (or process), here involves a connection (or communion) between the self and a greater reality, purpose or good. To return to the topic of class with which I began this introduction, then, I would suggest that, while Lawrence is *capable* of writing with a complexity and depth equal to that of any other modernist giant, from Joyce to Mann to Proust to Woolf, he is also (perhaps uniquely) able to combine these qualities with a deceptive and humble degree of accessibility. As a result, though he may not always command the same level of respect among the upper echelon of critics and readers, even the most deprived reader has a chance of finding some common ground in his work.

Notes

1 The figure of £20,000 equates to over £1,000,000 in 2020 (estimated using the UK Office for National Statistics composite price index); Weaver also donated a house to Joyce.
2 Huxley, Introduction. *The Letters of D. H. Lawrence* (1932, p. xvii); Forster, Letter to *The Nation and Atheneum*, 29 March 1930; Larkin (1992, p. 101).
3 In the year following its trial, *Lady Chatterley's Lover* reportedly outsold the Bible with two million copies (see: http://news.bbc.co.uk/onthisday/hi/dates/stories/november/10/newsid_2965000/2965194.stm).
4 While Millett's book was foreshadowed by Simone de Beauvoir's *The Second Sex* (1949), which includes a similar chapter on Lawrence, there followed a wave of feminist readings of Lawrence, with studies by Carol Dix, Sheila MacLeod and Carol Siegel all expressing varying degrees of dissatisfaction with Millett's take on Lawrence.
5 Camille Paglia likewise suggests that Millett's book in particular 'reduced complex artworks to their political content and attacked famous male artists and authors for their alleged sexism' ('Feminists Must Begin to Fulfil Their Noble, Animating Ideal', *The Chronicle of Higher Education*, 25 July 1997, p. B4).
6 Michael Bell suggests that such accusations have 'never been made by anyone who knows Lawrence's work well' (1992, p. 182).
7 The title of Williams' book is itself misleading in that it identifies Lawrence with a version of a phrase used by a fictional character in one of his novels (*Women in Love*).
8 Harris also notes that 'Millett implicitly defines the liberation of women as a redistribution of the cultural goods [. . .]. For Lawrence, the cultural goods were not worth having', and, 'as Norman Mailer gleefully pointed out, Millett suppresses contrary evidence, asserts unproved generalisations, quotes out of context, misinterprets quoted material, equates Lawrence with his fictional heroes, and sets up a distinctly misleading pattern of organizing Lawrence's work. Putting her thumb in the scale in this fashion is of course dishonest; but it is also an unnecessary expenditure of energy. [. . .] Lawrence's image of women, of men, and of their relationship to each other and to the universe is interesting enough as it stands' (pp. 524–9).
9 In *D. H. Lawrence: Language and Being* (1992), Bell places Lawrence's writing in a context of European modernist philosophy and anthropology, alongside Heidegger, Ernst Cassirer and Lucien Lévi-Bruhl, highlighting the enactivist relationship between language and being in Lawrence's novels, where there is 'a constant jostling of fundamentally different sensibilities', which renders the language 'inescapably philosophical' (p. 3). In *D. H. Lawrence, Science and the Posthuman* (2005),

Wallace counters the influence of Leavis by 'uncoupling Lawrence from a literary-critical tradition which continues, even in postmodern times, to limit what we can say about him' and provides a 'reassessment of Lawrence's reputation as an irrationalist' (pp. 6–7) by placing his work in a context of Bergsonian conceptions of thinking matter and more recent theories of the post-human. Although I have curtailed a broader survey of Lawrence criticism here for the sake of brevity, the next chapter does contain a detailed response to traditional studies of Lawrence's manuscripts and includes a discussion of recent critics such as Amit Chaudhuri, N. H. Reeve and Violeta Sotirova.

10 Others include Amit Chaudhuri, Rachel Cusk, Helen Dunmore, Richard Eyre, James Fenton, James Lasdun, Blake Morrison, Tim Parks, Louise Welsh and James Wood.

Part One

Critical frameworks

1

Anglo-American traditions, genetic criticism and recent developments

Introduction

Genetic criticism is a novel approach to the study of literature, which takes as its object of study the process rather than product of writing. It involves reading the drafts and alternative versions of a work, usually in the form of original manuscripts – where the author's writing and revision is directly on display, without editorial interference – and remaining open-minded about the contingent nature of writing: the creative process often leads to alternative versions and no single version is innately superior to another. To do this, a writer must have recorded at least some of their work in progress, and at least some of this work must have been preserved. Then, before a critic or reader can draw meaningful conclusions from the writing processes, it is necessary to establish the chronology of and relationship between the different drafts. Therefore, a thorough examination of the primary materials is an important part of any true genetic study.

Genetic criticism originally developed as a scientific discipline at the French National Centre for Scientific Research (CNRS), when, in 1968, Louis Hay was called upon to study the recently purchased collection of Heinrich Heine's manuscripts. Francis Lecompte provides the following history of the movement in France:

> The small Heine group, hosted by the École Normale Supérieure (ENS) in Paris, set to work in 1968. Their project marked the birth of the discipline that researchers would later call genetic criticism. It led in 1974 to the founding of the Centre d'Histoire et d'Analyse des Manuscrits Modernes. Renamed the Institut des Textes et Manuscrits Modernes (ITEM) two years later, it became a CNRS laboratory in 1982. In the meantime, the researchers, by then including several linguists, had begun investigating the manuscripts of Proust, followed by those

of Zola, Flaubert, Valéry, Sartre and many others, and genetic criticism became recognised as a fully-fledged branch of textual science. (Lecompte, 2018)

Along with some of the names originally studied (Proust, Zola, Flaubert, Valéry), which can be seen as representing a certain *type* of writer (a point to which I will return), the last phrase in this extract is important: a fully fledged branch of *textual science*. In spite of the name genetic *criticism*, then, French genetic critics are essentially engaged in 'a *science* of literature' (also the title of an essay by French geneticist Pierre-Marc de Biasi) – a theoretically informed codicology, using sophisticated technologies to date, categorize and study manuscripts – and researchers who historically identify themselves as genetic critics (often hailing from this specific research group at ITEM) have tended to adopt a similar approach.[1] One important output of this research has been the production of genetic editions, however, it is key to stress that genetic criticism is by no means restricted to genetic editing/editions.

The introduction of genetic criticism into the study of English literature has been slow, to say the least. This can partly be explained by the traditional and long-standing Anglo-American divide between the sciences and the humanities, as well as the further divide within Anglo-American literary studies itself, between literary and textual criticism (the interpretation versus the preparation of texts). The scientific aspect of genetic criticism has led some critics, even in France (e.g. Pierre Bourdieu), to scorn the movement as representing a return to philology, which neglects the development of critical theory (see Lernout, 2002), while other negative critics have taken almost the opposite stance by suggesting it encourages 'analysis interminable'. However, as the works of recent critics such as Dirk van Hulle, Sally Bushell, Finn Fordham and Hannah Sullivan suggest that genetic criticism of English literature is now steadily on the rise, this chapter attempts to explain the sluggish nature of the breakthrough in more detail, paying special attention to the study of D. H. Lawrence, clarifying the distinction between genetic and existing Anglo-American criticism, and mapping recent developments for the first time.

Anglo-American critical traditions

In his afterword to *Essais de critique génétique* (1979), Hay lists early precursors for genetic criticism in German and Anglo-American Romanticism; from Goethe and Schlegel, the latter of whom declared that 'one can only claim to have real understanding of a work, or of a thought, when one can reconstitute its becoming and its composition' (quoted in Hay, 2004, p. 18), to Coleridge (*Biographia Litteraria* (1817)) and Poe, whose influential essay 'The Philosophy of Composition' (1846) I return to later. To explain the gap between these early efforts and the development of genetic criticism itself, Hay explains two key preconditions necessary for proper genetic criticism:

> First, to analyse work habits, we must be able to 'go backstage', to enter into 'the workshop, the laboratory' of the writer. (Hay, 2004, p. 19)

The first precondition, then, is the existence of an archive. The prestige attached to great literary documents rose during the Romantic era (alongside national traditions) and encouraged their collection by wealthy benefactors. By the end of the nineteenth century, this led to the establishment of major literary archives, such as the Goethe and Schiller Archive in Weimar, and, as mentioned, genetic criticism developed from a research group assembled to study a particular archive at the CNRS. Florence Callu, a later director at ITEM, has described the modernist period as a 'golden age' of literary manuscripts (Callu, 1993, p. 64), and, as we will see in this book, there is certainly a wealth of extant manuscripts by D. H. Lawrence; these are housed in various collections across the globe, though predominately in the United States and the United Kingdom, with the single largest collection housed at Harry Ransom Humanities Research Centre at the University of Texas, where I conducted my own archival research. So much for the archive. What about the second precondition?

> Next, to be able to interpret the meaning of what we discover there [i.e. in the archive], we must also be equipped with sufficient theoretical intelligence about these 'internal mechanisms' [i.e. writing processes]. It is clear that these conditions have been fulfilled only relatively recently. (p. 21)

While the need for literary archives brings us to the end of the nineteenth century, this second, theoretical requirement, in Hay's own analysis, brings us up to the 1960s, with the emergence of structuralist and post-structuralist critical theory. The connection between genetic criticism and critical theory is contested, as suggested earlier. Nevertheless, it has been described as a 'decisive fertilizing influence (and necessary foil)' (Deppman, Ferrer and Groden, 2004) because, rather than tacitly viewing text as an immutable thing, critical theory (especially post-structuralism) suggests that text is intrinsically multiple, mobile, referential and intertextual. However, like genetic criticism, this type of critical theory did not originally develop in an Anglo-American context and has met with resistance. This delay and resistance to a key preconditions helps explain the delayed introduction of genetic criticism to English literature and can likewise be ascribed to opposing Anglo-American traditions. These include the aforementioned divide between textual and literary criticism, as well as an underlying focus on intentionality and formalism within Anglo-American traditions, and related concerns about involuntarism (loss of volition), deconstruction and interminable analysis (loss of form).

Despite heavy criticism of the relevance of an author's intentions to the study of English literature – represented in iconic essays by T. S. Eliot ('Tradition and the Individual Talent' (1919)) and W. K. Wimsatt Jr and M. C. Beardsley ('The Intentional Fallacy' (1946)), who form the backbone of 'New Criticism', a formalist approach, though such criticism is also variously implied by subsequent historical and sociological approaches – Anglo-American critics throughout the twentieth century and beyond have ironically[2] relied upon texts which are themselves edited according to an interpretation of the author's so-called final intentions. Forming the backbone of a respective movement known as 'New Bibliography', W. W. Greg set out the principles for editing according to an author's final intentions in an influential essay entitled 'Rationale of Copy-Text' (1950–1). This provided a basis for *eclectic* editing by developing R. B. McKerrow's notion of a 'copy-text' and adding a distinction between 'accidental' and 'substantive' readings. Though originally intended to help establish the most authoritative versions of works of English literature dating from 1550 to 1650 (a period dominated by Shakespeare), Greg's rationale was developed for more contemporary literature by Fredson Bowers (who founded the influential journal *Studies in Bibliography*) and was subsequently adopted by the Centre for Editions of American Authors (now the Centre for Scholarly Editions). G. Thomas Tanselle later defended the movement against the rise of critical theory (see bibliography).[3] These principles provide the basis for virtually all major Anglo-American editions, and the recently completed Cambridge Edition of D. H. Lawrence (first volume published in 1979) is a perfect example. It aims to create 'texts which are as close as can now be determined to those [the author] would have wished to see printed' (General Editor's Preface).

In contrast to this faithfulness towards an author's 'final intentions', modern German textual criticism, now a big influence on Anglo-American scholars, attempted to be faithful to each particular *version* of a text. Referred to as *documentary* editing, its principles were laid out in the German collection *Texte und Varianten* (1971) edited by Gunter Martens and Hans Zeller; Zeller also introduced these ideas to English readers a few years later in his essay 'A New Approach to the Critical Constitution of Literary Texts' (1975), which was published in *Studies in Bibliography* and which D. C. Greetham suggests 'proved a salutary balance to the prevailing intentionalist, or "author"-based predilections and "ideal," "clear-text" practices of Anglo-American scholarship' (Greetham, 1997, p. 285). Essays from *Texte und Varianten* were also later translated and collected in *Contemporary German Editorial Theory* (1991) by George Bornstein, Gillian Borland Pierce and Hans Walter Gabler. Here, Zeller spells out 'the subjective nature of editing' and criticizes the misleading way in which 'the texts of scholarly editions are largely understood and treated as if they were objective givens' (p. 19), emphasizing the fundamental point that, 'whether consciously held or not', editing 'is not immune to or a refuge from the discussion of literary theory; one can only make relevant literary statements and editorial decisions on the basis of theoretical premises' (p. 95).

These insights were hugely influential for Anglo-American textual critics and, aside from Gabler's own 'synoptic' edition of *Ulysses* (1984) and Bornstein's edited collection *Representing Modernist Texts: Editing as Interpretation* (1991), they led to a surge of publications addressing the problematic division between 'textual' and 'literary' criticism in the early 1990s, including a first critical appraisal of the Cambridge Edition of Lawrence: *Editing D. H. Lawrence: New Versions of a Modern Author* (ed. Ross and Jackson, 1995).[4] While these books were still ultimately concerned with editing (rather than interpreting) texts, French genetic criticism had continued to develop and now began making inroads in the Anglo-American world. The following journals dedicated special issues to the topic in successive years: *Romanic Review* (1995), *Yale French Studies* (1996) and *Word & Image* (1997), while van Hulle founded the e-journal *Genetic Joyce Studies* (2001) and went on to publish *Textual Awareness* (2004), a comparative study of the late manuscripts of Joyce, Proust and Mann, and the first true genetic study in English. The first English introduction to genetic criticism also appeared in the same year: *Genetic Criticism: Texts and Avant-Textes* (eds. Deppman, Ferrer, and Groden, 2004).

However, despite these breakthroughs, Joyce remained something of an outlier for English-language genetic criticism until very recently. Indeed, in the same 2006 volume of the journal *Text* (now *Textual Cultures*) in which van Hulle draws from his own research into the manuscripts of Samuel Beckett while discussing the ways in which 'genetic criticism can contribute to a richer understanding of the poetical, intertextual and semantic implications' of a text (p. 88), H. T. M. van Vliet suggested that what 'we urgently need [is] more interpretative studies of variants' (p. 77) and Peter Shillingsburg stated that, despite abandoning the quest for the 'archetype text, the one closest to the lost original text', and adding many new goals, 'what textual criticism has not done either well or ill is to develop the principles and practices of the interpretive consequences of its findings' (p. 63). In the same journal the following year, Sally Bushell likewise emphasized that 'a full critical engagement with textual process and the coming-into-being of the literary work has not yet occurred in any systematic way *within Anglo-American scholarship*' (Bushell, 2007, p. 100; my italics: an important qualification). While studies of English literary manuscripts have of course existed since at least the 1950s, as Deppman, Ferrer and Groden point out in their introduction to *Genetic Criticism*, and as I will explain in more detail later, these studies 'tended to be pragmatic and not theoretically self-conscious, to consider textuality and intention as unproblematic, and to see the manuscripts exclusively in relation to the subsequent published work' (p. 5); and Groden's own study *'Ulysses' in Progress* (1977) is included in their list of examples. The most influential critic in this respect with regard to Lawrence's manuscripts is undoubtedly Mark Kinkead-Weekes, and I dedicate a section of this chapter to clarifying the fundamental differences between Kinkead-Weekes's work and genetic criticism.

As Gabler points out in the indicatively entitled essay 'Unsought Encounters', many Anglo-American critics are simply unaware of genetic criticism and the fact that genetic critics have been 'developing theories and a discourse for some time' (1993, p. 158). It is partly in reference to this that van Hulle's landmark genetic study of Joyce, Proust and Mann was entitled *Textual Awareness*. This book aims to increase our awareness of genetic criticism by examining its ideas and mapping out recent developments, but it is also important to consider some of the causes for this lack of awareness, as resistance to textual theory more generally suggests a selective blindness, as well as addressing valid criticisms.

The question of whether the emotions and intentions of an author should feature in criticism of a text was debated by major critics throughout the first half of the twentieth century, from T. S. Eliot and John Middleton Murry's dispute as respective editors of *The Criterion* and *The Adelphi*, over terms such as 'romanticism', 'classicism' and 'impersonality' in the 1920s, to C. S. Lewis and E. M. W. Tillyard's debate over 'the personal heresy' in the journal *Essays and Criticism* in the 1930s (culminating in *The Personal Heresy* (1939)).[5] Those in favour were marginalized in the second half of the century following the aforementioned establishment of 'New Criticism', which undercut any reference to the private realm of the author by defining the 'proper' object of 'true and objective' criticism as the *language* of a text, which 'belongs to the public' (Wimsatt and Beardsley, 1946, pp. 470, 487). Wimsatt and Beardsley suggest that a text is separated from its author at 'birth' (p. 470) for this reason, and their essay on the intentional fallacy foreshadows Roland Barthes's similarly influential essay on 'the death of the author' (1967), which, through a similarly abstract focus on language, suggests that a text's embodiment in language cancels out any single point of origin (hence the author is erased); pushing this logic to its conclusion, in the same year, Derrida famously writes, 'there is no outside-text' (*il n'y a pas de hors-texte*) in *De la grammatologie*.

In his near-contemporary lecture on the question 'What Is an Author?' (1969), often read as a companion to Barthes's essay, Michel Foucault provides a less direct negation of the author's autonomy by highlighting the *function* of the author. He does so by sketching a new sociological and historical approach to literary works, which anticipates the New Historicist movement led by Stephen Greenblatt (as does the materialist criticism of Raymond Williams). Intentionality was also subject to sociological critique within the field of textual criticism, most famously in Jerome J. McGann's *A Critique of Modern Textual Criticism* (1983), which acknowledges the lectures of D. F. Mackenzie on the same topic. McGann argues that literary works are 'fundamentally social rather than personal or psychological products' and 'do not even acquire an artistic form of being until their engagement with an audience has been determined' (pp. 40–4). In a sociological approach to editing, then, we are asked to acknowledge 'a higher order of historical determinism', which, as Shillingsburg suggests, 'operates regardless of individual intentions' (1989, p. 63).

In the world of Anglo-American literary criticism, however, the author never really dies. Appearing in the same year as Barthes's essay, E. D. Hirsch's *Validity in Interpretation* (1967) provides a systematic defence of the importance of authorial intentions for literary interpretation. Hirsch recognized the problem of pluralism: as Morse Peckham observes, when critics rely solely on their own readerly response, it 'leads inevitably to the position that any interpretation is as good as any other' (1977, p. 803). Barthes and Derrida's erasure of origins, and focus on infinite textuality, are therefore seen as irresponsible gestures, a denial of origins. In 'The Problem of Textuality', Edward Said celebrates Foucault and Derrida for enabling critical work to avoid 'the self-confirming operations of culture and the wholly predictable monotony of the disengaged critical system', but warns that much contemporary criticism 'is lost in the "abysmal" element of textuality' and seems 'utterly blind to the impressive constitutive authority in textuality of such power as that of a broadly based *cultural* discipline, in Foucault's sense of the word' (1978, p. 713). Said suggests there is a tendency towards involuntarism in French textual theory, and resistance to such a tendency has indeed fuelled much of the ambivalence towards its import. Said's arguments are echoed by Eugene Goodheart in his critique of the sociological approach to textual criticism. While accepting that the author's role in textual interpretation is potentially tyrannical, Goodheart also points to the fact that publishers and readers 'may constitute their own tyranny', particularly when it comes to a heterodox writer like Lawrence (1993, p. 238). Goodheart argues that we 'diminish the audacious authority of Lawrence's work, its subversive message, if', as in sociological criticism and editing, 'we prematurely absorb it into an author-publisher-audience collaborative' (1993, p. 238). Goodheart's suggestion that power in contemporary society lies not with government but with 'public opinion: the publisher and the audience toward whom the book is directed' (1993, p. 238) is questionable, but is probably even more relevant in today's era of the internet and social media than ever before. Acknowledging the capability of writers to serve as critics of this prevailing power, Goodheart argues that the 'truly liberating critical act' is to preserve 'the intentions of the writer against the appropriating, bowdlerizing efforts of communities of readers to domesticate the intentions to the mere needs and desires of the readers' (1993, p. 238).

Valid points are raised by both sides in these debates around the role of the author in textual interpretation. However, one key point which unites both author-based and author-effacing forms of literary and textual criticism is the fact that both sides have neglected the *internal* history of the object of criticism itself, its textual genesis. While historicist, materialist or sociological criticism place textual products within a larger historical 'process', existing Anglo-American traditions have failed to move beyond the notion of a text itself as a product. Goodheart's representative attack on 'historicism' is symptomatic of this:

> Historicism is inimical to the individual will, or rather it transforms intention into an instrument of forces always greater than itself. [. . .] The interaction between history and self, between context and text, however, is possible only if the integrity of each term is preserved; in historicism the integrities are dissolved and absorbed into 'process', an appealing word with sinister potential. (p. 239)

Distinctions between history and self, text and context, are clearly valid and important, but what *is* a text? What *is* a self? And how are these things constituted? While 'publishers and readers may constitute their own tyranny', critics may also tyrannize texts by claiming to represent the author's intentions and by basing their interpretations on one particular textual product.

The author is to some extent erased even in intentionalist forms of criticism and editing by the presentation of single reading texts, which are produced and curated by the critic. Terms like 'authoritative' and 'final' are ultimately used to validate editorial interpretations which displace the author's actual process of writing. As Zeller has argued, an author's intention changes over time and can 'only speculatively be established on the basis of the written record' (1995, p. 25); hence his suggestion that editors should play a *documentary* role. While Anglo-American critics have traditionally focused on the author's so-called final intentions in order to overcome the issue of changing intentions, the concept inherently identifies text as product rather than process and (knowingly or unknowingly) leads to the teleological belief that each and every process or version of a work leads to the same end, the 'final' version, which therefore supersedes or even transcends the former.

As mentioned, the Cambridge Edition of Lawrence creates texts in a traditional Anglo-American style, merging multiple versions into a single eclectic text based on an interpretation of the author's final intentions, with variant readings relegated to an appendix at the back of volumes. In contrast, genetic editions directly transcribe the author's manuscripts and use editorial markings to indicate the different sources (i.e. the different manuscripts) and activities (e.g. deletion, addition and substitution), thus revealing the author at work, the contingent nature of texts, and allowing the reader to interpret specific processes of writing; the conventional 'apparatus' thereby becomes the main body of text. This provides a basis for genetic criticism, which, as Almuth Grésillon suggests, 'established a new perspective on literature by defining the axes of reading through the act of *production*' (1997, p. 106). While this form of presentation is less easily accessible for a general reader, it is also possible to present a single reading text on one page (the recto) and a genetic text on the facing page (the verso), as in Gabler's edition of *Ulysses*.[6]

As Paul Eggert has described, to read the Cambridge Edition of Lawrence for process, one would have to read *against the grain* of the edition, using the 'reading text to open up the textual apparatus', rather than, as is traditional, 'using the apparatus to check the validity of the editor's decisions for the text' (1995, pp. 29, 37). Interestingly, Eggert reflects on his own experiences as editor of the Cambridge edition of Lawrence's co-authored Australian novel *The Boy in the Bush* as follows:

> The conventional single-reading-text critical edition has reinforced what I believe was always an illusion: that the writer wrote a series of finished and thus essentially separate works in which his or her development or deterioration can be adequately studied. (1991, p. 65)

The common suggestion that even Lawrence's drafts represent a series of separate works is certainly misleading. As we will see, Lawrence rewrote 'Odour of Chrysanthemums', *Women in Love* and *The Plumed Serpent* on numerous occasions and usually followed the previous versions very closely while rewriting, changing some elements and leaving others intact.

Following his own study of the manuscripts of *The Rainbow* and *Women in Love*, Charles L. Ross suggested in the late 1970s that 'Lawrence's creativity has been misrepresented by even his staunchest admirers, who have gone to the extreme of presenting him as a "daimonic" novelist"', later adding that such views have 'had the unfortunate consequence of inhibiting critical appreciation of Lawrence' (1976, pp. 277–8; 1979, pp. 5–7).[7] In a later review of the Cambridge edition of *The Rainbow*, Lydia Blanchard suggested along similar lines:

> As additional volumes appear in the Cambridge University Press edition of the works of D. H. Lawrence, their significance for a re-evaluation of Lawrence begins to take shape [. . .] the cumulative impact of the emerging volumes [. . .] is close to revolutionary for Lawrence scholarship and criticism, creating new understandings of Lawrence as writer. [. . .] The textual apparatus of the Cambridge edition shows a flexible writer, one changing his mind, growing, evolving. (1990, p. 387)

Dennis Jackson explicitly suggested a few years later that the 'versioning' of Lawrence's writing 'represented in multiple texts in CUP appendixes' will 'surely make Lawrence's work the most intriguing, accessible laboratory for genetic studies in all of Western literature (with the possible exception of the Cornell Wordsworth)' (Ross and Jackson, 1995, p. 234). Despite this huge potential, genetic studies of Lawrence did not follow: none of the essays in *The Cambridge Companion to D. H. Lawrence* (2001) or *New D. H. Lawrence* (2009), two major edited collections on Lawrence which have appeared since the turn of the century, even reflect on the textual condition of Lawrence's work, let alone focus on genetics.[8]

The Cambridge Edition certainly provides a very valuable, comprehensive critical edition of Lawrence's work. The scholarly introductions, references and variants supply the necessary materials for research on Lawrence writings, while the removal of various 'corruptions' from previous editions, such as non-authorial errors, alterations and cuts, is equally valuable. The edition has also published alternative versions of works based on manuscript drafts, such as *Paul Morel* (2003), an early version of *Sons and Lovers*, as well as a complete version of Lawrence's unfinished novel *Mr Noon* (1984) for the first time (only the first volume – 140 of 407 manuscript pages – had previously been published). However, while the appendixes and alternative versions may appear to represent a 'laboratory for genetic studies', this is a slightly misleading claim given the underlying motivation for the edition, which is that of comprehensiveness rather than multiplicity; not to publish alternative versions based on drafts, for example, would have meant discarding large chunks of Lawrence's archive and leaving existing (and 'corrupted') publications as the main resource for future scholars (the Cambridge Edition is not the first to publish such versions: alternative versions of *Lady Chatterley's Lover*, for example, have existed for generations). The Edition itself does not set out any criteria for distinguishing between texts, works, versions and drafts (what do these words even mean in the context of the Edition?), nor does it reflect on the significance of multiple versions or develop any ideas about process. If the edition does encourage genetic work at all, then, it is inadvertently so, and, as Eggert suggests earlier, perhaps even against its own grain.

As in the wider culture of Anglo-American literary and textual criticism, then, there has been a general absence of ideas about textual process and a distinct lack of engagement with writing process in Lawrence studies (especially noteworthy given the amount of material available). In fact, the vast majority of critics who *have* researched Lawrence's manuscripts have collaborated on the Cambridge Edition, including John Worthen, Mark Kinkead-Weekes, L. D. Clark, Brian Finney, Helen and Carl Baron, Michael Squires, Paul Eggert and N. H. Reeve; Charles L. Ross also edited an edition of *Women in Love* for Penguin (1982). Since the 1960s, there has been a well-established tradition of criticism based on Lawrence's manuscript, the most influential origin of which is Mark Kinkead-Weekes's essay 'The Marble and the Statue: The Exploratory Imagination of D. H. Lawrence' (1968), which attempts to cover the compositional history of *The Rainbow* and *Women in Love*. However, this tradition contains the type of non-genetic work which Groden and Ferrer discuss in their introduction to *Genetic Criticism*: it is not theoretically self-conscious, it considers textuality and intention as unproblematic and it frames the manuscripts exclusively in relation to the final work. Like Ross's more detailed compositional history of *The Rainbow* and *Women in Love* (1979), published more than a decade later, Kinkead-Weekes's essay does not challenge the underlying Anglo-American assumption that the 'proper' task of a literary critic is to evaluate a *finished* work.

Kinkead-Weekes's essay has never received criticism from a genetic perspective and remains influential. Its ideas were recapitulated in Kinkead-Weekes's own introduction to the Cambridge edition of *The Rainbow* (1989) as well as in the relevant section of the second volume of the Cambridge tripartite biography of Lawrence (1996). A more recent critic has also suggested that Kinkead-Weekes 'encourages the study of Lawrence's manuscripts and letters that bear witness to his methods of composition' (McDonald, 2009, p. 4). It is therefore important for me to set out clearly the fundamental differences between Kinkead-Weekes's approach and genetic criticism.

The first important thing to note about Kinkead-Weekes's essay ('The Marble and The Statue') is its length, which is under fifty pages. In this short space, the essay attempts to cover the genesis of *The Rainbow* and *Women in Love* – both part of probably the longest and most complex compositional history of all Lawrence's novels, hence Ross's book dedicated exclusively to the topic and my own chapter here (Chapter 3) – while also discussing Lawrence's 'exploratory imagination' (which gives the essay its subtitle) as well as two other works: his book-length 'Study of Thomas Hardy' and the long essay 'The Crown'. These constraints mean that the essay does not have space for any detailed analysis of the drafts. However, Kinkead-Weekes is perfectly open about this and makes the essay's traditional viewpoint clear, arguing as follows:

> A full study of the manuscripts would show us the effort of imaginative exploration that went into the novel's growth; but only literary criticism of the finished work [. . .] could hope for adequate understanding. (p. 401)

The essay's main focus then is on the critic's broader argument about Lawrence's artistic 'growth', which he argues enabled Lawrence to transform the 'marble' of his early drafts into the 'statues' of his finished works. Kinkead-Weekes argues that Lawrence created a 'theology' of marriage (p. 384) in the final published versions of *The Rainbow* and *Women in Love*, and there is therefore a theological dimension to the way in which the finished versions transcend the earlier drafts. The essay concludes as follows:

> Lawrence aspired to, and achieved in the greatest moments of these novels, an imaginative vision inclusive enough to allow *all* opposites to play. [. . .] The aim of the exploratory theory and the finest achievement of the exploratory process, was to battle through partialities, to become objective enough to make his 'statues' stand free, complete. (p. 412)

Given this explicitly teleological view of the overall process of writing, Kinkead-Weekes does not discuss particular, contingent writing processes. A couple of passages from the early drafts are introduced, but only to demonstrate the apparent flaws in comparison to the final product. Likewise, rather than tracking the internal history of the novels themselves, Kinkead-Weekes argues that Lawrence's artistic breakthrough came by writing separate essays during a pause in composition from 1914 to 1915 ('only then could he write *The Rainbow*' (p. 384)). Ultimately, then, the essay is a biographical interpretation of Lawrence's own growth as an artist. When discussing the early drafts of *Women in Love*, for example, Kinkead-Weekes concludes that 'throughout the last draft, Lawrence had been liberating himself from the "leadership" theory which had been blocking his own, and not merely Ursula's, understanding of what marriage should be' (p. 402). The paradox here is that, despite suggesting elsewhere that 'we shall not respond fully to his best work until we learn to read in terms of process' (p. 407), the essay is essentially an exercise in how *not* to read in terms of process, with Lawrence's actual processes of writing overlooked throughout.

In the decades following 'The Marble and the Statue', a number of other critics focused on the period around 1914 when looking at Lawrence's manuscripts, and likewise portrayed this as a pivotal moment in Lawrence's life and career, a period marking his so-called progress to maturity (the title of a 1975 essay by Brian Finney, who claims there is an 'enormous gulf' (p. 322) separating *Sons and Lovers* and *The Rainbow*). J. C. F. Littlewood, who anticipated Kinkead-Weekes in some ways, suggests certain stories in *The Prussian Officer and Other Stories* (1914) – a collection which is problematically absent from 'The Marble and the Statue' – present 'the first moment of which it is possible to say that Lawrence is now truly himself and has found himself as an artist' (1976, p. 14), and supports this claim by comparing episodes in earlier and later works, or versions of the same work, while making judgements about the 'maturity' of respective passages.[9] In addition to those already mentioned, other critics who have produced studies in this vein include Keith Sagar, John Worthen and Keith Cushman. The teleological nature of this work is perhaps best summarized by the following passage from the latter's *D. H. Lawrence at Work: The Emergence of the* Prussian Officer *Stories* (1978):

> The progression from *The White Peacock* chapter ['The Scarp Slope'] to 'The Shades of Spring' is a study in Lawrence's growth to maturity, of his ultimate acceptance of his past and of himself. The special radiance of 'The Shades of Spring' also speaks clearly and directly to the fact that it is part of the emergent moment of *The Rainbow*. He had at last transformed something of a personal archetype into a first-rate work of short fiction. (p. 147)

Here, the internal process of writing is completely absent, as if the text simply drops from the pen (paradoxically so given the title of the study); a later 'version' is again seen to transcend an earlier one, and the critic switches between different works.

Genetic criticism

The manner in which the aforementioned type of criticism merely '*supplements criticism of the finished texts* with knowledge of their growth from seed into an organic whole' (Ross, 1979, pp. 3–4, my italics) must be placed in context: as emphasized, the purpose of traditional Anglo-American literary criticism is to evaluate *finished* works. In sharp contrast, as Groden and Ferrer point out, 'for geneticists, instead of a fixed, finished object in relation to which all previous states are considered, a given text becomes – or texts become – the contingent manifestations of a *diachronous* play of signifiers' (p. 5), and 'one could even say that genetic criticism is not concerned with texts at all but only with the writing processes that engender them' (p. 11). We can draw out at least two important points from this description. First, whereas in Anglo-American traditions the process of writing itself is seen as contingent (and hence subsidiary to the 'final text'), here we see how any individual *text* becomes a contingent manifestation of the more fundamental writing process (a concept which Lawrence himself echoes in letters describing his own composition of *Women in Love*, as we shall see). Second, by viewing a text *not* as something 'fixed, finished' but as a 'play of signifiers', focusing 'on the writing processes that engender' those texts and introducing the literary manuscript into the interpretation of literature, genetic criticism, rather than replacing individual agency with an abstract and potentially endless linguistic or textual system (encouraging involuntarism and effacing intentionality), actually concerns the concrete act and traces of writing, which provide a clearer and more complex source of individual agency. As Grésillon suggests:

> Manuscripts are not only an observation of the genesis of the work but also a place where the question of the author can be studied in a new light: a place of significant conflicts, a place of the genesis of the author. (1997, p. 123)

On the question of the death of the author, David Foster Wallace provides a basic human rebuttal: 'for those of us civilians who know in our gut that writing is an act of communication between one human being and another, the whole question seems sort of arcane' (1998, p. 144). Genetic criticism supports this rebuttal but allows us to be much less enigmatic and much more detailed about it.

In her book *Text as Process*, Sally Bushell has developed a complex theory of intentionality by applying it to the activity of writing. Bushell suggests that while 'it is easy to agree that intention should not be used as the fundamental basis for interpretation of a work of art [...] the question remains whether this is true in the same way, and to the same extent, for the interpretation of the coming-into-being of the work of art' (2009, p. 50). In response to the emphasis placed by New Criticism, as well as later theorists like Barthes and Foucault, on the public nature of language, Bushell suggests that 'although language as a thing existing beyond and above individual use denies agency, an individual sense of agency may be necessary in order to create' (2009, p. 50). In contrast, as Ferrer and Groden point out, an exclusive focus on the way in which texts are embedded within a discursive field (as in post-structuralist and intertextual theory) leads to a notion of the text 'as methodologically separate from its origins and from its material incarnation' and hence 'to a paradoxical sacralization and idealization of it as *The Text*' (Ferrer and Groden, 2003, p. 5).[10]

These observations are neglected in early critiques of genetic criticism in English by Laurent Jenny and Oliver Davis, with the latter going to the somewhat bizarre extreme of suggesting 'a jealous desire, to be alone with the author' becomes 'the very principle of the genetic critic's travails' (Davis, 2002, p. 100). The common bone of contention for both critics is the idea that genetic criticism 'does not have the effect of shoring up new interpretations, but of inventing a link with the text that suspends the hermeneutic relationship' and opens 'a corpus without closure' (Jenny, 1996, p. 11), offering a vision of 'exploration interminable' (Davis, p. 100). This is fuelled by a skewed perception of genetic criticism as a form of intertextual theory (I discuss the differences between genetic and intertextual criticism again later in the text when discussing Amit Chaudhuri's intertextual study of Lawrence's poetry). As in *any* reading, the possibility for subjective interpretation is itself endless. However, in genetic criticism, as in traditional criticism, the *avant-texte* (i.e. all the texts which feature directly in the process of writing) is *finite*; traditional criticism merely reads from a single text. Besides examining the author's concrete role in the production of text, therefore, genetic criticism also expands the pool of texts to read from, often opening new ground for interpretation where things might otherwise appear innocuous or obscure. As van Hulle suggests, the *avant-texte* 'opens up an enormous interpretative potential': it 'actively encourages and provides a textual basis for unlooked-for interpretations of underlying layers of meaning' and draws attention to 'the subdued poetical intensity and unexpected semantic pregnancy of even the most futile an adjective and the faintest idea' (2006, p. 94).

I believe a more valid criticism of genetic criticism can be made with regards to its limitations when viewed as a scientific discipline and the emphasis placed by some critics upon the systematization of texts. As mentioned, the term *avant-texte* (coined by Jean Bellemin-Noël) is used in French genetic criticism to denote all the relevant documents that feature in the genesis of a particular work, to frame those documents as texts and to consider all the texts together as part of a textual system. However, the notion of a textual system suggests that a work's genesis may be compiled into a massive synchronic text, thus erasing the 'vital' and contingent diachronic force of individual writing processes; this is suggested by genetic stemmata, or diagrammatic representations of the *avant-texte* (examples can be found in the chapters of this book on *Women in Love* and *The Plumed Serpent*). The extreme end of this approach is envisioned by de Biasi: computers 'should allow us to develop the basis for a real calculus in genetic matters' (Deppman, Ferrer & Groden, 66). While the categorization of the *avant-texte* is an essential part of genetic work, it is in a sense *preparatory* to the 'real', *critical* work of evaluating and interpreting particular drafts and writing processes. Schemas and stemmata therefore play a more peripheral role in recent English-language genetic studies by Bushell, Fordham and Sullivan, and the same applies to this book.

Another point of criticism can be made in relation to genetic criticism's response to *teleology*, which cannot simply be discarded. Teleology plays an important role in virtually all writing processes. As Fordham explains in *I do I undo I redo* (2010), 'the pressures and pleasures experienced by writers' are heavily influenced by 'the desire and need to disseminate and publish, or the attitudes and social facts and contexts around publication', all of which 'make teleological questions critical in any [genetic] study' (pp. 26–7). It is no coincidence therefore that the question of writing an *ending* forms a central theme in this book. That said, I would emphasize that teleology in writing is not always unidirectional, just as endings are not always singular. Bushell's phenomenological analysis of writing as 'a movement *between* a "spontaneous" (unwilled) engagement with language and a conscious return to that engagement' suggests a fundamentally circular, recursive pattern, while Fordham and van Hulle place equal emphasis upon 'creative undoing' as they do upon 'straightforward' creativity. Finally, as we will see with Lawrence, writers commonly revisit supposedly 'finished' works, often several years after their original 'completion' and publication, thus producing multiple valid endings. This type of revision can also function in a retroactive way: that is, a surviving piece of text may refer to something that existed in an earlier version of a work but has since been removed.[11]

Extending the scope of this survey for a moment, Bushell has suggested that 'a phenomenological account of being is partly responsible for a critical marginalizing of textual process and composition as an area of study' and discusses the ways in which Heidegger 'dwells on the self-sufficiency of the *completed* thing at the expense of the "coming-into-being" of the thing' (2009, pp. 215–16). This echoes the New Critical concept of the art object as an organic unity (an example of the latter is provided by Kinkead-Weekes's metaphor of the 'the marble and the statue'). Recapitulating the various forms of *Dasein* (or ways of being-there) set out by Heidegger in *Being and Time* (1931), Bushell suggests that the materials of process flit between dimensions, from 'ready-to-hand' objects, such as the pen while writing, and 'present-to-hand' equipment, such as the pen when it runs out of ink, to a more 'authentic' way of being, which modulates between the previous forms and exists in a state of permanent anticipation ('thrownness'), the example in this instance being the evolving manuscript itself during the process of writing. Bushell proposes that the latter exists as 'the displaced body or "textual self" of the writer, but also as an object existing through time and bearing witness to textual process and product' (p. 229). While Bushell, like any genetic critic, effectively undoes the traditionally subordinate status of the materials of process/manuscripts by treating them as objects worthy of study, we see here how it is possible to elevate their underlying ontological status.

Fordham also points out that 'the processes of writing and production have played scarcely any role at all' in phenomenological philosophy (2010, p. 60), but suggests that his own study of the textual genesis of selfhood poses a fundamental philosophical problem 'because the self that seeks knowledge', from Descartes to Heidegger, 'should be universal, whereas this idea argues that the form of the self is shaped by how a given culture relates to the modes of its symbolizing practices' (pp. 73–4). Whether philosophy *must* be universal, and hence anti-genetic, is not clear (is it not rather the case that classical philosophy, from ancient to present times, simply *has* aimed at universal truths?). In any case, individual writing processes (and particular 'symbolizing practices') undercut the universal concepts of being and selfhood found in traditional philosophical accounts, which have therefore tended to neglect 'the kind of room needed for particular accounts of formation due to some local and personal forms of experience' (2010, p. 59).[12]

It is worth noting that, whereas Bushell's 'Philosophy of Composition' concerns the *author's* experience (involving 'a movement into and out of self-awareness' (p. 231)), Fordham's comparative study of various modernist writers focuses on the particular writing processes themselves, 'for what they can say about the movements *within narratives* between conscious and unconscious, confederate and dissolute forms of selfhood [my italics]' (p. 25). Following on the latter point, it is also worth noting the increased pertinence of genetic criticism to modernist literature specifically (reflecting the way in which art/literature has itself changed over the last century or more). As Christine Froula suggests:

> The documents of a work's genesis only underscore what many a modernist experimental work already expresses: that the boundaries of its achieved form [. . .] are virtual, provisional, permeable by the evidences of its own history as by the known, unknown, and unknowable conditions of its making. (Froula, 1996, p. 114).

As we will see, the permeability of boundaries is echoed not only in Lawrence's narratives but also in his continual rewriting (and re-envisioning) of endings in particular.

Recent developments

More recently, genetic criticism has examined the ways in which writing processes provide not only a grounding for but also an *extension* of individual agency. Jean-Louis Lebrave and Denis Alamargot, for example, in their joint cognitive and genetic essay, suggest that writing processes form episodic memories: 'episodic memory stores events that are part of the writing process, and their reactivation probably plays a role in weaving the textual fabric' (p. 19). These memories can be reactivated externally through meta-discursive notes and, less consciously, through particular traces in the writing. The combination of text and memory enables a professional writer to sustain cognitive processes over long periods of time.

While Lebrave and Alamargot somewhat conservatively limit themselves to the observation that 'by serving as an external form of memory, the text produced so far can replace the author's own long-term memory', Bushell goes further, drawing on Maurice Merleau-Ponty's account of embodied cognition in *Phenomenology of Perception* (1945) to examine the ways in which 'the manuscript object might be understandably experienced as a kind of physical self-extension' (2009, p. 230). Bushell explores the permeable boundary between the embodied self and the material text through the writer's developing relationship with language, where 'the permanent present of the words is held in the material object but also constitutes a revisited and revisitable self for the writer' (pp. 230–1). The manuscript and the writing processes which it traces become a part of the writer's 'extended mind', and, like language, they serve as a mediator or leading edge for the writer's experiences.¹³

Van Hulle's recent work also draws explicitly on the post-cognitivist idea of the 'extended mind' – as well as Jakob von Uexküll's notion of an *umwelt*, which refers to an organism's internal model of the world – to argue that modern/ist manuscripts form an intrinsic part of the writer's extended mind. Van Hulle uses the analogy of a cane as used by a blind or visually impaired person (e.g. the blind piano tuner in Joyce's *Ulysses*) for how the writer uses a manuscript to navigate new linguistic environments.¹⁴ Van Hulle therefore questions the so-called inward turn associated with modernist literature and suggests that modernist manuscripts do not merely transcribe speech but rather form an integral part of cognition (functioning as an 'environmental vehicle' in the writer's own *umwelt* (2013, p. 229)).

As we will see in subsequent chapters, Lawrence frequently describes his own writing as something partly unconscious ('strange' or 'weird'): 'I am doing a novel which I have never grasped [. . .] it's like a novel in a foreign language I don't know very well – I can only just make out what it's about' (i. 543). The notion that writing facilitates the process of thinking is also suggested by Kinkead-Weekes's notion of 'exploratory imagination', while Worthen makes a similar point while observing the following in his biography of Lawrence:

> His writing, while liberating him from the tensions of his origins, was also a way of imagining (or dreaming) through his most disturbing experiences and so beginning to resolve them. He remarked in January 1912 how 'my dreams make conclusions for me. They decide things finally. I dream a decision. Sleep seems to hammer out for me the logical conclusions of my vague days, and offer me them as dreams' (i. 359). That was what his writing did, too. (2005, p. 83)

Here however we see a familiar teleological (and prescriptive) slant, which is also somewhat psychoanalytical ('liberating him from the tensions of his origins' and 'beginning to resolve them').

Aside from compiling an *avant-texte* or 'genetic dossier', genetic critics also divide the author's work into different phases: exogenetic (pre-compositional), endogenetic (compositional) and epigenetic (post-compositional), as in van Hulle's more recent book *Modern Manuscripts* (2013). These different phases vary in importance depending on the author or work being studied, although traditional genetic studies perhaps place a premium upon the first, which is another point of criticism for me and something which I will return to (after all, genetic criticism is supposed to be about writing processes themselves, i.e. the compositional phase). Genetic criticism also identifies two basic *methods* of writing: 'program writing' and 'process writing' (Hay, 2002). The former involves detailed planning on paper in 'a succession of preparatory phases', while the latter 'ignores programmed strategies and planning details' and 'consists of a succession of writing and revision phases until the author arrives at a stabilised manuscript' (Lebrave and Alamargot, 2010, pp. 14–15); Klaus Hurlebusch has offered a very similar distinction between 'constructive' and 'reproductive' writers, though Hurlebusch's terms highlight the fact that non-'program' writers (such as Lawrence) to some extent plan their work in their minds, and then 'reproduce' these ideas on paper. Grésillon similarly suggests that the most common metaphors for writing are either 'constructivist' or 'organicist', which draws roughly the same distinction, while, as Lebrave and Alamargot point out, there is also a parallel distinction in cognitive psychology between 'classical' and 'romantic' modes of writing.

These distinctions are non-binary, and the fact that 'process' writers may well plan in their minds helps explain why these distinctions are viewed not as pure opposites but as 'the opposite ends of a continuum' (Lebrave and Alamargot, 18).[15] However, to come back to my point about the focus in genetic criticism upon the exogenetic (pre-compositional) phase of writing, I would suggest that the paradigmatic writers traditionally studied by genetic critics are overwhelmingly drawn from the programme/constructive/constructivist side; to 'quite an extreme' extent, according to Hurlebusch (p. 78). The focus on 'exogenesis' is connected to the fact that the 'programme' type of writer produces a much greater quantity of pre-compositional material (notes, reading notes, plans, etc.).

Having laid out my main criticism of traditional Lawrence studies in terms of the common focus on 'final' texts and the teleological belief that these texts, like their author, 'matured' organically over time, I will now lay out more clearly my main criticism of traditional genetic criticism. As I have already suggested, the scientific status of French genetic criticism distracts from what should be its main focus, namely *criticism*: the interpretation and evaluation of manuscripts and writing processes (rather than their categorization only). I would also suggest that the richest vein of genetic criticism to date has heavily orientated itself around a particular *type* of writer, namely the 'programme' writer, someone who produces a large amount of paper planning and even explicitly views or approaches writing in a 'constructivist' manner. Two key examples are Flaubert and Joyce.

A major influence on Joyce himself (as well as on Henry James, Thomas Mann, Joseph Conrad, Marcel Proust, Ezra Pound, Samuel Beckett and doubtless many other major modernist writers, albeit with a clear male bias), Flaubert is heavily identified with the idea (or ideal) of self-conscious craftsmanship, the iconic reference point being the mot juste. As in Poe's 'Philosophy of Composition', which discusses the apparently reverse-engineered composition of his famous poem, 'The Raven', this involves a view of writing as a métier or profession, something trained and controlled, the result of an 'apprenticeship', not an inherited or inspired gift, and goes hand in hand with the historical rise of the 'professional' writer (Poe and Flaubert were both early professional writers). I adopt the term 'constructivist' to describe this type of writer/writing in this book because it is more obviously used as a metaphor and has the broadest connotations.

'Constructivist' metaphors – which fundamentally refer to the idea that something (i.e. a text) is *constructed*, fabricated, the result of self-conscious artifice – are hugely influential in the very modern (and postmodern) world. They have a strong connection to cities (the modern environment) – where the majority of writers dwell and where the entire landscape is literally constructed – as well as to the wider zeitgeist of post-romantic, self-conscious cynicism or irony, and are usually emphasized exclusively for their liberating potential (in opposition to essentialist ideas). Notions like sincerity and spontaneity are easily scoffed at or met with fear or suspicion in this context and some of Lawrence's hypothetical ideas (such as 'blood consciousness') seem intentionally exaggerated in order to challenge or even upset a modern sensibility. Such fear is partly a response to the worst ideological beliefs, where the underlying idea is that some things just *are* in essence (e.g. human races 'are' superior/inferior and humans 'are' a certain sexuality). However, it is easy to forget that the worst ideological crimes have been committed by *organized* states with *institutionalized* beliefs; that is, ultimately, by design. I would suggest that, whereas ideological beliefs (be they organic, class-based or any other category) are basically delusional – and any delusion is potentially dangerous – design is a credible and often extremely useful principle, yet it has a radically more dangerous potential (a nuclear weapon is clearly the result of design, less clearly the result of ideology or delusion).[16] This is partly why I find Bertrand Russell's infamous slur about Lawrence and fascism – in his autobiography, published after Lawrence's death – frustrating: while Russell was a philosopher and co-authored a bible of classical logic (*Principia Mathematica* (1910–13)), most of Lawrence's ideas are opposed to control.[17] Besides providing a critique of wilfulness throughout his work, Lawrence responds specifically to Flaubertian craftsmanship in an early review of Thomas Mann (1913), which draws out the connection between constructivism and the desire for mastery (I discuss this review in more detail in

Chapter 4); Lawrence also goes much further by identifying the aesthetic desire for mastery with a wider social desire for control, present in Germany at the time (on the eve of the First World War).[18] By studying an avowedly non-constructivist writer in detail, this book therefore aims to provide some balance.[19]

However, the apparent alternative to constructivism, which Grésillon defines as *organicism*, is problematic in other ways. Lawrence's less controlling approach to writing is not simply a reflection of a belief that things should to some extent grow unselfconsciously. The key issue with control for Lawrence is that it binds the self to itself, to the ego (the extreme consequence of which is delusion). The key for Lawrence was to remain open to external forces, to the unknown, but also, less mystically and above all else, to *otherness* (other people, other animals, other places). Both constructivist and organicist metaphors, taken as a whole, perhaps suggest a single, monistic process or self. I therefore set out genetic *dialogism*, which involves an exchange between self and other (or multiple selves), as an alternative metaphor for writing, based on Lawrence's writing processes, and in opposition to both constructivism and organicism.

As I have so far criticized traditional approaches to studying Lawrence, before I move on to consider Lawrence's manuscripts, it is important to mention some recent developments within Lawrence studies which do make a form of inroad for genetic criticism.[20] In *D. H. Lawrence and 'Difference'* (2003), for example, Amit Chaudhuri offers a critique of traditional approaches to Lawrence's poetry and, instead, situates individual poems within a larger, intertextual poetic discourse where different cultural values can be affirmed:

> It seemed that to 'lift' single masterpieces, or 'finished' works, from this discourse, in order to preserve them by either anthologizing them or studying them (in effect, reading them), and to take the occurrence of the often unwieldy, repetitive, and overwritten discourse in which they were located as redundant or unfortunate, would be to rob those poems of a certain dimension of meaning, and, indeed, to elide the significance that Lawrence himself assigned to such a discourse. Was there a way, then, in which the redundancy and 'unfinishedness' of this discourse could be addressed positively, in a reading that had other values to affirm than ambiguity, meaning, felicity of expression, and complexity of treatment and subject matter? (p. 2)

Chaudhuri suggests Lawrence's poetic discourse, like the non-logocentric language of Derrida's 'grammatology', 'disrupts the centrality of the image, its chronological "development", and destroys frames around individual poems' (p. 5). Emphasizing Lawrence's unusual working-class origins, Chaudhuri argues that Lawrence's resistance to the centralizing and monopolistic trends of

Western aesthetic culture is a form of post-coloniality and cultural 'difference', and suggests that there are parallels between this critique of Anglo-American reading practices and 'Lawrence's own critique of Western assumptions about "primitivism"' (p. 115).

Interestingly, Chaudhuri also likens the traditional praise of Lawrence's poetic genius to 'the admiration of the "civilized" man for the savage [. . .] thrilling to his spontaneity and oneness with life [. . .] in a manner remarkably similar to Orientalist scholarship', where 'Lawrence's "difference" is held to be somehow mysteriously fixed and essential' and thus 'no attempt is made to work towards a critical language that could address and describe that difference' (pp. 115–16). This book follows Chaudhuri's lead by working towards a critical language that can address and describe Lawrence's writing processes, including their difference from the 'constructivist' patterns more commonly described in modernist literature. However, Chaudhuri's contrasting intertextual approach is open to the aforementioned criticism of a potentially endless chain of inter-texts, some of which offer radically different and even contradictory readings. The entire chain of texts (in an intertextual reading) could also be seen as representing one gigantic static text. Although the resulting 'mega text' may be plugged into an endless series of other discursive formations, including those formed by each new, 'participatory' reader, the discursive totality is itself as restrictive as it is liberating. The absence of time, a linear temporal dimension, also leads to paradoxical consequences. Chaudhuri suggests, for example, that Lawrence's early poem 'End of Another Home-Holiday' is 'haunted by and *reminiscent of* a late poem, "Bavarian Gentians"', and 'what we seem to witness is the early poem's amnesiac evasion of the theme of the later work' (p. 27).

Another more recent critic, for whom the temporal dimension is central, and who actually looks at instances of *revision*, is N. H. Reeve, each of whose commentaries in *Reading Late Lawrence* (2003) 'has been prompted by a particular piece of revision, one which seems to me to reveal something of the textual impulse both in Lawrence's original conception and in its subsequent development' (p. ix). As we can see in the following summary, Reeve focuses on types of revision which exemplify what Ferrer labels 'retroaction' and 'persistence':

> I am interested in the phantom imprints, as it were, left by Lawrence's first thoughts upon the thoughts that replace them. I am also interested in watching for signs of this across and between works as well as within one work, given that virtually everything Lawrence wrote, especially in his later years, was a form of reengagement with something he had already written. (2003)

However, unlike Chaudhuri, Reeve does not suggest that his work offers any innovation to existing traditions and he does not therefore offer a critique of previous approaches to the study of Lawrence's revision, nor does he discuss the ideas behind his own approach in any great detail. It is also important to note that *Reading Late Lawrence* is not a study of manuscripts: the book predominantly focuses on previously published versions of works, especially *Lady Chatterley's Lover*, early versions of which were first published in the 1940s.

Though Reeve does point to recent interest in Bakhtin and dialogism as conducive to a critical climate in which Lawrence 'could come to be read more for the processes than for the outcomes or ostensible messages of his writing' (p. ix), his own readings are essentially psychoanalytic, often focusing on Lawrence the man.[21] As Reeve explains, he is interested in the provisional elements in Lawrence's writing for 'the signals they send out of something more vulnerable, less confident, more psychologically defensive' in the author, with the suggestion that there is an effort 'to face up to the persistent survival in him of feelings that ought, in theory, to have been long superseded' (p. x). Reeve suggests his haunted readings are mainly owing to the late stage of Lawrence's career which he looks at, but I would suggest their implicit genetic dimension is also a factor. Take, for example, the following question, which Reeve poses in response to a question called out by a character in Lawrence's story 'Glad Ghosts':

> When Lady Lathkill calls out, 'Are you here, Lucy?', is it not possible to hear [. . .] the defiant, even rather majestic pathos of one for whom the world is momentarily enriched by the echoes of the past vibrating in it? (p. 121)

Reeve focuses on the biographical resonance of this passage: Lawrence's children-in-law had recently re-entered his and Frieda's lives (Frieda had been denied access to the children after leaving her first husband). However, there is also an implicit genetic dimension to Reave's question here ('the past vibrating in it'), which a genetic study might draw out.

Other critics who have recently made indirect use of Lawrence's writing processes include Russell McDonald, who does so in order to reassess Lawrence's collaborations with women in the context of modernism and feminist criticism. Taking issue with Hilary Simpson's notion of Lawrence as a 'literary trespasser' (set out in *D. H. Lawrence and Feminism*), McDonald demonstrates that there is 'superb textual evidence' of how Lawrence used collaboration to 'install real gendered conflict' in his work (2010, p. 22). Elsewhere, Violeta Sotirova outlines the relevance of a dialogical, intersubjective model of language and of self for Lawrence – where 'freezing personality in a stale form is antithetical to human essence' (2012, pp. 5–6) – and uses a mixture of statistical analysis and evidence from the manuscripts – comparing *The Trespasser* and *Sons and Lovers* – to argue that Lawrence *intentionally* developed dialogical stylistic features during this pivotal phase in his career. While novel in its purpose, we see how Sotirova approaches Lawrence's manuscripts in a familiarly teleological and constructivist (or intentionalist) manner; there are strong echoes of traditional Lawrence manuscript studies, and Sotirova explicitly supports a chronology of Lawrence's 'progress to maturity' set out by Keith Sagar in the 1960s.

Despite recent developments, then, manuscripts and writing processes (in particular) remain subsidiary subjects within Lawrence studies. This book represents the first dedicated genetic study of Lawrence. As we look 'behind the scenes' at 'Odour of Chrysanthemums', *Women in Love* and *The Plumed Serpent*, we will gain a clear picture of just how complex and multifarious Lawrence's writing processes are: how Lawrence frequently rewrote entire drafts, and produced original, rough drafts with the express intention of doing so (a form of preparation for subsequent work); how the tension between the flux of writing and the static nature of the finished text grounds a central thematic opposition between flux and stasis, incompletion and completion, the present and the past, life and death; how a common stylistic and narrative counterpoint between descriptive rest and dialogic strain are echoed in the rhythms of revision; and how perhaps the greatest writerly dilemma for Lawrence was how to write an ending.

Notes

1 For a recent survey of genetic criticism, see Cislaru (2015).
2 This irony has been observed by many critics before (including Greetham, 1989, Groden, 1991, and Cohen and Jackson, 1991).
3 Gabriel Egan's *The Struggle for Shakespeare's Text* (2010) provides a recent overview of Anglo-American editorial theory and practice.
4 See *Devils and Angels: Textual Editing and Literary Theory* (ed. Cohen, 1991) and *Palimpsest: Editorial Theory in the Humanities* (ed. Bornstein and Williams, 1993), in particular.
5 On the debate between Eliot and Murry, see Goldie (1998); on Lewis and Tillyard, see Bruce L. Edwards's 'Introduction' in Heck (2008).
6 For a more detailed discussion of the synoptic mode of editing, see Elisabeth Hopker-Herberg, 'Reflections on the Synoptic Mode of Presenting Variants, with an Example from Klopstock's *Messias*' (Bornstein, Pierce and Gabler, 1991).

7 Aldous Huxley, for example, suggested 'it was characteristic of [Lawrence] that he hardly ever corrected or patched what he had written. [. . .] In other words, he gave the *daimon* another chance to say what it wanted to say' (1932, p. xvii).

8 Andrew Harrison does reflect on the publication and material history of *Sons and Lovers* in 'Dust-jackets, blurbs and forewords: the marketing of *Sons and Lovers*' (Booth, 2009).

9 The quotation is from Littlewood's book *D. H. Lawrence, I: 1885-1914* (1976), which is based on articles published in *The Cambridge Quarterly* in the 1960s, at least one of which predates Kinkead-Weekes's essay (see Littlewood, 1965 and 1969).

10 Louis Hay deconstructs this notion of 'the text' in his essay 'What is the Text?' (1988).

11 Daniel Ferrer discusses these topics in 'Clementis's Cap: Retroaction and Persistence in the Genetic Process' (1996) and 'Variant and Variation: Toward a Freudo-bathmologico-Bakhtino-Goodmanian Genetic Model?' (2009). N. H. Reeve has also provided a Lawrentian example of this in the three Lady Chatterley novels (see *Reading Late Lawrence* (2003), Chapter 4, 'Parkin's Wedding Photograph').

12 In contrast, in his comparative study of modernist texts, Fordham aims to remain 'alive to the fugitive movements within processes rather than favouring and making an aesthetic principle out of any one state' (p. 25).

13 See Andy Clark and David J. Chalmers's essay 'The Extended Mind' (1998) as well as Richard Menary's edited collection of the same title (2010).

14 See Stewart et al.'s (eds) *Enaction: Toward a New Paradigm for Cognitive Science* (2011) and Jakob von Uexküll's *A Foray into the Worlds of Animals and Humans* with *A Theory of Meaning* (2010).

15 As Daniel Ferrer explains, all writing in some way anticipates and/or projects its completion, hence 'process writing appears to be a particular case, or minimal form, of programmatic writing', while, at the same time, as the 'project' or 'intention' always to some extent 'shapes up along the way, in the course of the elaboration of the work', program writing likewise 'becomes a special case of process writing' (1996, pp. 225–7).

16 In a modernist context, consider the respective impact of control and delusion in Conrad's *The Secret Agent* (1907), where a 'fully cognizant' adult tricks a young person with learning difficulties into committing a (failed) terrorist atrocity.

17 'He had developed the whole philosophy of fascism' and 'his mystical philosophy of "blood" [. . .] led straight to Auschwitz' (1953; 1968, II, pp. 21–3), quotations which should not be read without at least some context: Russell, son of the Viscount and Viscountess of Amberley, was so affected by his personal acquaintance with Lawrence, son of a collier and pupil teacher, that he confessed to being suicidal when Lawrence broke off their short-lived friendship.

18 Michael Black also discusses Lawrence's opposition to Flaubert in 'Revision and Spontaneity as Aesthetic' (1999), although the essay does not present genetic examples.
19 Lebrave and Alamargot acknowledge process/romantic writing as an 'under-researched' topic (p. 18).
20 I have provided a short, general overview of Lawrence studies in the book's Introduction.
21 Paul Eggert (ed.) discusses dialogism in the introduction to *D. H. Lawrence and Comedy* (1996).

Part Two

'Odour of Chrysanthemums' (1909–14)

2

Setting the scene

A 'mature' text?

We now reach the primary chapters of this book, which re-evaluate some of Lawrence's major works of fiction on the basis of original genetic study. While subsequent chapters focus on two long novels dating from the early to middle and middle to late stages in Lawrence's career, the present chapter makes an initial foray into Lawrence's writing processes by looking at an example of short fiction dating from the early stage of his career, in the form of the short story 'Odour of Chrysanthemums'.

This choice is not incidental. In December 1909, when Lawrence was just twenty-four years of age, an early version of the story was accepted by Ford Maddox Ford (*né* Ford Hermann Hueffer) for publication in *The English Review*, along with another short story entitled 'Goose Fair', which helped launch Lawrence's career.[1] Founded the previous year, *The English Review* published some of the leading writers of its day, including major influences on Lawrence, like Thomas Hardy, Joseph Conrad and H. G. Wells. Though 'Odour of Chrysanthemums' did not publish in the journal until June 1911, under new editorship (Austin Harrison) and following heavy revisions, it stimulated the publisher Martin Secker to offer Lawrence the chance to publish a book of short stories. It also formed a major part of the traditional narrative in Lawrence studies of the author's so-called progress to maturity, which I challenge. Finally, Lawrence also rewrote the story's ending at every opportunity, which is symptomatic of his general struggle to write an ending; not, I argue, due to a failure of imagination, but because of a resistance to closure and stasis.

The story has been widely studied and praised, with many critics focusing on its rich textual history, which includes its dramatization by Lawrence into the play *The Widowing of Mrs Holroyd*, written and published during the same overall time frame ('Odour' was revised over several years, from 1909 to 1914). I will discuss the story's reception in more detail later, but one important thing to note is that previous critics have focused almost exclusively on the story's closing section and have focused their praise on the final version of that ending. This chapter effectively does the opposite: I find the main body of the story, in the early versions, to be of greater merit and I reserve some criticism for Lawrence's later edits, which detract from the story's central drama and are arguably motivated by external factors.

Though Lawrence's novels often overshadow his short fiction, the stories have had their own admirers from the start, particularly 'Odour of Chrysanthemums'. Ford Madox Ford famously claims to have accepted 'Odour' in December 1909 and declared Lawrence a 'genius' after reading just the opening page (quoted in Nehls, 1957, p. 107). Despite titling his renowned study *D. H. Lawrence: Novelist*, F. R. Leavis also suggests that 'of the shorter forms of prose fiction – short story and longer tale – Lawrence is surely the supreme master. His genius manifests itself there with an authority of original power, and an astonishing maturity, from the start' (p. 77). According to Con Coroneos and Trudi Tate, Leavis's discussion of Lawrence's stories 'remains one of the finest accounts of Lawrence's tales' (2001, p. 104), but it is important to emphasize Leavis's reference to 'maturity'. While Keith Cushman and Victor Schulz also label 'Odour' a 'masterpiece of short fiction', as I demonstrate later in the text, these and other critics essentially champion the *final version* of the story, which emerged following heavy revisions from 1910 to 1914, while also placing the revisions in a *biographical* context, as evidence of Lawrence's own 'progress to maturity'.[2]

Writing before Cushman and Schulz, in an essay on 'Lawrence's Early Tales', J. C. F. Littlewood concurs with Leavis's suggestion that Lawrence first achieved artistic 'maturity' in his short fiction, but refines the argument by suggesting that it was Lawrence's revisions of 1914 that constituted the 'breakthrough' moment. Littlewood fleshes out this point by comparing a handful of early and late versions of scenes from stories in the *Prussian Officer* collection and using *The Rainbow* as a high-tide marker of Lawrence's artistic maturity. On 'Odour of Chrysanthemums', while conceding that the first published version of 1911 contains 'the vivid, first-hand portrayal of the miner's world', Littlewood suggests that, in the 'last few pages', the story 'collapses into an unfelt conclusion of weak moralising-cum-psychologising' (1965, p. 120). By contrast, Littlewood suggests that 'the grafting on of the new ending [in 1914] seems entirely successful' (note the external connotations in the term 'grafting') and, in a typically teleological reading of the story's genesis, that 'comparison of the two versions makes the reader feel that in the second the author discovered the meaning that had always been waiting to be found in the story' (p. 123). Like the critics who come after him, Littlewood's analysis focuses on the story's ending, in which its protagonist, Elizabeth Bates, confronts the dead body of her husband, Walter, who is carried home at night having suffered a fatal accident at work in the local colliery. According to Littlewood, Elizabeth's new 'intuition of the "other" reality of the other person' in the 1914 climax unifies the story and is 'of the essence of Lawrence, and in the central line of his development', repeating an insight 'first realised [by Lawrence] in the Tom Brangwen part of *The Rainbow*' (pp. 123–4).

James T. Boulton deploys a very similar argument when discussing the cuts made by Lawrence in 1910 and 1911, in preparation for the story's publication in the June 1911 edition of *The English Review*:

> The focus of the writer's attention has notably shifted from the beginning to the end; from, that is, the evolving situation in the Bates's house in which the circumstantial details of the mother and children awaiting Bates's return are central, to the adult emotions associated with the preparation of the dead man's body for burial. Lawrence's relative immaturity in the story printed here is manifest; the revisions recorded in the textual apparatus equally testify to his growth in self-criticism. (1969, p. 8)

While Boulton is unique in suggesting that 'maternal love' (p. 11) serves as a unifying principle for the story, rather than the perception of otherness, which Littlewood and other critics focus on, Boulton here praises the writer's apparent maturity in switching the focus from the 'circumstantial details' at home, in the early versions, to the 'adult emotions' of the later versions, experienced while the wife and mother confront the body.

In probably the most detailed study of the story, which he describes as 'a moving statement about the human condition' (1978, p. 47), Keith Cushman likewise focuses on the concluding section, rather pessimistically arguing that Elizabeth's response to her husband's body provides 'a lesson in human isolation' and a 'revelation of our irredeemable loneliness' (p. 69).[3] Like Littlewood, Boulton and others, Cushman reads Lawrence's revisions in a teleological way and places them in an almost exclusively biographical context:

> the successive versions are one of the best available mirrors of [Lawrence's] artistic and emotional growth during his first years as a writer [...] the successive revisions of the original story – in connection with Lawrence's biography – allow

us to date with some precision the moment a central Lawrentian belief assumed its mature form. The culmination of the story is one of the starting points for the Lawrence of *The Rainbow, Women in Love*, and the 1920s. (p. 76)

Pushing the biographical lens to something of an extreme, however, Cushman also suggests that 'Mrs. Bates's reverie in successive versions of the tale is conditioned by Lawrence's own feelings about his parents as he grew older' (p. 69). Likewise, having eloped with and married Frieda Weekley in the meantime, in the final 1914 version of the story Lawrence was apparently able to pass 'beyond the personal question of his mother and father to express an insight into man's fate' (p. 69).

Rounding off this trend, in the Cambridge edition of *The Prussian Officer and Other Stories* (1987), John Worthen suggests that 'Lawrence's short stories allow us to see him revising, transforming and frequently transcending his early work' and that 'the history of the stories [. . .] is also the history of Lawrence's remarkable development as a writer between 1907 and 1914' (p. xix). Likewise, in *The Vicar's Garden and Other Stories* (2009), a more recent Cambridge edition of early and draft versions of many of the same stories, including 'Odour', N. H. Reeve echoes Worthen by suggesting that 'this volume demonstrates, as no other brief collection of Lawrence's work could, [Lawrence's] extraordinary development as a writer of fiction between 1907 and 1914, and his growing mastery of the short story form' (p. xvii).

Before moving on to examine the story's actual genesis and offer a counter interpretation of its development, it is worth highlighting Howard J. Booth's general criticism of the traditional focus on 'maturity' by critics of Lawrence's early writing processes:

> Critics have not questioned sufficiently the model for interpreting the early life and work that Lawrence himself first laid down. Heavily teleological, the claim is that a 'real' Lawrence emerged [. . .]. This narrative is organised around a breakthrough, or series of breakthroughs, that allowed the 'mature' Lawrence to emerge [. . .]. An 'advance' in terms of relationships is linked to a breakthrough in writing, where an outdated interest in late nineteenth-century forms of writing gives way to a more modern writing-style. (2011, p. 37)

Though he does not focus on Lawrence's actual writing processes, Booth challenges this influential narrative by considering the early versions of Lawrence's stories on their own terms and for their own merit (rather than as bridges to an inevitable final version which surpasses them). It is also worth pointing out that, from a genetic point of view, traditional critics essentially read Lawrence's early stories *backwards*. Emphasizing an apparent absence of maturity and suggesting that this lack is later filled in (in this case by cutting early passages and rewriting the story's conclusion), critics overlook the ways in which this perceived absence is a projection on their own part, arising from a prior knowledge of the final, 'mature' version of the text, which influences their subsequent (and retrospective) reading of the earlier version.

Compositional history and alternative versions

The story's compositional history officially begins on 9 December 1909, the date on which Lawrence sent an early version to *The English Review*, though it was most likely written the previous month (see i. 147).[4] Page proofs for this version were prepared by 10 March 1910, and Lawrence revised these proofs on more than one occasion between that date and April 1911. During this time, Lawrence rewrote the ending twice and, following a request by Harrison to cut 'five pages' (i. 172), he also removed a substantial amount of material from the early parts of the story (discussed later). Lawrence began revising the story again in July 1914 when working on proofs for *The Prussian Officer and Other Stories*, extensively rewriting the ending again, before making a final set of revisions in October 1914, during which the story's ending was revised once more.

With references provided to Roberts and Poplawski's bibliography of Lawrence, as well as the two aforementioned Cambridge editions, the story's extant materials can be divided into *five* levels (though each document may contain multiple versions due to revision):

(1) A six-page holograph fragment forming the conclusion to an early version of the story (Roberts E284a), published as 'Appendix I' in *PO* (pp. 201–5) and later labelled 'Version One' by Reeve in *VG*

(2) Corrected proof sheets for *The English Review* numbering twenty-seven pages, with a further eight pages of holograph corrections and insertions (Roberts E284c), published in *VG* in two forms: the pre-revision text as 'Version Two' (pp. 75–99) and the post-revision text as 'Version Three' (pp. 101–21)

(3) A thirty-nine-page fair copy of the heavily revised *English Review* proofs, completed by Louie Burrows in April 1911 (Roberts E284b) and containing hundreds of errors and alterations which Lawrence subsequently adopted and revised, and which forms part of the textual apparatus in *PO*

(4) The corrected page proofs of *PO* (Roberts E326.6), which contains the July 1914 version of the ending, the latter published as an 'Appendix' in *VG* (pp. 211–16) where it is labelled 'Version Four'
(5) The first edition of *PO* (Roberts A6a), containing subsequent revisions completed in October 1914 (labelled 'Version Five')

As I discuss again in later chapters, the neat labelling of each manuscript as a particular 'version' by the Cambridge Edition adds to the misleading idea that alternative versions of Lawrence's work stemmed from 'separate processes of creation' (1987, p. xxv), a term L. D. Clark uses to describe the relationship between the different versions of *The Plumed Serpent* and *Lady Chatterley's Lover*. In fact, there is a high degree of continuity between alternative versions, and Lawrence tended to rely directly upon earlier drafts while rewriting: some sections are revised and rewritten (often multiple times), while others remain intact. As we will see, Lawrence certainly cut and condensed sections in the early parts of 'Odour of Chrysanthemums' when revising the story between 1910 and 1911, and yet, despite these alterations, much of the opening four-fifths of the story remain unchanged throughout all the phases of revision. Likewise, though Lawrence rewrote the story's ending at least half a dozen times between 1909 and 1914 (*The English Review* page proofs alone contain three different versions of the ending), there are still matching points where the story's ending can be 'tagged together' across alternative versions.

In the rest of this chapter, I provide references to the Cambridge Edition, where transcriptions of each manuscript have been published (as outlined earlier).[5] As a rough guide, allusions to *VG* refer to earlier drafts (1910–11) whereas *PO* refers to the later versions (July and October 1914).

Networks and emotions in the 'immature' early sections

While critics have reserved special praise for the existential climax to 'Odour of Chrysanthemums', the main section of the story is generally regarded as a conventional realist depiction of domestic colliery life, albeit meticulously crafted and containing subtle symbolism. The opening paragraph, for example, provides a deft account of the spread of industrialization: the fields are 'dreary and forsaken', 'flames like red sores' rise from the 'ashy' sides of a nearby pit bank and a 'small locomotive engine, Number 4' appears in the opening line and comes 'clanking, stumbling' down the line with 'slow inevitable movement'; nevertheless, a colt, which the train startles from some gorse beside the track, is still able to outdistance the engine 'at a canter' (*VG* p. 77). Similarly, chrysanthemums are seen as symbolizing the Bates's marriage: at the start of the story, Annie is impressed by a chrysanthemum tucked in Elizabeth's apron band, and the mother explains (in lines which go virtually unrevised): 'it was chrysanthemums when I married him, and chrysanthemums when you were born, and the first time they ever brought him home drunk he'd got brown chrysanthemums in his ~~coat~~button-hole' (*VG* p. 84; *PO* p. 186); when the men carry Walter's body into the parlour at the end of the story, a vase of chrysanthemums is also knocked onto the floor and smashes.[6] Generally though, critics pass fairly quickly over the early sections (and in fact the majority) of the story and praise Lawrence's cuts in revision. Boulton describes the activities at home as 'circumstantial detail' (as mentioned earlier); Mara Kalnins suggests Lawrence pared away 'superfluous detail in the early part of the tale' (p. 472); while Cushman suggests 'the detail is lovely, but it distracts from the central situation' (p. 57).

In opposition to this consensus, if we ignore the final version of the story and consider the internal logic of these early 'details' – even down to the level of syntax, which is often more complex in the early (1910) version – we notice that the story's primary drama involves the emotional dynamics at home, as Elizabeth and her two young children, Annie and John, await the arrival of the husband and father, Walter, a coalminer, whose physical absence and increasingly overdue return from work creates and increases the tension as the story unfolds. Walter's apparent absence is a big negative presence in the narrative, and we begin to notice how, in the early parts of the story, Lawrence establishes a whole network of objects which emphasize this ambiguous boundary between absence and presence (including the boundary between inner and outer and public and private spaces).

The first example of the latter is the railway lines themselves. These are alluded to several times, and we are told they stretch 'down from Selston' and 'up [...] to Underwood' (*VG* p. 77). The railway lines provide a network for local activities, trafficking miners between neighbouring towns and the pits, where Walter works. The tracks provide Elizabeth with status updates on the local activities, and she 'reads' them in this way on more than one occasion, for example to see when the last group of workers have left the pits. The tracks are also overwhelmingly close to home: the Bates's 'small cottage' is 'squat beside the great bay of railway-lines', there are steps leading directly down 'from the cinder-track to the threshold of the house', and these steps are actually made out of 'old sleepers' (*VG* p. 77; i.e. physical components from the track). The Bates family's intimate connection with the lines is also indicated when a second engine comes to a halt 'opposite the gate' and is driven by Elizabeth's father, who leans down from the driver's seat to receive a cup of tea from the door. In the ensuing dialogue, the father tells a tale of Walter bragging in a local pub the previous Saturday. While gossip is itself a form of *network*, which renders absence present, it is also a famously *unreliable* form of information (telling us as much about the teller) and this draws our attention to the fact that other signals may also be false; later, when the last train passes without bringing Walter home, Elizabeth falsely assumes that he has gone to the pub, for example. Other entanglements around the cottage include a 'large bony vine', which scrambles over the roof 'as if trying to claw [it] down', and 'a tree-hidden brook course' at the bottom of the garden (*VG* p. 78).

Chrysanthemums also feature in the story's ambiguous network of absent presence. Besides their symbolic connection to the Bates's marriage, which Elizabeth outlines to her daughter, the story's title suggests that the flowers are symbolic in a more 'meta' sense, yet they also appear as ordinary objects within the narrative itself, which hints at the ambiguous relationship between words and things: the flowers are simultaneously linguistic (symbolic), imaginary (memorial) and real (contingent, physical objects). 'Dishevelled pink chrysanthemums' (*VG* p. 78) are spotted growing in the back garden when Elizabeth goes to fetch John at the start, the flowers then follow the pair towards the house as John picks and scatters them along the garden path, while Elizabeth also deposits some 'into her apron band' (p. 79), thus taking them inside, where Annie later spots and comments on them. This *material* connection between past and present is echoed elsewhere in the early parts of the story. For example, John's clothes, 'too thick and hard', were 'evidently cut down from a man's clothes' (*VG* p. 78), which not only indicate the family's working-class status (the old clothes are recycled) but also remind us of the absent father, presumably their original owner. The father is also evoked in the boy himself later on when Elizabeth reflects on her son as an amalgamation of his parents: 'very much like herself', but with 'his father's brutality' (p. 81).

The children also make use of a variety of objects, including clothes, as part of their games, which, in the early version, are again highly charged reminders of the absent father. Before dinner, John sits carving a piece of wood into the shape of a tram, or 'little truck such as is used down pit' (*VG* p. 81), while, after dinner, the children first play a game called 'gipsies', where John uses 'a pair of the father's stockings' (*VG* p. 85) as an imaginary dinner item, then they play at 'pit', where John lies under the sofa 'on his side as his father had taught him' and pretends to hack at a coal face while Annie drags up 'a little box on wheels', as though 'loading a wagon' (*VG* pp. 85–6). If you re-read the story, it is hard not to be struck by the sad juxtaposition of the children impersonating their father by 'playing at pit' and recreating an imaginary coalface in their living room, when all the while Walter lies dying or dead in a real one.

Before moving on to look at the ways in which Lawrence revised the story, another key dramatic element is the intense emotional sensitivity of the female characters, particularly Elizabeth. While the children play at 'pit', the mother sits 'all this time' making a singlet for her husband, and we are told 'her anger wearied itself of pacing backwards and forwards like an impotent caged creature' (*VG* p. 86). The strain of waiting becomes increasingly unbearable, but Elizabeth's intense emotional life blurs distinctions between inner and outer activity as her feelings effectively mirror the threading of the needle ('pacing backwards and forwards') as she makes a new piece of clothing; as we will shortly see, emotions are frequently caricatured as physical creatures in the story. Once Annie arrives home in the early part of the story, the family are whole except for Walter, whom they initially wait for to begin dinner. His prolonged absence suggests either insult or neglect, and the tension increases: 'the mother let loose, now, the silent anger and bitterness that coiled within her. She said little, but there was the grip of "trouble", like the tentacle of an octopus, round the hearts of the children' (*VG* p. 82). The three decide to eat dinner alone and, like the children's games and the mother's sewing, laying and clearing the table, the activity provides some respite: 'actively engaged she could endure, but as she sat still her fury seemed to sway like fighting imps within her, and to break out of her control' (p. 85). Annie is also very sensitive to her mother's feelings and begins 'almost feverishly chattering', as 'anything was better than the clouds of silence that would settle on them' (p. 85). She then suggests playing games with her brother, feeling 'almost unequal to the struggle with the pressure of the trouble' and 'in childish dread of abnormal states, in terror of an approaching climax, she forced herself to play' (p. 85); this sense of 'an approaching climax' is key and I will return to it at the end. Later, while Elizabeth reads the children a bedtime story, Walter still having not returned, silence itself becomes a menace: as a noise outside interrupts the reading, 'the old silence woke up' and 'bristled in the room, till two people had gone by outside' (p. 86).

Like the networked objects discussed previously, the female characters' keen sensitivity adds to the drama of expectation, and the two layers are often interwoven, with Elizabeth's emotional life driving her to look for signs of a climax. Elizabeth gazes obsessively at the clock and provides a running commentary on the agonizing passage of time throughout by deciphering this and other signals, like the lighting of the 'yellow lamps [. . .] along the highway' and the traffic of the miners: 'the men trooping home, fewer now, and fewer' (*VG* p. 81).

Economic cuts

How did Lawrence's cuts and revisions for publication in *The English Review* affect the story's central drama, as outlined earlier? One of the most dramatic changes is the complete removal of the children's games, as Lawrence replaces a detailed description of their activities with the following short passage:

> While, for an hour or more, the children played subduedly, intent, fertile of invention, united in fear of their mother's wrath and in dread of their father's homecoming, Mrs Bates sat in her rocking-chair making a 'singlet'. (*VG* p. 109)

Here, there is no connection between the children's games and the absent father, while John's identification with his father and Annie's emotional sensitivity towards her mother are blunted: the children are 'united in fear' and 'dread' of their parents. This change marks a pattern in Lawrence's edits from 1910 to 1911, as he worked to accommodate the substantial cuts requested by Austin Harrison for publication.[7]

Consider the following passage in the revised 1911 text, as the children are taken up to bed:

> The children had their hands and faces wiped with the flannel. They were very quiet. When they had put on their nightdresses, they said their prayers, the boy mumbling. The mother looked down at them, at the brown silken bush of intertwining curls in the nape of the girl's neck, at the little black head of the boy, and her heart burst with anger, at the father, who caused all three such distress. The children hid their faces in her skirts, for comfort. (*VG* pp. 109–10)

This fairly dense descriptive passage makes use of parataxis, which enacts the narrative tension in the accumulative flow of syntax. Some of the details are ornate and slow the reader down, like 'the brown silken bush of intertwining curls in the nape of the girl's neck', but the plurality of details, like the commas and the syntactic rhythm, which switches between long and short sentences, encourages the reader along and helps intimate the blind dependency between the children and their mother. However, compared to some of the foregoing passages, the mother's 'burst with anger' is quite restrained, restricted to her 'heart', while she is quite able to apportion blame to the father, 'who caused all three such distress'.

Now compare the aforementioned passage with the earlier version of the same passage in the 1910 text:

> The children had their hands and faces wiped with the flannel, and were undressed on the hearthrug. They were very quiet. When they had put on their nightdresses, they kneeled down, and the girl hid her face in her mother's lap, and the boy put his face in his mother's skirt at the side, and they said their prayers, the boy mumbling. She looked down at them, at the brown silken bush of intertwining curls in the nape of the girl's neck, and the little black head of the boy, and in front of her eyes shone love and pity, and close behind pity stood anger, with shadowy hate, like a phantom, and scorn, glittering and dangerous; all these on the darkened stage of the mother's soul, with pity and love in front. The children hid their faces in her skirts, and were full of comfort and safety, and they prayed to her, for she was the God of their prayers. Then she lighted the candle and took them to bed. (*VG* p. 87)

The syntactic features highlighted earlier (long and short sentences, plural details, parataxis) are much more pronounced in this earlier version, and they in turn heighten the drama of the narrative. The specific units of text that were subsequently removed by Lawrence also increase the sense of dependency between the mother and children, which is more intense in the earlier version: the children press their faces against the mother and pray 'to her, for she was the God of their prayers'. Likewise, the absent father is not alluded to in the earlier version and remains instead a more keenly *absent* presence. This places more emphasis on the mother's emotions, which are themselves more volatile: 'close behind pity stood anger, with shadowy hate, like a phantom, and scorn, glittering and dangerous'. There is also a psychoanalytic overtone in the earlier version, as the mother's soul is characterized as a 'darkened stage', with 'shadowy hate' lingering 'close behind' and 'pity and love in front', and the reference to a 'phantom' suggests not only the mother's 'shadowy hate' but also the shadowy figure of the husband.

My argument then is that, driven by Harrison's economic request for cuts, Lawrence polished away some of the tension and volatility of the early version and in doing so produced a less dramatic (and perhaps more conventional) realist text, with an existential climax later attached to the end. Consider the earlier (1910) version of the following passage, which follows immediately after the above extract, as Elizabeth goes downstairs after putting the children to bed:

> When she came down, the room was strangely empty, with a tension of expectancy. The mother took up her sewing and stitched for some time without raising her head. Meantime her anger was accumulating. She broke the spell sharply at last, and looked up. It was ten minutes to eight. She sat staring at the pudding in the fender, and at the saucepan to the inside of which bits of dried potato were sticking. Then, for the first time, fear arrived in the room, and stood foremost. The expression on her face changed, and she sat thinking acutely. (*VG* 87)

The same syntactic features, along with an abundance of present participles ('sewing', 'raising', 'accumulating', 'staring', 'sticking', 'thinking'), help the syntax enact the increasingly feverish tension of the narrative. The 'tension of expectancy' is tangible, and Walter's absence is projected into the emptiness of the room. Elizabeth is keenly aware of the uneaten and untidied remainders from dinner, as though time has frozen. The mother's sewing is again an active distraction, her obsessive recording of time sharpens the tension, and the characterization of emotion as a physical creature again suggests the intensity of emotion, although here in a more explicitly disembodied and violent manner as fear arrives 'in the room' (rather than being 'caged' inside her, as in a previous example); this arrival is also, again, a kind of reflection of Walter's non-arrival. Compare this with the revised (1911) version:

> When Mrs Bates came down, the room was strangely empty, with a tension of expectancy. She took up her sewing and stitched for some time without raising her head. Meantime her anger tinged with fear. (*VG* 110)

The suggestive details are cut and even the seemingly innocuous revision of 'she' to 'Mrs Bates', an intimate pronoun for a distant proper noun, suggests an economic drive towards determinacy. However, the most emphatic example of reductive revision is the handling of Elizabeth's emotional life, with the scene transformed into a kind of stale watercolour, as 'her anger tinged with fear'.

Before moving on to consider the story's famous conclusion, I will give one final example of Lawrence's revisions for *The English Review*. In a passage taken shortly after the earlier extract, Elizabeth having thrown down her sewing and stepped outside to seek her husband, the revised (1911) text reads as follows:

> The night was very dark. In the great bay of railway-lines bulked with trucks there was no trace of light, only away back she could see a few yellow lamps at the pit-top, and the red smear of the burning pit-bank on the night. She hurried along the edge of the track, and, crossing the converging lines, came to the stile by the white gates, whence she emerged on the road. Then the fear which had led her shrank. (*VG* p. 110)

The passage contains an almost compulsive rhythm, which leads the reader along like Elizabeth's 'fear'. However, when we compare the earlier (1910) version, we see these features were originally deployed in a much more emphatic style:

> The night was very dark. In the great bay of railway-lines where the black trucks rose up obscurely there was no trace of light, only away back could she see a few yellow lamps at the pit-top, and the red smear of the burning pit-bank on the night. She could see the street lamps threading down hill beyond the railway and the field, shining large where the road crossed the lines, and tangling like fireflies in a blur of light where she looked straight down into Old Brinsley. She hurried along the edge of the track, stepping carefully over the levers of the points, and, crossing the converging lines, came to the stile by the great white gates near the weighing machine, whence she emerged on the road. Then the fear which had led her by the hand unhesitating loosed its hold, and shrank back. (*VG* 88)

As in the previous examples, parataxis is here more extensively and skilfully used, and the resulting drama is heightened. Elizabeth's emotional life is also more powerful: whereas, in the revised version, fear leads her along and then shrinks back vaguely, here it leads her 'by the hand unhesitating' and then 'loosed its hold, and shrank back'.

Having emphasized the economic nature of the early cuts to 'Odour of Chrysanthemums', it is important to note that, while Ford Maddox Ford accepted the original story for publication, it was *The English Review*'s Austin Harrison, a far more business-orientated editor, who often requested writers shorten their work in order to increase the magazine's profit margin, and who, having taken over in 1910, requested Lawrence make substantial cuts in order to proceed with the publication.[8]

'Culmination' and the problem of endings

As the work of previous critics demonstrates, a detailed discussion of the ending to 'Odour of Chrysanthemums', which Lawrence heavily rewrote on numerous occasions, warrants a chapter in itself. However, while the present chapter is more focused on the main body of the story, having reassessed the earlier version, it is important to highlight the ways in which the dramatic tension and interplay between absence and presence discussed earlier anticipate and provide an internal dramatic context for the conclusion, in which Walter finally returns home: rather than an existential excursus, therefore, the story's ending first and foremost provides an emotional culmination to the drama.

In the short Foreword to *Women in Love*, in which he suggests that 'the sensual passions and mysteries are equally sacred with the spiritual mysteries and passions', Lawrence concludes by suggesting that 'every natural crisis in emotion or passion or understanding comes from this pulsing, frictional to-and-fro, which works up to culmination' (*WL* pp. 485–6). The crisis in 'Odour of Chrysanthemums' is the 'tension of expectancy', as Elizabeth awaits the return of her husband, and it does indeed 'work up to culmination'. Whereas Annie, in her 'childish dread of abnormal states', dreads the 'terror of an approaching climax' (*VG* p. 85) (in the early version), Walter's return, regardless of his fate, brings an end to Elizabeth's agonizing uncertainty, that is, a release.

Tracking back a moment, when Walter's mother finally arrives at the Bates's cottage 'at a quarter to ten' and obscurely repeats 'Whatever shall we do, whatever shall we do!' and 'I don't know [. . .] I don't know' (*VG* p. 92), Elizabeth's strain reaches its limit:

> 'Is he dead?' she asked, and at the words her heart swung violently, though she felt a slight flush of shame at the ultimate extravagance of the idea. The question sufficiently startled the old lady, **almost brought her to herself**. (*VG* pp. 92, 113; *PO* p. 191)

Though her heart swings 'violently' at the suggestion of a fatal accident, Elizabeth ultimately desires the relief of a definitive answer (is her 'slight flush of shame' not also a guilty acknowledgement of this?) and the story's climax provides this. It is significant to note therefore that, aside from adding the extra clause describing the mother-in-law at the end in 1914, this passage remained intact throughout the various phases of writing.

From a genetic perspective, as Lawrence generally did not edit particular units of text at different points in time (as in a 'constructivist' mode) but rather went through whole texts from beginning to end during one major phase of writing or rewriting (a mode which I will describe as 'dialogical' in subsequent chapters), the story's conclusion also represents an end to the process of writing for Lawrence. Lawrence's tendency to rewrite his work as a whole (regardless of genre) is well known; he often did so on numerous occasions, as in 'Odour of Chrysanthemums'. However, I interpret this tendency as a form of resistance to stasis and endings, hence his less well known though equally strong tendency to rewrite *endings* in particular. If we consider a text in process as something fluid and 'alive', endings represent the point at which the text solidifies and 'dies', transitioning into something static: a textual product. Given the positive emphasis placed on vitality and flux in Lawrence's writing, Lawrence's apparent resistance to endings seems logical. Unlike traditional critics who regard his finished works as complete and self-sufficient, hence the prominent metaphor of 'maturity', Lawrence was generally opposed to self-sufficiency and completion, and his longer works of fiction (like *Women in Love* and *The Plumed Serpent*) are largely driven by conflict between characters who are striving either to be or not to be self-complete. Lawrence's own social and cultural criticism of the West often tackles this fixation on completion, self-sufficiency and perfection (attacking concepts like monumentality).[9] It also explains Lawrence's nonplussed treatment of his own manuscripts and physical copies of his own books, which he seemed to regard as the dead material remainder of his creative life.[10] Without wishing to overly aestheticize human life and death, it is worth considering the ways in which the dead male body – a diegetic object of contemplation not only at the end of 'Odour of Chrysanthemums' (and the interrelated play *The Widowing of Mrs. Holroyd*) but also *Women in Love* (where Birkin reflects at length on the dead body of Gerald, a scene which formed the conclusion to the 1916 version of the novel,[11] and was also rewritten by Lawrence on numerous occasions, as discussed later in the book) – symbolizes the same phenomenon in Lawrence's fiction.

The writerly context for both death and endings has been neglected by previous critics. Though Cushman hints at a strong literary context for the climax to 'Odour of Chrysanthemums' in the form of J. M. Synge's play *Riders to the Sea* – in which a mother's youngest and only surviving son is brought home dead – like most traditional critics, Cushman's primary reading is biographical: 'the main creative impulse came from Lawrence's own experience' (1978, p. 50).[12] However, rather than interpret Lawrence as an autobiographer, biography should be treated as one pool of 'inter-texts' *alongside* literary texts, as well as (and predominantly) from a genetic perspective, early and alternative versions of the same text.[13] Lawrence's letters also provide overwhelming evidence that Synge's play (*Riders to the Sea*) was hugely influential: he first mentions reading the play (and wanting to read more by Synge) in a letter to Blanche Jennings on 1 November 1909 (i.: 142), which is precisely the time he is most likely to have written the first draft of 'Odour of Chrysanthemums', while his next allusion to the play, which he describes as 'about the genuinest bit of dramatic tragedy, English, since Shakespeare' (i.: 261), comes in a letter to Sallie Hopkin on 26 April 1911, just a few weeks after he finished rewriting the story for *The English Review* (suggesting that Lawrence re-read the play for this reason).

Lawrence saw 'Odour of Chrysanthemums' itself in 'finished' form when it was published in *The English Review* in 1911. Hence, when he came to revise the story again, three years later in 1914, Lawrence was in a sense gazing at the corpse of his own literary work. Elizabeth's reassessment of her relationship with Walter in the rewritten endings of July and October 1914 can also therefore be read within the context of writing, as both character and author gaze across the divide between process and product, re-reading the past from a point of completion: 'the horror of the distance between them was almost too much for her – it was so infinite a gap she must look across' (*VG* p. 216; *PO* p. 199). Rewriting in 1914, Lawrence introduced the story's eventual final line, in which Elizabeth 'winced with fear and shame' from death, 'her ultimate master' (*VG* p. 216; *PO* p. 199). While this recoil echoes Lawrence's own resistance to endings, the story's climax, though tragic, also provides *relief*, relieving Elizabeth of her agonizing uncertainty, and this relief extends to the writer as well, who is ultimately relieved of the potentially endless process of writing. Lawrence introduced a noteworthy repetition in this respect during the same late phase of writing. In the early 1910 version of the story, after Elizabeth and her mother-in-law finish washing Walter's body, the first sentence of the subsequent paragraph is simple: 'At last it was finished' (*VG* p. 98).[14] This line was never altered by Lawrence during subsequent rewritings, and, in 1914, he repeated it when writing the story's concluding paragraph, which begins with the same words: 'At last it was finished'.

Notes

1 Lawrence's first publication was a short story entitled 'A Prelude', which won a Christmas competition and was published by the *Nottingham Guardian* in December 1907 (under the name of 'Jessie Chambers', Lawrence's close friend and erstwhile lover).

2 See Cushman, 1978, pp. 47–76, and Schulz, 1991, pp. 363–71; Schulz, for example, argues that 'the author's main objective in this story is to explore the widow's complex response to her husband's death' (p. 366).

3 Schulz qualifies this reading by suggesting that the story's moral is not universal but is relevant to these particular, 'unsuitable spouses' (p. 367). Schulz in fact suggests the story ends on a positive note, with 'Mrs. Bates turning away from the irreparable failure of her married life toward a vague hope of finding fulfilment as a mother' (p. 368). One other critic who has studied Lawrence's revision of the story is Mara Kalnins, whose conclusions in 'D. H. Lawrence's "Odour of Chrysanthemums": The Three Endings' (1976) echo those of Cushman.

4 For a more detailed account of the story's compositional history, see the respective Cambridge introductions by Worthen and Reeve's referenced earlier.
5 There is also a genetic hypertext and study-guide edition of 'Odour of Chrysanthemums', hosted by the University of Nottingham and lead by Sean Matthews, which can be access via the following URL: http://odour.nottingham.ac.uk.
6 For Schulz, this episode symbolizes the start of a new and more hopeful phase in Elizabeth's life (p. 368).
7 Lawrence also completely cut a brief episode in which Elizabeth reads the children a bedtime story; Bryan Rivers discusses the significance of the episode in '"No Meaning for Anybody": D. H. Lawrence's Use of Hans Christian Andersen's *The Fir Tree* in the Original Version of *Odour of Chrysanthemums* (1910)' (2014).
8 For more on *Austin Harrison and the English Review*, see Vogeler (2008).
9 See Lawrence's Foreword to *Studies in Classic American Literature* (pp. 379–86).
10 See Lawrence's '"The Bad Side of Books": Introduction to *A Bibliography of the Writings of D. H. Lawrence*, edited by Edward D. McDonald' (2005, pp. 73–8).
11 See *The First Women in Love* (p. 443).
12 Another noteworthy inter-text which Cushman alludes to is the depiction and dressing of the dead body of Christ in the gospels. Cushman also refers to Lawrence's uncle James, who died in a mining accident before Lawrence's birth, as well as his older brother Ernest, who died of pneumonia and erysipelas while Lawrence was a teenager in 1901 and whose body was brought home and placed in the parlour. Pushing the biographical reading to its extreme, however, Cushman suggests that Lawrence's parents 'are the real prototypes of Walter and Elizabeth Bates' (p. 49) while, as discussed, Lawrence's 1914 revisions are connected to his marriage with Frieda Weekley.
13 Stanley Sultan argues the same in his essay 'Lawrence the Anti-Autobiographer' (1999–2000), minus the genetics.
14 Weaving in another literary/biblical inter-text, this phrase echoes Jesus's last words as related in John 19.30: 'It is finished'.

Part Three

Women in Love (1913–21)

Table 1 Stemmatic table for *Women in Love* adapted from Farmer, Vasey and Worthen (1983), with references to Roberts and Poplawski's bibliography (2001); I have added 'version seven' – the surviving page proofs for the first English edition of the novel – as Lawrence inserted chapter titles as well as a new chapter division at this stage

Bibliographical Notes		Version	Date
Pp. 291–6 in Warren Roberts's *Bibiliohraphy of D. H. Lawrence*, MS Catalogue no. E441a	MS ?296pp. 'The Sisters I'	One	March – June 1913
Unfinished; pp. 373–80 in Roberts E441a	MS ?380pp. 'The Sisters II'	Two	August 1913 – January 1914
Not extant	MS ?600pp. 'The Wedding Ring'	Three	February – May 1914
Typed by Dunlop; TCC pp. 219–75, 279–84 in Roberts E331a	TS ?500pp. TCC ?500pp. 'The Wedding Ring' 'The Wedding Ring'		
Roberts E331a	MS & TCC 811pp. *The Rainbow*		November 1914 – March 1915;
Unfinished first draft; Roberts E441b	MS 55pp. 'The Sisters III'	Four	April 1916;
Pp. 650–863 in Roberts E441C	MS 863pp. 'The Sisters III'		April – June 1916
Pp. 1–368 typed by DHL, pp. 369–666 typed by Pinker: Roberts E441d & e	TSIa 666pp. TSIb 666pp. *The First* 'Women in Love'	Five	July – November 1916
Roberts E441f	TSII 766pp. *Women in Love*	Six	March 1917 – September 1919
Roberts E441g	English Proofs (DHL's set) 508pp. *Women in Love*	Seven	October – November 1920

3

Re-evaluating the compositional history

The compositional history of *Women in Love* is a well-trodden territory, and I must acknowledge several previous accounts before presenting my own.[1] While building on existing coverage, however, my own account reveals a number of uncertainties in the record and suggests that Lawrence completed more drafts than has previously been suggested. I also reflect on Lawrence's methods, starting with his peculiar *preparations* for writing. Before beginning, I have included the (slightly adapted) stemmatic table (see Table 1) from the Cambridge edition of *Women in Love* as this can be used as a basic reference map throughout. However, it should be noted that the labelling of each manuscript as a particular 'version' in this table, as well as the addition of hypothetical titles ('Sisters I', 'Sisters II' and 'Sisters III'), suggests a clearer division between drafts and a greater overall certainty about the writing processes than my own account which follows.

Pre-genesis: Lawrentian preparations for writing

In March 1913, towards the end of his stay in Gargnano, Lake Garda, where he had lived with his soon-to-be wife Frieda Weekley since September 1912, Lawrence began writing a draft for a novel, subsequently entitled 'The Sisters'. This work would evolve through perhaps a *dozen* major phases of writing, resulting initially in the publication of *The Rainbow* in 1915 (though this book was banned within a few weeks), and, finally, of *Women in Love*, which was published privately in the United States in 1920 and then publicly in England, with some important amendments, in 1921, some eight years after its inception, a period covering over a third of Lawrence's relatively short career. Despite the many, many revisions, rewritings and alternative versions which form the subject of these chapters on *Women in Love*, as we will see in the next chapter, most of the central characters, character dynamics and themes are already represented in the very earliest drafts.

However, while the manuscripts themselves provide evidence of Lawrence's actual writing processes, prior to and in the act of penning the very first draft, there is already evidence of what I label Lawrence's *dialogical* method of writing (a term used not in a pure Bakhtinian sense but in a more specific genetic sense, in opposition to more popular, constructivist and organicist metaphors for writing).[2] Unlike fellow modernist giants like Joyce, Mann and Proust,[3] all of whom admired Gustave Flaubert and his notion of the writer as a sort of craftsperson, and, like Flaubert, made direct and often prodigious plans, outlines, notes and sketches in preparation for writing, Lawrence's 'preparations', though similarly prodigious, were more indirect and diffuse.

Having finally 'completed' his third novel, *Sons and Lovers*, in November 1912,[4] and having already 'thought of a new novel – purely of the common people – fearfully interesting' (i. 431) in August that year, Lawrence followed it up by conceiving and beginning work on *three* separate novels between December 1912 and March 1913, abandoning each one in turn before starting the next (these are summarized later in the chapter). Lawrence's almost comic level of creativity was not in the least restricted to these projects, however, as, in the period between conceiving 'a new novel' in August 1912 while completing *Sons and Lovers* and beginning 'The Sisters' in March 1913, Lawrence also wrote the following: several pieces of travel writing on his recent journey on foot across the Alps; two plays, one of which was *The Daughter-in-Law*, which both Kinkead-Weekes and Worthen have suggested is possibly Lawrence's best; a philosophical foreword to *Sons and Lovers*; a short story entitled 'The Overtone'; a review of Edward Marsh's anthology of *Georgian Poetry 1911–1912* (1912); and a second set of travel writings set 'By the Lago di Gada'.[5] This level of activity was actually fairly normal for Lawrence throughout his entire career, and, in a simple sense, it suggests a rare creative genius. 'Drilling down' into the 'nuts and bolts' of it though, it suggests more specifically that the actual act of writing was itself a major spur for his creativity, and that writing was *itself* a kind of preparation. This is something Lawrence seems to have been aware of. Following an interruption in order to travel while writing a later draft of 'The Sisters', Lawrence wrote to his editor: 'I am just getting sufficiently unrooted to begin work again. I was a fool to move in the midst of a flow. If the Sisters is late, it'll be my fault this time' (ii. 99).

What of Lawrence's projects for a novel? The first, a novel 'purely of the common people', appears to have been abandoned virtually before it began, with the title 'Scargill Street' mooted in October 1912 but never repeated (i. 466).[6] Having posted *Sons and Lovers* to Garnett in the intervening month, Lawrence then mentions a new project in December 1912: part history, part fiction, based on the life of legendary Scottish poet Robert Burns but set in the English Midlands. There are surviving draft fragments, but Lawrence appears to have abandoned this second project after only a month or so as, towards the end of the year, having 'stewed my next novel inside me for a week or so', Lawrence began 'dishing up' (i. 496) a new and unspecified novel of which very little is known.[7] However, Lawrence ditched the third project even more rapidly than the Burns novel and, continuing the culinary theme, by 12 January 1913 he was 'simmering a new work' (i. 501). Lawrence suggested this fourth project 'may not come off' (i. 501) either, but, by 17 January, he had already 'written 80 pages' (i. 505), and, despite his reservations, he described it as 'a most curious work' (i. 505), 'a weird thing' (i. 525) and 'a most fascinating (to me) novel [. . .] so new, so really a stratum deeper than I think anybody has ever gone, in a novel' (i. 526). Lawrence's plan on 11 March 1913 was to 'stick at it, get it done, and then write another' (i. 526). Despite completing '200 pages' and describing it as 'a novel I love', however, this work was apparently '*too* improper', and so, a few days later, Lawrence claimed to have 'put it aside to do a pot-boiler' (i. 536).[8] It was a case of fifth-time lucky: by 22 March, Lawrence had completed '46 pages' of what he rather coyly described as a 'new, lighter novel' (i. 530). By 5 April 1913, he had reached 'page 110' (i. 536), and, despite intending it to be 'absolutely impeccable' (i. 526), the novel had 'developed into an earnest and painful work – God help it and me' (i. 536). Less than three months after beginning work, Lawrence completed a first full draft of this novel in early June 1913, and, writing to Garnett on 10 June to confirm safe receipt (ii. 20), he entitled the work 'The Sisters'.

In the Cambridge biography of Lawrence, Kinkead-Weekes provides a teleological reading of Lawrence's work during these months: 'the newly imagined sympathy with "the common people"' alluded to by Lawrence in his first idea, 'Scargill Street', was not diminished but 'was merely coming out now in anti-bourgeois form' with 'a heroine who must escape the deathly enclosure of class and money' (as in *The Lost Girl*), while the foreword to *Sons and Lovers* is described as a prelude 'to a deeper fiction, still to be written, about both marriage and integration' (i.e. to *The Rainbow*).[9] While making some order out of Lawrence's creative chaos, this neat overview removes some of the contingency, which is present in all historical processes, but especially so in writing. How does Lawrence's second effort, a fictionalized life of Burns, for example, fit into these schemes? While it may relate tangentially to both ('the common people' or 'marriage and integration'), as we saw with 'Odour of

Chrysanthemums' and Synge's play (see Chapter 2), a more immediate context (or trigger) is literary: Lawrence's contingent reading material at the time, namely, a biography of Burns.

Perhaps a better way of finding wider meaning in Lawrence's frenzied activity is to consider his general method of writing. Michael Black, who was the publisher at Cambridge University Press involved in founding the Cambridge Edition of Lawrence, and who has written several books on Lawrence's early and early to middle career, has described Lawrence's method as follows:

> Lawrence found himself working on a number of works which he had initially composed, often very rapidly, in a free improvisatory mode. He always wrote fast, and could produce a draft in days or weeks rather than months. He then often laid aside what he had written for a future reworking, while he embarked on something else. In this way he had at any given time a number of works in progress, at different stages of composition. His normal procedure was to bring them towards eventual publication by revising them more than once, sometimes very radically, taking them through a number of manuscript and, after 1912, typescript drafts, and then later revising again in proof. So the scholar who wants to pursue the writing life in detail would not only have to move from draft to draft of any one work, but from this draft of one work to that draft of another, and then perhaps to the inception of a third or fourth distinct work before returning to the next draft of the first work. (1999, p. 150)

Black captures several key features here: Lawrence writes in an 'improvisatory mode', with very little paper planning; he writes 'rapidly', able to produce a draft in days or weeks; he has multiple 'works in progress' at any given time; he usually revises or reworks a first draft 'more than once' and 'sometimes very radically'. However, Black's account also contains some weaknesses owing to its traditional Anglo-American (rather than genetic) approach to writing: by pursuing a generalized 'writing life' – jumping from work to work – a critic would overlook the specific writing processes which can only be traced by following the evolution of one work across one series of manuscripts. Connected to this avoidance of specific processes is the slightly exaggerated sense of speed: Lawrence did complete drafts of poems and short stories in a matter of days or weeks, but, as we have just seen, it took at least a few months to complete a draft of a *novel* (and often several years to complete a novel in its entirety).

Whereas, in this genetic study, we find Lawrence repeatedly reworking old material by retaining some passages and rewriting others (as witnessed already in Chapter 2), Black also suggests elsewhere (echoing L. D. Clark's comments) that there is often a 'rift between draft versions, which is so drastic, one has to go beyond the notion of detailed revision of a steadily evolving text, and to posit a process of returning to a source' (Black, 1995, p. 154). While I agree one has to 'go beyond' the notion of a steadily *constructed* text, Black's notion of 'returning to a source' refers not to a specific source text (i.e. the previous draft or version of a work) but to the critic's own general concept of Lawrence's 'writing life'. In opposition to a steadily evolving text, Black uses (similarly restrictive) *organicist* metaphors to explain this 'process of return': 'the growth and flowering of a perpetual plant was his own model [. . .] producing first these flowers, then those. Yet they are all from the same originating organism'; 'Lawrence at these points began again, dived back into the pool of spontaneity where he always started, and which he always trusted more than second and third thoughts'; 'Lawrence seeded and flowered for a score of seasons; and while each flower was unique, they are all from the parent plant, identifiable and comparable, unique and generic' (Black, 1999, pp. 151–2; 154; 165). Rather than view writing as in any way self-conscious or as containing a specific, contingent history (as I do in this genetic study), these metaphors aestheticize the writing process and give the texts an inscrutable, cosmic origin.[10] We could say that Black falls into the trap of 'primitivizing' Lawrence (as Chaudhuri and Ross separately warn).

Lawrence's string of false starts certainly appears erratic, but the way in which he continues to work through one project after another until settling on the 'right' one is itself methodical in a probing sense: rather than wilfully changing course, perhaps Lawrence was experimenting, working through trial runs. Likewise, as he proceeded, Lawrence actually seems to have been *shedding* basic levels of planning: he started with a title and a theme ('Scargill Street' and 'the common people') and apparently never began writing, and ended with a complete draft which was only retrospectively titled and themed: 'I am doing a novel which I have never grasped. Damn its eyes, there I am at page 145, and I've no idea what it's about' (i. 544).

Of course, Lawrence's ability to plan his work *mentally* should not be underestimated. Before beginning 'The Sisters', Lawrence expressed a tongue-in-cheek desire to produce a 'potboiler'; this owes something to his financial vulnerability having recently resigned his post as a teacher, but it also indicates a basic plan: a romance novel.[11] However, Lawrence's most revealing comment is made while working on the penultimate project ('The Insurrection of Miss Houghton') and concerns his general method of writing: 'I shall write it as long as I like to start with, then write it smaller. I must always write my books twice' (i. 517). While this suggests both freedom ('I shall write it as long as I like') and restraint ('to start with, then write it smaller'), and it should also be noted that Lawrence's mental picture solidified as a draft developed – he was able to note that he had 'written more than half' (i. 526) of 'Miss Houghton' once he had reached two hundred pages of the first draft and he was likewise able to forecast that the first draft of 'The Sisters' would 'only have 300 pages' once he had reached '180 pages' (i. 546)[12] – the key point is that *redrafting* was a conscious method ('I must always write my books twice'). A consequence of this, which previous critics have tended to overlook, is the fact that it renders Lawrence's first drafts intrinsically *provisional*; comparable in themselves to an extremely detailed plan. This method undermines both constructivist (i.e. self-conscious) and organicist (i.e. spontaneous) metaphors as it involves both intentionality *and* spontaneity. Above all perhaps, it emphasizes the importance for Lawrence of creating a *dialogue* between multiple drafts.

Rewriting: Multiple drafts

Having already suggested 'I must always write my books twice', responding to criticism from Garnett in a letter dated 17 May 1913, Lawrence expresses his intention to write a second draft of 'The Sisters' before having finished the first: 'I was glad of your letter about the Sisters. Don't schimpf, I shall make it all right when I re-write it. I shall put it in the third person' (i. 550).[13] By implying that the first draft of 'The Sisters' may have been written in the *first* person ('I shall put it in the third person'), this letter also draws attention to the first major uncertainty in the compositional history of *Women in Love* as the earliest extant fragment ('The Sisters I') is written in the *third* person.[14] Unlike *Sons and Lovers*, where Garnett made direct and substantial cuts, Garnett's influence upon the early drafts of *Women in Love* is more intangible, yet his disapproval clearly encouraged Lawrence to rewrite. However, Lawrence's characterization of the first draft as 'a first crude fermenting' which he would 'make right' and 'make into art' in the same letter perhaps reflects Garnett's criticisms more than his own views.

What we do know is that Lawrence began work on a second draft of 'The Sisters' in August 1913 in Irschenhausen, where he stayed until late September, having spent the intervening months in England. In another initially misfiring burst of creativity, Lawrence reported 'two false starts' (ii. 67) in August, but the new draft had 'quite a new beginning – a new basis altogether' (ii. 68) by early September and he had completed 'a hundred pages' (ii. 74) by 15 September.

Writing was then interrupted for a month or so as Lawrence travelled across the Alps and then waited several weeks for the postal service to forward his manuscript from Munich; it was after this interruption that Lawrence updated Garnett about 'just getting sufficiently unrooted to begin work again' and being 'a fool to move in the midst of a flow' (ii. 99), again suggesting a self-conscious spontaneity as he works to get himself 'sufficiently unrooted' in order to restart the 'flow' of writing.

False starts and interruptions made slow work of the second draft, but Lawrence was clearly committed to the project. In a letter to Garnett on 30 December 1913, in which he also indicates a new title, Lawrence anticipated sending 'the first half of the Sisters – which I should rather call The Wedding Ring – to Duckworths' in 'a few days' (ii. 132). Lawrence also begins to sound more defensive in this letter. As well as suggesting that he will send the new draft to his publisher (Duckworths) rather than Garnett (his editor), Lawrence intimates he will 'be sorry if you don't like it, but am prepared' (ii. 132). Likewise, after dispatching the first half a week later, Lawrence reported on 6 January 1914 that, although 'there may be some small weeding out to do', and again anticipating Garnett 'may not find it as exciting', he was confident 'this will be the final form of the book. I really think it is good' (ii. 134). Lawrence expected to 'finish it in six weeks – perhaps in eight' and hoped they might 'rush quickly into print' (ii. 135), while, in terms of length, on 19 January he reported having done '340 pages' (ii. 137), meaning the second full draft was already longer than the first prior to its completion (in terms of manuscript pages, at least).

Over the next few weeks, however, Lawrence appears to have decided to abandon work on the well-advanced second draft and start over again, partly due to renewed criticism from Garnett. Lawrence had received another disappointing response from Garnett, who appears to have written a more detailed critique in response to the new material, by 29 January, and, in a remark which seems deeply understated, Lawrence suggests in his reply that 'I am not very much surprised, nor very much hurt by your letter' (ii. 142). We can only reconstruct the content of Garnett's critique through Lawrence's letter, which summarizes and agrees with 'two main criticisms': 'that the Templeman [probably a prototype of Anton Skrebensky in *The Rainbow*] episode is wrong, and that the character of Ella [i.e. Ursula] is incoherent'.[15] While Lawrence purportedly agrees with these points, he also distinguishes a more general criticism 'about the artistic side being in the background'. Lawrence essentially rejects this latter suggestion, which appears to register an emerging split between Lawrence and Garnett: Lawrence is unwilling to condemn 'the new style', which he had previously suggested was '*very* different from *Sons and Lovers* [. . .] another language almost' (ii. 132). Lawrence does however plan to 'go over it all again' (ii. 142), acknowledging that he 'must write to live' and initially suggesting he will 'abandon the exhaustive method entirely' and 'write pure object and story' (ii. 143) if the second half of the new draft also disappoints Garnett.

Despite his initial intention to persist with the second draft, then, by 7 February 1914 Lawrence had indeed 'begun it again' (ii. 144), and he worked on a new full-length draft between February and May (ostensibly the third full draft). Lawrence appeared to have a stronger conviction in the work on this occasion, however, as he had the British Consul in Spezia, Thomas Dunlop, type the draft up as he went (ii. 152). This conviction is also reflected in a letter to Garnett on 22 April: 'I am sure of this now, this novel. It is a big and beautiful work' (ii. 164), and, while still acknowledging the ultimate exigency of publishers and readers ('I *must* have money for my novels, to live' (ii. 166)), he suggests he will no longer accept rejection from Garnett: 'if Duckworth is not really *keen* on this novel, we will give it to [literary agent J. B.] Pinker' (ii. 166).

Lawrence completed the third full draft in May 1914. Having already changed the title to 'The Wedding Ring', Lawrence now re-christened the novel 'The Rainbow' – 'a better title than the Wedding Ring, for the book as it is' (ii. 174) – and he described the work as 'a magnum opus with a vengeance' (ii. 173). Like the previous manuscript drafts of 'The Sisters', the majority of this typescript draft is lost; a fragment, which was interpolated into a subsequent manuscript of *The Rainbow*, survives. Although Lawrence was now committed to the novel and probably had a complete typescript, his work on the book was to be interrupted first by other projects and then by greater historical events, after which nothing would be quite the same.

The outbreak of war

Lawrence's work on the novel initially stalled as, having posted the typescript to Garnett in May 1914, he and Frieda left Italy the following month, initially visiting family in Germany and England, before getting married in London. They intended to return to Italy in September (cf. ii. 166 and 170), and Lawrence probably planned to complete the novel upon their return. In the meantime, Lawrence received a very substantial offer of £300 for the novel's rights from literary agent J. B. Pinker, as well as yet another hostile response from Garnett.

In a famous letter of 5 June – in which he reflects on futurism,[16] criticizes 'the old-fashioned human element' and 'the certain moral scheme' for characters in traditional fiction and advises Garnett not 'to look in my novel for the old stable ego' but for 'allotropic states' and 'some other rhythmic form', which is 'not perfect' but 'takes lines unknown' and is 'the real thing' (ii. 182–4), points which I return to in later chapters – Lawrence finally rejects Garnett's position: 'I don't agree with you about the Wedding Ring' (ii. 182). Lawrence decided to take the English rights elsewhere and signed an agreement with Methuen in late June 1914 (ii. 189). Although Garnett regretted this decision (ii. 189), Lawrence had made Pinker's interest as well as his own financial situation clear, while, as the aforementioned letter suggests, and perhaps more importantly, his trajectory as a writer was drifting away from Garnett, who probably viewed *Sons and Lovers* as the benchmark, while Lawrence was seeking a new direction of travel.[17]

However, to make up for the withdrawal of his novel, Lawrence offered a book of short stories to Duckworth instead (an idea first mooted by Martin Secker, the eventual publisher of *Women in Love*, in June 1911 after reading 'Odour of Chrysanthemums' in *The English Review*). Work on the novel was therefore laid aside while Lawrence gathered and revised his short fiction. This collection was closely edited by Garnett and published rapidly in November 1914 under a topical title (*The Prussian Officer and Other Stories*), much to Lawrence's chagrin: 'Garnett was a devil to call my book of stories *The Prussian Officer* – what Prussian Officer?' (ii. 241). Aside from working on these stories, the period from June to November 1914 does not so much represent a 'break' in the external history of the novel as a *rupture*, for, between stopping and restarting work, Britain had declared war on Germany. To say the least, the Lawrences' travel plans were irrevocably altered.[18]

During this break, Lawrence also made a host of new acquaintances who would have a major impact on the rest of his life (as well as his posthumous legacy), including Catherine Carswell, Amy Lowell, Richard Aldington, H. D., S. S. Koteliansky, Lady Ottoline Morrell (who would later introduce Lawrence to E. M. Forster, Bertrand Russell and Aldous Huxley, among others), Compton Mackenzie, John Middleton Murry and Katherine Mansfield. Besides the *PO* collection, and in typical fashion, Lawrence also wrote or worked on a number of other things, including the book-length 'Study of Thomas Hardy' ('in reality a sort of Confessions of my Heart' (ii. 235)). As discussed in Chapter 1, these two books (in particular) have been studied at length by previous critics of the compositional history of *Women in Love*, who seek to pinpoint a 'breakthrough' moment in Lawrence's progress as a writer. While I have criticized this approach for being too external, and teleological, I don't think we can ignore the wider impact of the war upon Lawrence and society itself during the summer months of 1914 and beyond.[19]

Lawrence wrote a lesser-known piece entitled 'With the Guns' during the same break, published in the *Manchester Guardian* (now *The Guardian*) on 18 August 1914, exactly two weeks after Britain entered the war, which provides a brief snapshot of this impact.[20] It begins with an account of a recent journey through Barrow train station in Cumbria (Barrow-in-Furness), where Lawrence witnessed young male reservists 'leaving for London by the nine o'clock train [. . .] some of them drunk'. He recalls a woman who 'stood before the carriage window' with her sweetheart and cried: '"Well, so-long!" [. . .] as the train began to move', and, 'When you see 'em let 'em have it', to which the man replied: 'Ay, no fear', and then 'the train was gone, the man grinning'. In the rest of the article, Lawrence, who, the previous autumn (in the break between the composition of the first and second full drafts of 'The Sisters'), had 'followed the Bavarian army down the Isar valley and near the foot of the Alps', reflects on 'what it would really be like, "when he saw 'em"':

> I could see what war would be like – an affair entirely of machines, with men attached to the machines as the subordinate part thereof, as the butt is the part of a rifle [. . .] the unnatural suspense and suppression of serving a machine which, for ought we knew, was killing our fellow-men, whilst we stood there, blind, without knowledge or participation, subordinate [. . .] this was the glamour and the glory [. . .] who would have been torn, killed, no one would have known. There would just have been a hole in the living shadowy mass; that was all. Who it was did not matter. There were no individuals, and every soldier knew it. He was a fragment of a mass, and as a fragment of a mass he must live and die or be torn. He had no right, no self, no being. [. . .] It is a war of artillery, a war of machines, and men no more than the subjective material of the machine. It is so unnatural as to be unthinkable.
>
> Yet we must think of it.[21]

Outside a consulting room and before the terms 'shell-shock' or PTSD had been coined, Lawrence anticipates the traumatic nature of the First World War, 'so unnatural as to be unthinkable', and then, in a way summative of Lawrence's entire project as a writer, the article not only lays bare the traumatic kernel of mechanized warfare but also compels its readers to *confront* this 'unthinkable' reality ('Yet we must think of it'). As the use of the plural pronoun ('we') indicates, this urgent call to thought is a societal responsibility. The article also suggests that history and time are themselves dragged into the disturbance:[22]

> I remember standing on a little round hill one August afternoon. There was a beautiful blue sky, and white clouds from the mountains. Away on the right, amid woods and corn-clad hills, lay the big Starnberg lake. This is just a year ago, but it seems to belong to some period outside of time.

We might wonder whether Lawrence experienced a similar feeling when returning to the typescript draft of 'The Wedding Ring'/'The Rainbow' in November 1914.

Having completed work on the *PO* collection, Lawrence reported to Pinker on 31 October, 'I don't feel quite in the humour for tackling the novel just now' (ii. 227), although he did intend to 'go over the whole thing thoroughly' (ii. 228) and work was well under way by 5 December 1914, when he sent Pinker 'the first hundred or so pages' (ii. 240). Lawrence referred to the process variously (and indicatively) as 'rewriting' (ii. 239), 'writing over' (ii. 240) and 'revising' (ii. 255), but a new full-length draft which he now referred to exclusively as *The Rainbow* was clearly under way. Lawrence originally intended to 'finish the thing by the end of January – perhaps earlier' (ii. 240) and by 5 January 1915 he had completed '300 pages' (ii. 255). However, there was a drastic change of plan by 7 January, when Lawrence sent Pinker 'another hundred pages of the novel' and announced a new intention: rather than complete a single novel, he would 'split the book into two volumes: it was so unwieldy. It needs to be in two volumes' (ii. 256). Reflecting the external rupture produced by the war, then, Lawrence decided to split the novel in two in January 1915.

Tracing back a moment, it seems that Lawrence's original solution to Garnett's criticisms of January 1914 – 'that the character of Ella is incoherent', and his insistence that 'I *must* have Ella get some experience before she meets her Mr Birkin' (ii. 142) – was to develop Ella/Ursula's prehistory by introducing two further generational levels to the Brangwen family saga while working on the draft of February–May 1914.[23] Despite initially rewriting the resulting 'magnum opus' as one, from November 1914 to January 1915, Lawrence then split the novel in two by suspending the narrative after Ursula's 'experience before' and saving the introduction of 'her Mr Birkin' for a subsequent volume. Having set aside the originally titular relationship between the sisters, Ursula and Gudrun, as well as their respective romantic relationships with Birkin, Gerald and Loerke, which occupy most of the eventual narrative of *Women in Love*, there was then a gap of just over a year in the former novel's compositional history while Lawrence completed work on *The Rainbow* (making substantial revisions to manuscript and typescript drafts, as well as the page proofs), which was published in September 1915, and then worked on a fresh array of shorter projects.[24]

Return to 'The Sisters': *Women in Love* and the travails of typing

Following a short break from novel writing after the completion of *The Rainbow*, which, it should be stressed, was acrimoniously seized by the police and banned, with Methuen blankly refusing to defend it,[25] it was not until the end of April 1916 that Lawrence returned to his original project, 'The Sisters' (ii. 599). Having arrived in London in June 1914, Lawrence had lived in and around the capital (moving from Kensington to Chesham to Greatham to Hampstead) until December 1915 when he moved to the extremity of England's rugged southwestern tip in Cornwall, where he would remain for nearly two years, until October 1917.

The build-up to the rebirth of *Women in Love* in April 1916 echoes its original inception in March 1913, with Lawrence producing an array of prior work and then mooting a different idea for a novel, suggesting in March 1916 that he was 'not quite sure' what to do but would probably get to work on 'The Insurrection of Miss Houghton' (ii. 580; i.e. *The Lost Girl*), another draft laid aside years before, if he could retrieve the manuscript from Germany. Instead, on 26 April, Lawrence reported that he had begun 'a new novel' (ii. 599). Given the amount of ground that had been covered – geographically, historically and in terms of literary output – since writing the initial drafts from 1913 to 1914, as well as the decision to syphon off some material for *The Rainbow*, it is unsurprising that, in a bid to produce what he described to Barbara Low on 1 May 1916 as 'the second half of the *Rainbow*' (ii. 602), Lawrence decided to write a new draft. However, despite Lawrence labelling the work a 'new novel' and describing it a few days later as 'a thing that is a stranger to me even as I write it. I don't know what the end will be' (ii. 604), as we will see, the narrative (at least) of the latest draft was closely based on the previous versions. As Lawrence would also go on to produce *another* series of drafts for *Women in Love*, this new draft of April 1916 was itself another kind of plan for subsequent versions.

Having restarted work, Lawrence reported at the end of May, barely a month later, that 'two thirds of the novel are written', claiming 'I have not travailed over it' (ii. 614) and later that 'it has come rushing out' (ii. 617). However, it was not until a month later, on 30 June, that Lawrence declared 'I have finished "The Sisters", in effect', and pondered returning to Duckworth ('I like him because he treats my books so well' (ii. 619)). Lawrence's qualification about finishing 'in effect' is noteworthy, and he expands on this a few days later: 'I have finished my novel – except for a bit that can be done any time' (ii. 621). Five months later, when finishing a subsequent version of the novel in November 1916, Lawrence reported the same problem in slightly more detail: 'I have finished my novel – save the last chapter, which, a sort of epilogue, I shall add later on' (iii. 25). While critics have previously accepted this as a purely practical point, these repeated hesitations clearly point towards Lawrence's underlying reluctance (or resistance) to consider his work 'finished'.

Having 'finished' this particular draft in June 1916 (in a series of notebooks, which I discuss in more detail in Chapter 5), and having 'only six pounds [GBP] in the world' (ii. 630), Lawrence decided he would 'try to type it' (ii. 627) himself the following month. However, the history of composition from July to November 1916 is confusing to say the least and involves a comical debacle with the typewriter itself. As previous commentators have only distinguished a single new draft from the latter period, I will describe these few months in more detail as there in fact appear to be *at least two* separate drafts produced.

Lawrence reports that he 'gave up typing the novel' and 'began scribbling out the final draft in pencil' after only a week or so in July as 'it got on my nerves and knocked me up' (ii. 637). But, wasn't he supposed to be 'typing up' the notebooks? So what was there to 'scribble out'? Lawrence had clearly been using the opportunity to *rewrite* the existing new draft on the typewriter, producing a second new draft, which also explains his almost self-willing reference to this new handwritten draft as 'final'. In the same letter to Pinker (21 July 1916), Lawrence describes this latest version as 'the fourth and final draft' and claims it is '⅘ done' (ii. 637). As we will see, Lawrence's numbering of drafts (like his numbering of pages within drafts) is unreliable, but, if we wanted to frame this latest draft as a 'fourth' version, it would probably be in the following series: (1) March–June 1913; (2) August 1913–May 1914 (combining two versions, the first left unfinished in January 1914); (3) April–June 1916; (4) July 1916.

Despite vowing 'never will I type again' (ii. 638) in July, Lawrence rather bewilderingly reported to Amy Lowell – who had herself donated the typewriter to Lawrence as a gift in November 1914 (ii. 234), as Lawrence was quite poor throughout the war – on 23 August 1916, at which point he had probably finished the aforementioned handwritten draft, that he was 'typing out a new novel' and that his typewriter had 'at last become a true confrère'; in a comic echo of Birkin's offer to Gerald in *Women in Love*, Lawrence goes on to suggest that 'I and the typewriter have sworn a Blutbrüderschaft' (ii. 645). In the same letter to Koteliansky in which Lawrence had expressed his intention to type the novel himself, back in July, Lawrence had also requested a new 'black ribbon' (ii. 621), suggesting that the typewriter was faulty. After much confusion, with Kot twice sending the wrong type of ribbon and Lawrence twice returning it ('all I want is an ordinary half-inch black ribbon. Can you solve the mystery for me?' (ii. 636)), it seems Lawrence finally received a new ribbon at the start of August (ii. 638), which may have spurred him to use the machine again.[26] Therefore, having originally completed a new draft in June, which he began rewriting on a faulty typewriter in July and finished by hand in early August, Lawrence appears to have begun 'typing up' the now rewritten draft in earnest in mid-August.

However, typing up himself, Lawrence again appears to have been unable to resist his inclination to rewrite. He remained 'typing away' (ii. 647) for several months, and his letters become increasingly exasperated with the process. While previous critics have focused on the physical labour, I would focus instead on the likelihood that Lawrence was again substantially revising the previous draft and hence his travails were also writerly (concerning the content of the novel itself). This is hinted at in a report to Lady Ottoline Morrell in September: 'I only want to finish this novel, which is like a malady or a madness while it lasts' (ii. 656), while, on 12 October, Lawrence clearly distinguishes between the physical and creative labour: 'I am still typing away at my new novel: it takes a tremendous time: and *the novel itself* is one of the labours of Hercules' (ii, 665, my italics). To confuse matters even more, however, the very next day (13 October) Lawrence reports having given up typing with 'about two-thirds' (ii. 666) completed and proceeds to write out the rest by hand (mirroring the stuttered, multi-layered process of the previous draft). This second bout of handwriting was finished by 31 October, at which point Lawrence sent 'the untyped [section of] MS' (ii. 669) to Pinker for typing.

This Gordian knot of handwritten and typed drafts from July to October 1916 appears to have flummoxed previous critics: Ross misses these steps completely, which produces a slight jump in his account (1976, pp. 102–14), while the Cambridge editors only take one of two or three steps into account and offer a similarly confusing account, with Lawrence's work again seen as continuous during this period (*WL*, pp. xxix–x).

Before moving on to the full typescript drafts, it is worth noting that there was a degree of fluidity regarding the novel's title in 1916. While Lawrence seems to have decided by August 1916 that the novel was 'to be called *Women in Love*' (ii. 645), and it was this title that he used when dispatching the aforementioned manuscript to Pinker for typing, he initially refers to it as both 'the second half of the *Rainbow*' (ii. 602) and 'The Sisters' (ii. 619), and offers Pinker *Women in Love* as a question on 13 July: 'Shall I call the novel *Women in Love*?' Adding, 'I'm not good at titles – never know if they're good or bad' (ii. 631). Lawrence also toyed with 'The Latter Days' (ii. 659) and 'Dies Irae' (ii. 669) in October (the latter appears in the surviving notebook drafts). Finally, in letters to friend and fellow writer Catherine Carswell in August, Lawrence first explains why the original title was abandoned: 'It was "The Sisters", but May Sinclair having had "three Sisters" it won't do', while reiterating his uncertainty about the eventual choice ('I thought of calling this of mine *Women in Love*. But I don't feel at all sure of it' (ii. 639)), and then provides a glimpse into his ludic associative thought processes by suggesting a seemingly endless series of possible titles for Carswell's own novel ('The Wild Goose Chase', an apt title for Lawrence's own work in progress; 'Never The Land of the Living'; 'The Rare Bird'; 'The Love Bird'; 'Cuckoo!'; 'Cuckoo, Cuckoo'; 'Loose strife'; 'Had'; 'The Pelican in the Wilderness'; 'The Lame Duck'; 'The Kingfisher'; 'Ducks and Drakes').

Returning to the compositional history, Lawrence received duplicate typescripts (TSI) from Pinker on 6 and 13 November and immediately carried out numerous fairly extensive revisions. With the assistance of Frieda, these revisions were copied onto both copies and completed by 20 November, at which point Lawrence dispatched one to his agent, Pinker, and sent the spare copy to Carswell for her and her husband (a lawyer) to read through. On a side note, this latter copy was ultimately circulated to a large group of people including the likes of Aldous Huxley, H. D., and probably Vanessa Bell (Virginia Woolf's half-sister),[27] hence the influence of *Women in Love*, which I would wager has been grossly underestimated by literary historians, can be traced back to well before the novel's eventual publication in 1920 and 1921 (not to mention the possibility of others having read drafts of 'The Sisters' from 1913 onwards, via Lawrence or Garnett).

Factoring in the aforementioned revisions to TSI, Pinker then produced a second typescript (TSII), of which Lawrence received copies between 28 March and 1 April 1917. TSII was then extensively revised by Lawrence over the following two and a half years, though the majority of changes (in blue ink) were carried out sometime between May and December 1917, probably completed by October 1917 when the Lawrences left Cornwall, with a second, lighter set of changes (in reddish-brown ink) completed sometime before

September 1919 – probably in late August to early September 1919 – when Lawrence sent TSII to his American publisher Thomas Seltzer.[28]

Evicted from Cornwall in October 1917 and no longer permitted to live by the coast (due to his wife being German, an episode fictionalised in the 'Nightmare' chapter of the later novel *Kangaroo*), the Lawrences had continued to move around in England – initially staying in London before moving back and forth between Berkshire and Derbyshire – until November 1919, when they were finally able to leave for Italy. Due to protracted discussions with his prospective English and American publishers, it was another *year* before Lawrence received page proofs for Thomas Seltzer's American edition in Italy in October 1920 (see iii. 613), though it was too late to include any of Lawrence's minor corrections to those proofs in the private edition of *Women in Love* published in New York on 9 November 1920. Lawrence also received proofs for Martin Secker's English edition in October and November 1920, along with Secker's request to insert chapter titles and alter certain passages (such as character names) due to a very real threat of libel.[29] Following these alterations, the first public edition of *Women in Love* was finally published in England on 10 June 1921.

Coda

Aside from the surviving manuscripts, which are patchy, the only traces of the vast amount of work Lawrence completed for *Women in Love* are recorded in the letters. Whenever there are gaps in the manuscript record and uncertainty in the letters, a degree of guesswork is therefore involved. Whereas the later typescript drafts (1917–19) are complete and correspond with the letters, there are a number of unknowns during the two original phases of writing, from March 1913 to May 1914 and from April to October 1916.

Prior to the Dunlop typescript of May 1914, of which only sixty-three pages remain, there are only two surviving manuscript fragments, which total just *fourteen pages* in length altogether. To put this into context, the early typescript alone is estimated to have totalled 600 pages; while we can only guess at the exact quantity of material produced prior to this, we know that the first full draft of 'The Sisters' totalled around 300 pages and the second at least 400, while Lawrence's comment on 3 April 1914 gives us a good idea: 'Oh, I tried so hard to work, this last year. I began a novel seven times. I have written quite a thousand pages that I shall burn' (ii. 161). The latter estimate would mean that the surviving material accounts for only around 1 *per cent* of the earliest drafts.

The existing critical consensus suggests that Lawrence completed just two early drafts of 'The Sisters', and the two earliest fragments are seen to correspond with these; hence, they are labelled 'The Sisters I' and 'The Sisters II'. Of course, Lawrence's suggestion in April 1914 that he began the novel 'seven times' may be hyperbolic. He used the same figure two months earlier in February ('I have begun my novel again – for about the seventh time' (ii. 146)) but then suggested in March that he had begun the novel 'for about the eleventh time' (ii. 153). However, Lawrence does report two 'false starts' in August 1913, and, given his ability to write rapidly, the results may have been substantial. He also suggested in May and June 1913 that he would rewrite the very first full draft in 'the third person' (whereas 'The Sisters I' is already written in the third person).

It is likewise suggested that Lawrence completed just two drafts between April and November 1916. Longer fragments survive from this period: a fifty-five-page handwritten manuscript containing an incomplete version of two opening chapters ('Prologue' and 'The Wedding'); ten handwritten notebooks containing approximately the last third of *Women in Love*, some of which (7–10) have traces of an earlier pagination and appear to have been removed from a previous manuscript,[30] corresponding to the second 'half' of TSI (pp. 369–666); the first 'half' of the latter (pp. 1–368), which is less professionally typed, contains many more words per page (370 compared to 260), and likewise appears to have been taken from an earlier manuscript; there is also a note on the first page of one of the aforementioned notebooks which appears to tie the earlier notebook and typescript chunks together ('continued from p. 368 (type)'). The current explanation is that the early fifty-five-page fragment represents a false start abandoned from April; a hypothetical 863-page manuscript (of which the earlier notebooks form the concluding section) represents Lawrence's work from April to June; and a composite manuscript made up of the first half of TSI and all ten of the notebooks represent the work completed from July to October. However, while this helps make some sense of the material itself, it doesn't stack up with Lawrence's letters: Lawrence doesn't mention a false start or an abandoned draft in April 1916 (as he had done in the early period from 1913 to 1914), and, as outlined earlier, he also suggests that three separate drafts were completed from April to October 1916.

In summary, traditional accounts have downplayed what is in reality an incredibly complex compositional and textual history, containing several unresolved and perhaps unresolvable questions, which make it impossible to be precise when framing the surviving materials. There is also a considerable amount of chance surrounding the 'final' form in which *Women in Love* was published, with many of Lawrence's later changes made to facilitate the publication of a novel which had already existed in manuscript form for around eight years. The most dramatic examples of this are the changes introduced to the proofs, partly at Secker's request: these include a new chapter division (producing the eventual thirty-two chapters) and *all* of the chapter titles (four of which were themselves revised by Lawrence before returning the proofs). Like the chapter titles, the many chapter divisions lend the final novel its distinctive crystallized form, yet these too were introduced by Lawrence at a late stage, when revising the second typescript draft (TSII); the earlier manuscript and typescript drafts contained just thirteen chapters (less than half the eventual amount). These factors have perhaps been downplayed due to a general scholarly ideology in which incomplete knowledge and guesswork are concealed, but we can also see it as a by-product of the traditional literary critical focus upon a series of finished texts, rather than on writing and textual process.

Notes

1 See Kinkead-Weekes, 1968, 'Introduction' (Lawrence, 1989), and 1996; Ross, 1976; Farmer, Vasey and Worthen's 'Introduction' (Lawrence, 1983); and Worthen and Vasey's 'Introduction' (Lawrence, 1998).
2 See Chapter 1 for a discussion of these metaphors and other terms used by genetic critics.
3 For a comparative genetic study of these authors, see van Hulle (2004).
4 It was not published until May 1913, following extensive work by its editor Edward Garnett.
5 Kinkead-Weekes praises *The Daughter-in-Law* in *From Triumph to Exile* (p. 60) and Worthen likewise in 'Drama and Mimicry in Lawrence' (p. 21). For a more detailed account of the works listed here, see Kinkead-Weekes's *From Triumph to Exile* (pp. 55–68); there is also a chronology of Lawrence's writings during this time in Appendix 1 of the same volume.
6 The 'common people' theme and the biographical setting (Scargill Street is a street in Lawrence's home town of Eastwood) do however relate to the two plays written around the same time (*The Fight for Barbara* and *The Daughter-in-Law*) and may have also fed into subsequent novels, including *The Lost Girl*.
7 The surviving fragments of 'A Burns Novel' are published in Nehls (1957, pp. 184–95). Critics suggest that the subsequent unspecified novel was probably based on the Cullen family of Eastwood (Florence Cullen nursed Lawrence's mother on her deathbed, while she and her father, George Henry Cullen, provided a basis for

James and Alvina Houghton in *The Lost Girl*), making use of material removed from 'Paul Morel' (a work in progress later retitled *Sons and Lovers*) and traceable to the 'Elsa Culverwell' fragment housed at Southern Illinois University; see James T. Boulton's suggestion in Lawrence's letters (i. 496) and Kinkead-Weekes in *Triumph to Exile* (p. 59).

8   Lawrence didn't mention a title for the deserted work until May 1913, when he referred, 'provisionally', to 'The Insurrection of Miss Houghton' (i. 546). Lawrence eventually returned to this work after having completed *Women in Love* and it was published as *The Lost Girl* in 1920.

9   *From Triumph to Exile* (pp. 59–64). Kinkead-Weekes also incorporates the short story written by Lawrence during the same period ('The Overtone') in this anticipatory scheme: 'not much of a story, and perhaps over-lyricised – but it marks yet another step behind mere stories of character, motive and blame' (p. 66).

10 In the essay from which these extracts are taken, Black does point to a helpful distinction between Lawrentian and Flaubertian methods of writing. Black also points out that Lawrence's more flexible approach to 'planning' avoids the problem of pre-determination: if a plan is too detailed and rigid, the author is prevented from following new leads and is ultimately no wiser at the end of a process of writing than they were at the beginning. I concur with both points.

11 I discuss the 'pot-boiler' tag in more detail in Chapter 4.

12 The length of 'The Sisters' can be gauged by Lawrence's final update in June 1913: 'I have nearly finished The Sisters – p. 283' (ii. 20).

13 Lawrence repeats this in another letter to Garnett a couple of days later (May 19): 'I wonder how you like 'The Sisters'. Not much, I am afraid [. . .]. Never mind, you can tell me what fault you find, and I can re-write the book' (i. 550).

14 Lawrence may have been speaking metaphorically of course, although he repeats the suggestion in another letter to Garnett (June 1): 'I am rather keen to re-write it in the third person' (ii. 20).

15 Ben Templeman is an early lover of Ella, the original name for Ursula (whose name was revised in the first manuscript of *The Rainbow*). Both characters feature in the second earliest surviving fragment, which I discuss in Chapter 4.

16 Andrew Harrison examines the impact of Marinetti and Futurism on Lawrence in *D. H. Lawrence and Futurism* (2003).

17 Lawrence reported: 'I've got just over £50 now, in the bank. It must last into May' (ii. 143) in a letter to Garnett in January 1914 and notified Garnett of Pinker's interests in April of the same year (ii. 166). According to Kinkead-Weekes, Lawrence 'now realized he was "after" no less than a revolutionary break with the classical European novel; and that this meant inevitable difficulty, even for the most intelligent and sympathetic of readers whose sensibilities had been developed within nineteenth-century concepts of character and of form' (*Triumph to Exile*, p. 152).

18 They weren't granted passports for the best part of five years (until 1919).
19 A few months later, in a letter attaching the first hundred pages of a new draft of *The Rainbow* (5 December to Pinker), Lawrence suggests that the war 'kicks the pasteboard bottom in the usual "good" popular novel. People have felt much more deeply and strongly these last few months, and they are not going to let themselves be taken in by "serious" works whose feeling is shallower than that of the official army reports' (ii. 240).
20 Kinkead-Weekes discusses the article briefly in *Triumph to Exile* (p. 151), to which I owe the reference to Barrow Station. Philip Skelton has also discussed this piece in his thesis 'D. H. Lawrence: Lawrentian Politics and Ideology' (pp. 1–5), submitted to the University of Nottingham in 2002. Both authors use the article as evidence of Lawrence's response to the war.
21 D. H. Lawrence, 'With the Guns' (1994, pp. 81–4). Also accessible online via *The Guardian*: https://www.theguardian.com/world/2014/aug/18/first-world-war-dh-lawrence-1914-with-the-guns.
22 For a discussion of this theme in relation to modernist culture more generally, see Armstrong (*Modernism*, pp. 6–23).
23 The content of the 'Wedding Ring' typescript is indicated by Alfred Kuttner reader's report, which can be found in 'Appendix III' of *TR*, pp. 181–8.
24 In mid to late 1915 and early 1916, Lawrence wrote several short stories including 'England, My England' and 'The Thimble'; he also made plans to lecture on the topic of social reconstruction with Bertrand Russell and set up a short-lived magazine on a similar topic with John Middleton Murry and Katherine Mansfield, entitled *The Signature*, which put out three issues between October and November 1915; for the latter, Lawrence wrote a series of allegorical essays entitled 'The Crown'; he then wrote a similar essay entitled 'Goats and Compasses' (now lost); worked on numerous pieces of travel writing, resulting in the publication of *Twilight in Italy* in June 1916; and, finally, completed his second collection of poetry, entitled *Amores*, which came out in July of the same year.
25 In a solemn description reaffirmed by the majority of Lawrence critics, Kinkead-Weekes suggests 'it is impossible to exaggerate the effect on Lawrence himself, on his conception of his audience and therefore on the nature of his work, of the destruction of *The Rainbow* in the England of 1915' (*TR*, p. li). For reinforcement of the argument that Lawrence's relationship with his audience radically altered after *The Rainbow*, see Bell's *D. H. Lawrence: language and being*, Eggert's Introduction to *Lawrence and Comedy*, and Worthen's 'Drama and Mimicry in Lawrence' in the same collection.
26 Geoff Dyer provides a comic account of 'the episode of the typewriter ribbon' in *Out of Sheer Rage*, pp. 161–2.
27 For a discussion of the full list of probable readers, see *Women in Love* (p. xxxii).

28 For more on the chronology of these two sets of revisions, see Ross (1978, pp. 117–23) and *WL* (pp. xxxv–ix).
29 For a fuller discussion of the novel's publication and the preparation of proofs, see *Women in Love* (pp. xxxix–li). Ross's suggestion that 'in comparison to the substantial and pervasive revision of *The Rainbow* proofs [...] the corrections of *Women in Love* are slight and infrequent' (1978, p. 126) may be correct in a quantitative sense, but the insertion of chapter titles alone is very significant in a qualitative sense.
30 Notebooks 7–10 carry the earlier title of 'The Sisters', which has been crossed out and replaced with 'Women in Love' and 'Dies Irae', as well as an earlier pagination of pp. 650–863, which has likewise been crossed out and replaced by pp. 220–36.

4

Early fragments and multiple drafts

This chapter looks at each of the early fragments in the compositional history of *Women in Love* in turn. It starts with the two earliest fragments ('The Sisters I' and 'The Sisters II'), which date from March 1913 to January 1914, before moving on to the second, longer fragment of typescript from 'The Wedding Ring' draft, which dates from February to May 1914 (thus predating Lawrence's decision to split the work in two (*The Rainbow* and *Women in Love*)), and finishes by following Lawrence's return to *Women in Love* in April 1916 (after completing *The Rainbow*) to look at the so-called 'Sisters III' fragment and comparing it to the opening section of the first full draft of the novel (TSI).

Though rich literary documents in their own right, these early manuscripts have hardly been studied by previous critics. I remedy this by providing a clear account of each fragment and picking out and tracking the development of prominent thematic and stylistic features, many of which provide a clear grounding for the final novel. Tracking Lawrence's own reflections on the work in progress in his letters from 1913 to 1916, I also clarify the *status* of these fragments as drafts, that is, as self-consciously provisional documents.

Genesis I (1913–14): Plotlines, rough drafts and 'real being' as process

Although the two earliest fragments are difficult to place precisely, they do demonstrate that familiar characters, plotlines and themes for *Women in Love* were established at an early stage. Both fragments contain primary sets of relationships (Gerald-Gudrun-Loerke, Birkin-Ella(Ursula)-Templeman(Skrebensky) and Ella(Ursula)-Gudrun), while also revealing a central theme: the struggle for the self, away from a known and complete or static past, towards an unknown and incomplete or fluid future.

'The Sisters I' fragment sets the tone immediately, beginning with a brief account of Gerald Crich's mother (Christiana Crich in *Women in Love*), who, alienated from her husband (the industrial magnate Thomas Crich), 'lived alone, a blind, unconscious resistance', and for whom 'the world outside did not really exist' (SI 291). There follows a brief exchange in a schoolroom between Gerald and his younger sister, Winifred (the schoolroom is 'now her workroom' (SI 291), though in *Women in Love* a studio for Winifred and Gudrun is constructed at the Crich's estate of Shortlands) in which Gerald shares his intention to marry Gudrun Brangwen. Gerald then visits Gudrun (who has her own 'lodgings' in the fragment), but finds 'the sculptor', Loerke, who has just arrived from Germany having been 'sent for' (SI 292) by Gudrun. There follows a heated exchange, during which Loerke condemns Gerald, apparently alluding to his fratricidal past: 'you trust to your position to play with *her*, you trust to your muscles to threaten me, just as you would threaten an unarmed man with your loaded gun' (SI 293). Loerke departs in grief, his face 'broken into lines of real agony, all distorted' (SI 293), and there is a brief interruption from Winifred, before Gudrun and Gerald are ostensibly reconciled, though Gudrun merely submits to Gerald's proposal of marriage: Gudrun, we discover, is pregnant and Gerald senses 'this aloofness of hers – she came to him as the father of her child, not as to a lover, a husband' (SI 296).

The second fragment, 'The Sisters II', is slightly longer and contains more narrative than the first, but is again dominated by an intense climactic exchange, this time between the other lead couple of *Women in Love*, Ella (later renamed Ursula) and Birkin, and likewise culminates in a marriage proposal. It begins with Ella departing (apparently from Birkin's lodgings) following a dispute with Birkin, who, like Gerald's mother in 'The Sisters I', is cut adrift, though more repressed: 'leaving him silent, impassive, but inside himself raging, only denying it all' (SII 373). August having arrived, the Brangwen family then go on holiday to Scarborough, though Ella and Gudrun stay at home. As Gudrun had her own lodgings in the first fragment, Lawrence has either altered the narrative so that Ella and Gudrun live at home throughout the later draft (as they do in *Women in Love*, Gudrun having recently returned from living in London), or she has not yet moved out (the second fragment begins on manuscript page 373, eighty-two pages ahead of the first fragment, but the drafts appear to have gotten longer and longer, hence Lawrence's eventual decision to split it into two separate works). The majority of the second fragment then involves a climactic exchange between Ella and Birkin, the latter visiting the house while Gudrun is out (at 'a tennis party' (SII 373)). Anticipating Birkin's proposal perhaps,

Ella experiences an agony of uncertainty about herself and Birkin and swings between being 'crouched together on the floor like some wild animal in pain' (SII 376) one moment and detached with pride the next, while Birkin, whose more repressed 'mind was blank' (SII 376), reacts by declaring his love and proposing. The scene is then interrupted by Gudrun's return and Birkin swiftly departs, inviting the sisters to visit him at 'Wamsley Mill' (SII 378) (in *Women in Love*, Birkin takes up lodgings at a mill beside 'Willey Water'). Ella and Gudrun are then called away to the family in Scarborough and the fragment's penultimate episode contains correspondence between Ella and Birkin. Ella self-consciously explains: 'I am really not hysterical [. . .] it takes a long time to get rid of the old things [. . .] it is working the old strain off that makes one so upset' (SII 379), while Birkin describes himself as 'entangled in the ruins and fragments of my old life, and struggling to get out' (SII 380). The fragment ends with the sisters on a walk by Flamborough Head, where they catch sight of Ella's former lover Ben Templeman and Ella experiences 'a wave of terror, deep, annihilating' (SII 380).

Both fragments are composed in Lawrence's typically neat and compact handwriting on long sheets of paper, approximately the length of A3 and width of A4 paper. Both are also very lightly revised, 'The Sisters I' containing around two to three minor revisions per page and 'The Sisters II' only one or two; the revisions consist of the deletion or substitution of a word or phrase (with replacements written superscript), and may well have taken place during the original writing process. Lawrence seems to have produced around thirty pages a week, which, on such large sheets of paper represents well over 10,000 words. Combined with the lightness of revision, this phenomenal speed suggests a spontaneous flow, which is reinforced by Lawrence's own description of his need to get 'sufficiently unrooted' in order to work.

There is however a deceptive amount of craft going on here, most obviously qualified by Lawrence's prior intention to rewrite, as discussed in the previous chapter. Lawrence notes his intention to rewrite his second draft while writing it, in a letter to Garnett on 29 January, and it is worth noting Lawrence's general description of his writing at this stage in the same letter:

> I write with everything vague – plenty of fire underneath, but, like bulbs in the ground, only shadowy flowers that must be beaten and sustained for another spring. [. . .] I do not try to incorporate it very much – I prefer the permeating beauty. (ii. 143)

The drafts are therefore invisibly layered, with the first entirely provisional and each subsequent draft a slightly less provisional rewritten version of the previous. Lawrence actually declares a preference for 'the permeating beauty' of this provisional style of writing, but goes on to acknowledge the financial necessity of making the provisional final: 'I must write to live, and it [the writing process] must produce flowers' (ii. 143).

Given the status of these fragments as drafts ('bulbs' or 'shadowy flowers'), Kinkead-Weekes's bald dismissal of the first ('even from a bald account, one can see what Lawrence meant by saying the novel was "for the *jeunes filles*", and the style is still a little novelettish' (1968, p. 375)) seems wayward. As does the emphasis placed by Farmer, Vasey and Worthen, in their respective introductions to the Cambridge editions of *Women in Love* and *The First 'Women in Love'*, on Lawrence's use of the phrase 'potboiler'. The editors suggest that this phrase 'cheerfully refers' to the first draft itself at page 110 (*WL*, p. xxi; *FWL*, pp. xix–xx), when, in actual fact, Lawrence uses it in reference to his *original* intention ('to do a potboiler'), before describing the draft *itself* as 'an earnest and painful work – God help it and me' (i. 536). Both of the phrases which the various critics highlight ('*jeunes filles*' and 'potboiler') are misleading, having essentially been used in jest by Lawrence to refer to a hypothetical intention – his earliest report that 'it will be decent' (i. 530) is followed by the playful parenthesis 'D.V.' (god willing) – whereas his descriptions of the drafts themselves are sincere. The most telling comment comes in May 1913 when 180 pages into the first draft (and still a hundred pages short of the first fragment itself):

> It was meant to be for the 'jeunes filles', but already it has fallen from grace. I can only write what I feel pretty strongly about: and that, at present, is the relations between men and women. After all, it is *the* problem of today. (i. 546)

Here Lawrence directly rubbishes the 'jeunes filles' tag and follows it up with a famous remark summing up one of his main motivations for writing the novel.

Returning to the question of spontaneity, Lawrence's own reflections support the argument that his writing was only partly autonomous. Consider his allusion to 'The Sisters': 'damn its eyes, there I am at page 145, and I've no notion what it's about [. . .] like a novel in a foreign language I don't know very well' (i. 544). Lawrence refers to the writing process and/or drafts in the third person, but he is clearly following in its wake and making sense of it as it unfolds: gradually learning the foreign language. In an oft-quoted passage in his introduction to *Collected Poems* (1928), Lawrence describes rewriting his early poems in similar terms: 'I have tried to let the demon have his say [. . .] the young man interfered with his demon' (2002, p. 620). The author may be interfering but the demon is equally '*his* demon' and the author a necessary medium. Lawrence actually expands on this point in a much earlier letter forewarning his then fiancé Louie Burrows, in December 1910 (near the outset of his career):

> It is the second me, the hard, cruel if need be, me that is the writer which troubles the pleasanter me, the human who belongs to you. Try, will you, when I disappoint you and may grieve you, to think that it is the impersonal part of me – which belongs to nobody, not even to myself – the writer in me, which is for the moment ruling. (i. 240)

While traditional critical theorists may have dismissed this suggestion of multiple selves, 'impersonal parts' or 'demons' as ideological, romantic or mystifying, I would emphasize that human agency is complex and is especially altered during creative and/or artistic processes.[1] As Fordham points out, genetic criticism needs to take account of the fact that 'writers thus express an experience of their own conscious agency being replaced by the agency of writing' (2010, pp. 24–5), and I refer the reader to the discussion of Bushell's Philosophy of Composition, the contributions of genetic criticism to cognitive psychology (where the activities of writing are seen to alter and supplement 'normal' cognitive processes) and the notions of textual selves and the extended mind discussed in Chapter 1.[2]

While writing 'The Sisters' drafts, Lawrence was soon to become the author of his third, and most successful novel, *Sons and Lovers*, having also published a collection of poems and numerous short stories. Lawrence effectively became an established writer during the early compositional history of *Women in Love*, therefore, and his fascination with his own writing processes reflects the fact that he is experimenting with literary form and attempting to give his writerly self more freedom. Hence the emerging split with his early editor Garnett, which is anticipated in Lawrence's report to Garnett in December 1913: 'in a few days I shall send you the first half of the Sisters [. . .] it is *very* different from *Sons and Lovers*: written in another language almost. I shall be sorry if you don't like it, but am prepared [. . .] the Hueffer-Pound faction seems inclined to lead me round a little like one of their show-dogs' (ii. 132–3). Like Garnett, the Ford Maddox Ford and Ezra Pound 'faction' was, in Lawrence's eyes at least, seeking to establish a fixed aesthetic form (whether that be Naturalism, Imagism, Vorticism or any other-ism).

In seeking to capture something *real* (like the provisionality of the 'bulbs' or 'shadowy flowers' alluded to earlier), Lawrence's writing was, like the characters of 'The Sisters' fragments, seeking to escape from fixed forms. In a letter to Garnett in April 1914, written while Lawrence was working on the third full draft of 'The Sisters' (i.e. 'The Wedding Ring') and having had several months to reflect on Garnett's disapproval of the previous drafts, Lawrence suggests an ontology of *process* as the deepest form of reality:

> I was upset by the *second* letter you wrote against it ['The Sisters'], because I felt it insulted rather the thing I *wanted* to say: not me, nor what I had said, but that which I was trying to say, and had failed in. [. . .] But it is no good unless you will have patience and understand what I *want* to do. I am not after all a child working erratically. All the time, underneath, there is something deep evolving itself out in me. And it is *hard* to express a new thing, in sincerity. [. . .] And this is why I didn't like the second letter you wrote me about the failed novel [. . .] because you seemed to insult my real *being*. (ii. 165–6)

The repeated assertions of 'I' suggest a coherent writerly self, expressed in the ongoing process of writing and withstanding these antagonisms between real and unreal dimensions of being. However, while Lawrence also suggests a teleology in which 'something deep' may eventually 'evolve its self out' in the final version of the work, 'real being' here appears as an effect of process, of something 'working' and 'evolving'. There is a conflict between the idealized (product) and the actual (process), and this provides a fundamental theme not only in the two early fragments but also the later published version/s of *Women in Love*. Real being, then, is not what is established ('not me, nor what I had said'), but what is in process ('what I *want* to do [. . .] something deep evolving itself out in me').[3]

When Lawrence returned to 'The Sisters' in 1916, his reports on the writing process closely echo the early letters. Lawrence writes to Lady Ottoline Morrell in May 1916: 'I have begun a new novel: a thing that is a stranger to me even as I write it. I don't know what the end will be' (ii. 604). The writing process is again invoked as an autonomous process, while the apparent sense of autonomy (and spontaneity) should be qualified not only by our knowledge of Lawrence's policy to 'always write my books twice', but also by the fact that this 'new novel' is itself a second overall attempt to write 'The Sisters'. In lines which closely echo the descriptions of Gerald's mother in the first fragment and Birkin's letter in the second, Lawrence also remarks elsewhere in the same letter: 'it is only in my individual self, which struggles to be free of the greater social self, that I live at all. One is at best only a torn fragment, a torn remnant of a man. It remains to trust that this remnant is the living essential part, otherwise one is already as good as dead' (ii. 603).

Lawrence's more fatal tone in the later letters should be read in the wider context of the First World War. In an earlier letter to Morrell, on 9 September 1915, Lawrence reported:

> Last night when we were coming home the guns broke out, and there was a noise of bombs. Then we saw the Zeppelin above us, just ahead, amid a gleaming of clouds [. . .]. So it is the end – our world is gone, and we are like dust in the air. (ii. 389–90)

However, we should also bear in mind those themes already evident in the early fragments (and the letters). While the war inflects Lawrence's more apocalyptic tone in these letters and in the later versions of *Women in Love*, there was already a framework in place to understand its impact on public and private notions of the self, and an underlying continuity of vision across the drafts and letters, which focuses on the conflict between flux and stasis, completion and incompletion, established thing and process. Prior to his report of the Zeppelin raids in the aforementioned letter, Lawrence had suggested: 'first there is the shedding of the old, which is so slow and so difficult, like a sickness' (ii. 388). Compare this and the previous quotation with Ella and Birkin's correspondence in the 'Sisters II' fragment:

> it takes a long time to get rid of the old things [. . .] it is working the old strain off that makes one so upset [. . .] it seems that everything has come toppling down, like an earthquake, since I have known you, and here I am entangled in the ruins and fragments of my old life, and struggling to get out. (SII 379–80)

The Sisters I: 'he would empty every drop of blood out of his veins, to warm her'

As mentioned, the first fragment begins with Mrs Crich, who appears alienated by the bonds attaching her husband, the industrial magnate, to society:

> She had let society bind her down, and had gone ~~stiff~~ **half-paralysed** in bondage. She began to write, or rather to compose, her various letters on the subject of her eldest son's marriage. The world outside did not really exist for her. She might as well have written letters to some mythological place of her own creation. But she wrote fictitiously, taking the tone of the usual, correct British nation. (SI, 291)

There is a critical edge towards societal norms here which I would suggest is sharp enough to place Lawrence at odds with Garnett: writing in 'the tone of the usual, correct British nation' is so detached from what Lawrence describes elsewhere as 'real *being*' that it 'might as well' be addressed to 'some mythological place'; the desire of the 'real' self is to escape stasis. It is also significant that Mrs Crich's letters concern her son Gerald's marriage, as her plight foreshadows the choice offered to Gudrun in her relationships with Gerald and Loerke: (for Gudrun, at least) Gerald essentially represents 'the usual, correct British nation', whereas Loerke represents experimental avant-garde art.[4]

In a cursory reading, the early fragments might also be viewed as less 'mature' or 'modernist' (than the later versions of the novel) due to the central theme of love and marriage, as in a more conventional romance. However, the marriage institution is challenged by the critical edge evident in the aforementioned quotation, while love and emotions generally are narrated with such intensity – 'this complete tenderness of love' – that the texts transgress conventional narrative boundaries. Certain passages in the fragments would have seemed obscene to 'the usual, correct British nation' of 1913, presenting an element of trauma which the (pre-First World War) public was not yet prepared to confront.

Following Gerald's delayed proposal, Gudrun informs him that Loerke 'ought *never* to have been allowed to come' and 'I shall always hate you a bit, for this' (SI 293). When Gerald approaches Gudrun, 'very hesitating', and, trembling 'with fear', draws her face 'against his chest' and bends over her in a dominating posture, Gudrun 'merely submitted [. . .] like a wild thing hiding itself from fear and misery against him' (SI 294). Gudrun's submission reminds Gerald of one of Winifred's rabbits, who had hurled itself at Winifred for protection after being 'attacked by a cat' (SI 294). This had 'hurt [Gerald] deeply, for nothing would come to him to be sheltered and loved' (SI 294), hitning that Gerald's desire for Gudrun is sadistic (the rabbit is attacked by a cat before it seeks comfort), while Gerald's desire to comfort Gudrun is also masochistic in its intensity: he 'felt he would empty every drop of blood out of his veins, to warm her and comfort her' (SI 295), and 'it cut him' to be reminded of his previous treatment of Gudrun; once attained, Gudrun also becomes all-consuming for Gerald: leaving him 'unable to realise anything else than just her' (SI 295).

The sadomasochistic bond between Gudrun and Gerald is simply made more explicit in *Women in Love*. There, in a new episode, Winifred's rabbit (Bismarck) actually scores the arms of Gudrun and Gerald in a frenzy, drawing blood. This leads to an acknowledgement of the nature of their bond, which is worth tracing through both typescripts of *Women in Love*: 'they looked at each other with half-smiling eyes of unconfessed knowledge, as if recognising a blood-brotherhood' (TSI 297). We see here how the invisible layering of the drafts works: an allusion to Winifred's rabbit in 'The Sisters I' becomes an episode in its own right in *Women in Love*; the allusion to blood-brotherhood in the passage in TSI is another invisible layer: later erased from that passage, it then becomes an episode in itself with the imagined pact between Birkin and Gerald. In TSII, Lawrence rewrites the passage with the most direct and obscene experience yet, where the traumatic extremity of feeling becomes clear: 'the long, shallow red rip seemed torn across [Gerald's] own brain, tearing the surface of his ultimate consciousness, letting through the forever unconscious, unthinkable red centre of the beyond, the obscene beyond' (TSII 385).[5]

To return to the opening point, Mrs Crich foreshadows Gudrun's own potential confinement at Shortlands. This is made evident in a passage following Gerald's proposal: 'something in [Gudrun] had shut up, or had gone frozen, during that time, and was now unresponsive to him, dead to him' (SI 295). As we see in miniature form earlier with the passage involving Winifred's rabbit, while relying heavily on the earlier drafts, Lawrence opens up and explores the dynamic between Gudrun and Gerald in more detail in later versions.

The Sisters II: 'Do you love me?'

The main episode in 'The Sisters II' fragment closely mirrors that of the first, involving a climactic emotional exchange between two of the lead protagonists, in this case Ella and Birkin, with the same added suspense of a looming marriage proposal. The second fragment is also marked by the conflict between established form (whether that be literary form or 'correct' behaviour) and 'real *being*' (in this case the contingent life of emotions). This is evident at the very start of the fragment when Ella departs Birkin leaving him 'silent, impassive, but inside himself raging, only denying it all, because he was a gentleman', while Ella 'felt her life was going on rich inside her' and 'could not concern herself with outside things' (SII 373).

There are however some noticeable differences in the second draft. Though similarly intense, the dynamic between Ella and Birkin is less sadomasochistic and (ultimately) destructive than that of Gudrun and Gerald. The second fragment also lacks the added strains of Gudrun's pregnancy and the involvement of a second love interest (in the form of Loerke); Ella's own secondary romantic interest, Templeman, does appear later in the fragment, though at a remove. The setting is also more significant in the second fragment, involving ambiguous lighting and porous inner and outer spaces, features which are quickly entangled in the ambiguity of the characters' own experiences.

The context, as mentioned, is Birkin's visit to Ella at home. As Ella is singing at the piano, and the doors and windows are open, her voice floats out to the street where Birkin hears it before arriving. Birkin arrives 'in the half light' and then remains 'standing rather hesitating in **on** the door **threshold**' after knocking. Birkin's introduction is also ambiguous: '"I wondered if you would be at home", while Ella's response is even more unclear: "I am alone", she said, half to keep him from ~~entering~~ **coming in**, half inviting him'. Inside, 'the house seemed very silent and ghostly about them, in the twilight, with doors and windows open' (SII 374), and the ambiguity of the narrative, the porousness between external scene and internal life, increases as the characters are brought into closer proximity. Birkin first sits 'in the shadow near the door' where, 'wearing grey', he is 'almost invisible', though Ella perceives his 'thinly modelled' head 'faintly yet distinctly' through the 'grey *clair-obscur*'. Confronting both the awkward lighting and physical distance, Ella goes to fetch some matches to light the fire while Birkin follows her 'insidiously' and offers his own matches, breaching a final, haptic boundary as, 'hesitating', her fingers 'twitched' his. Once a fire is lit, the visual clarity introduces a new *existential* ambiguity, as Birkin's face is illuminated but indecipherable: 'intent, hard, without expression', leaving Ella 'half-terrified', as 'the steady hardness of the eyes was dreadful to her'. At this pitch of sensitivity, Birkin's (physically intrusive) voice resonates with 'a hard, vibrating quality', and Ella feels increasingly 'powerless against him, and yet not with him' (SII 375). Battling this tension, Ella summons 'all her self-restraint' and puts 'her hand on [Birkin's] arm', saying 'pleadingly, pathetically: "No – no"', but Birkin's 'living arm beneath his sleeve' is 'a torture to her'. Closely mimicking the gesture of Gudrun in the first fragment, though perhaps inverting the sentiment, Ella reacts by catching Birkin to her, hiding 'her face on his breast' and 'crying, in a muffled, tortured voice, "Do you love me?"' (SII 375).

The expressionistic form may be evidence that Lawrence put more craft into the second draft, but it may also simply reflect the greater openness of Ella and Birkin's relationship, as evidenced by their subsequent, confessional correspondence. Gudrun and Gerald's relationship is more all-consuming, while the presence of Loerke also provided an extra dynamic in the first fragment. While this proviso should also be applied to the following point, and it is impossible to know whether the second fragment is not a revised version of the first draft/s of 'The Sisters', the second fragment does appear to explore the characters' inner lives more extensively than the first, as the following extract demonstrates:

> But [Birkin's] breast was strange to [Ella] [. . .] he was quivering, rigid [. . .] he was strange to her. He was strange to her, and it was almost agony. He was cold to her [. . .]. She felt he was cold to her. And the quivering man stiffened with desire was strange and horrible to her. She got free again, and, with her hands to her temples, she slid away to the floor at his feet, unable to stand, unable to hold her body erect. She must double up, for she could not bear it. [. . .]

Her womb, her belly, her heart were all in agony. She crouched together on the floor, crying like some wild animal in pain [. . .] a sound she was unaware of, that come from her unproduced, out of the depths of her body in torture. (SII 375–6)

The language (Ella's inability to 'bear' her feelings, which reach all the way down to 'her womb') and obvious use of repetition in this passage are extremely reminiscent of *The Rainbow*; however, the intensity of emotion, the 'wild animal' simile and Birkin's subsequent sense of detachment ('he knew she did not feel him any more. He knew he had no part in her, that he was out of place' (SII 376)) are also anticipated in the first fragment.

Tracking back briefly to Ella's earlier, blunt and almost defensive question to Birkin: 'Do you love me?" (SII 375), it is worth noting that the 1916 versions of *Women in Love* did not initially contain a passage in which Ursula questions Birkin in this way. Lawrence did however insert such a scene when revising TSII from 1917 onwards, so that, following the episode with Birkin's cat Mino, in a completely rewritten section of dialogue, Ursula says: '**Say you love me, say "my love" to me** [. . .]. **Say "my love" to me**' (TSII 245). This plea, or command, is itself a climactic moment, and it is interesting that in inserting the passage Lawrence was essentially returning to the earliest drafts.

The Wedding Ring: 'It was a shell now'

At sixty-three pages, the next surviving fragment is significantly longer than the previous two. It comes from 'The Wedding Ring' typescript, completed in February–May 1914, and survived because Lawrence inserted it (in two segments) into the first manuscript of *The Rainbow* (MSI, November 1914–March 1915). The two key identifying features of the fragment are the original pagination (pp. 219–75 and 279–83, revised to pp. 548–604 and 608–13) and the name of 'Ella', which is revised to 'Ursula' throughout.

Unlike the two earlier fragments, Lawrence heavily revised this third fragment by cutting passages throughout, most dramatically towards the end. There appear to be two levels of revision: the first in pencil and the second in pen. As the original pagination is altered in pencil (from that of 'The Wedding Ring' typescript, to that of *The Rainbow* manuscript), and pen is occasionally used to re-revise the revisions made in pencil, it is likely that both levels of revision were made when Lawrence was writing MSI of *The Rainbow*, six to ten months after completing 'The Wedding Ring' draft.

Early Fragments and Multiple Drafts   95

As the first two fragments are so short, one can only speculate on whether the overall nature of each draft was significantly altered. However, I discussed how the setting was more prominent in the second fragment, and continuing in this trajectory the third fragment appears to move away from the isolated conflicts presented in the earlier fragments to present a much broader critique of modern English society; this may simply be down to the section of narrative which survives in the fragment, in which Ella enters the world of work (Chapter 13, 'The Man's World', in *The Rainbow*). The very first paragraph repeats Ella's depth of feeling but signals this shift to her wider place in society:

> **She was** shut in ~~about~~ **with** the wet, silent, morning-sombre people, of whom she was one. The conductor came down issuing tickets, and each little ring of his clipper ~~seemed to sentence another person~~ **sent a pang of dread through her**.
> They were all going to work: she too was going to work. The fresh, slim girl sat trying to feel as they felt, to fit in with them. And fear was at her bowels. She was in the grip of some unknown force. (WR 219)

Though Ella is 'going to work', and the bulk of the fragment deals with her struggles to adapt to the harsh social realities of the school, the extract also echoes 'The Sisters II' with Ella's intensity of feeling, which stretches all the way to 'her bowels' and provides an existential edge to the narrative.

Worthen and Vasey in their introduction to *The First 'Women in Love'* (based on TSI) concur with Lawrence's own suggestion that, unlike *The Rainbow*, *Women in Love* 'does contain the results in one's soul of the war' (iii. 143), and suggest that the later novel 'came to reflect [Lawrence's] new attitude towards his society' (p. xxvi). However, the novel's textual genesis suggests far greater continuity across pre and post-war drafts. While Worthen and Vasey conclude that the 1917 publication of *Women in Love* 'would have reinforced strongly the extent to which Lawrence saw it as a novel which 'knocked the first loop-hole in the prison where we are all shut up' (ii. 663)' (p. lv), we can already make out this vision for the novel in the paralysis experienced by Mrs Crich at the very opening of the first fragment, and in Ella and Birkin's battle against the 'old life' in their letters towards the end of the second.

The trope of the prison takes shape most clearly in the third fragment, as Ella's sensitive, emergent self clashes brutally with the rigid system of discipline required to survive at the school, as well as with the schoolmaster's perverse pleasure in maintaining a system of power. This is made clear immediately upon

Ella's arrival, as Mr Brunt beckons her into the teacher's room 'as from a prison cell' and speaks to her without 'one touch of the colour of chivalry or gallantry in his voice, he spoke to her as if she were not a person at all, and particularly, not a woman' (WR 221): 'she had never been treated like this before, as if she ~~were a thing~~ **did not count**.' As these passages suggest, the third fragment also appears more self-conscious than the previous two, with greater theoretical depth. In a development that mirrors the later drafts of *Women in Love* (as we will see in the following chapters of this book), Lawrence's revisions and additions are often theoretical explorations of the preceding narrative, as in the following addition to the initial descriptions of the schoolroom: '**in the gas-light and gloom and the narrowness of the room all seemed unreal** [. . .] **it seemed that neither morning nor weather really existed. This place was timeless**' (WR 220). We also saw earlier how the teacher's room was directly likened to a 'prison cell', and this trope is repeated elsewhere: the schoolroom, in 'its rigid, long silence ~~was rigid and chilling~~ **reminded her of a prison** [. . .] because of the horrible feeling of being shut in [. . .] the prison was round her now!' (WR 223). While it may seem a romanticized image, Ella is self-conscious of this, too, which only emphasizes the cruel reality of the school: 'she winced, feeling she had been a fool in her anticipations [. . .] this prison of a school was reality [. . .] here she would realise her dream of being the beloved teacher bringing light and joy to her children~~,~~!' (WR 224).

It is worth noting that, although, as I discuss in the following, the 'prison' trope gives way to a more complex trope of the 'shell' as the third fragment progresses, the former does recur in *Women in Love*. As, for example, when Birkin spends a night at Hermione's stately home Breadalby early on in the novel:

> How lovely, how sure, how formed, how final all the things of the past were – the lovely accomplished past – this house, so still and golden, the park slumbering its centuries of peace. And then, what a snare and a delusion, this beauty of static things – what a horrible, dead prison Breadalby really was, what an intolerable confinement, the peace! (TSII 112)

This example also shows how Lawrence's tropes connect disparate strands, from state education to traditional forms of beauty, through the central thematic opposition of creative flux and deathly stasis.

The schoolroom provides Lawrence with a model of modernity, where an almost military level of discipline is applied to deal with mass society in an organized and efficient way ('the long rows of desks, arranged in a squadron') (WR 224), and where the realms of the human and the individual can seem 'out of place' (WR 224) in face of the abstract and the collective. Consider the following long extract during Ella's first day in the schoolroom, where Lawrence's revisions again add theoretical depth:

> The desks before her had a hard **an abstract** angularity that was impervious to sentiment. She knew **crystallised her sentiment into hard impersonality. She winced, feeling** she had been a fool in her anticipations. This hard shell of a school showed her very well what the spirit was: something hard and calculated. **was not meant for love and personal feeling: it had a hard purposiveness that she could not understand.** She had brought her feelings and her generosity where neither generosity nor emotion held good **were wanted**. And already she felt rebuked, ashamed of herself **troubled by the new atmosphere, out of place**.
>
> She slid down, and they returned to the teachers' room. It was queer to feel that the placed denied **one ought to alter** one's personality. Ella seemed to herself dumb, neutral. This experience was strange to her. She was nobody at all. She had no reality of her self, the reality was all outside her, extinguishing her. **She was nobody, there was no reality in herself, the reality was all outside of her, and she must apply herself to it.** (WR 224)

Lawrence was a schoolteacher himself (and before that a pupil teacher) for many years, and education is perhaps a unique social institution due to the level of authority invested in the teacher and the importance of leadership within the pedagogic relationship. Though Birkin is himself a school inspector, the schoolroom is only glimpsed at in the eventual novel (following its divorce from *The Rainbow*), and the long 'Industrial Magnate' chapter of *Women in Love* provides a different example of industrialized social organization where leadership and authority are prominent. However, there is another, completely different context in which we can place Ella's experiences in the schoolroom, and that is in relation to writing itself.

As the many descriptions of strangeness and foreignness indicate, the protracted process of writing *Women in Love* (over many years) was an absorbing and educational process for Lawrence in itself. However, Lawrence was not working in a vacuum, and his frequent reflections on other writers during the period help us contextualize his work. While his *Study of Thomas Hardy* has been widely discussed by critics, his earlier, much shorter and more antagonistic review of Thomas Mann, written in June 1913, only a month after the first draft of 'The Sisters' was finished, helps us place Ella's schoolroom experience of 'hard impersonality' in the third fragment in a writerly context:

Germany is now undergoing that craving for form in fiction, that passionate desire for the mastery of the medium of narrative, that will of the writer to be [. . .] undisputed lord over the stuff he writes, which is figured to the world in Gustave Flaubert. (1913, p. 200)

Lawrence here expresses his clear opposition to those Flaubertian tenets of writing admired by so many of his contemporaries, including Garnett. Lawrence's projection of 'a craving for form in fiction' onto the entire German nation is less outlandish when we place it in the context of the Prussian military training which Lawrence himself had witnessed that same summer of 1913 (as discussed in his article 'With the Guns'), a year before the country's invasion of Belgium. Furthermore, Lawrence suggests that 'this craving for form is the outcome, not of artistic conscience, but of a certain attitude to life', and that, for the Flaubertian school, 'form is not a personal thing like style. It is impersonal like logic. And just as the school of Alexander Pope was logical in its expressions, so it seems the school of Flaubert is, as it were, logical in its aesthetic form' (200). Lawrence therefore views logical form as inhuman – a desire for mastery, an imposition of logical standards on human individuality – and poses his fundamental concern with Flaubertian, Modernist form as a question: 'Can the human mind fix absolutely the definite line of a book, any more than it can fix absolutely the definite line of action for a living being?' (200).

To return to the schoolroom, we find the individual are pupils grouped into classes and the classes ranked into 'Standards', which are then ordered to 'fall in' and file to their desks while the school piano plays 'a march tune' (WR 226–7). In the same massive room as Ella, Mr Brunt leads his class 'like a machine, always in the same hard, high, inhuman voice [. . .] oblivious of everything' (WR 228), while Ella's own becomes 'this ~~innumerable class~~ **inhuman number** of fifty children depending on her [. . .] this class of fifty ~~unknown~~ **collective** children, depending on her command [. . .] she could not speak as she would to a child, because they were not individual children, they were a ~~collection of scholars.~~ **collective inhuman thing**' (WR 228). We see here how abstract, logical form renders individuality superfluous, while, with the pupils thus abstracted, the masterful teacher becomes the (Flaubertian) writer or conductor:

> The class was his class and ~~felt with him~~ **he asserted it.** ~~It did not matter how he thrashed or bullied, nor how he was hated.~~ **She was a wavering substitute. He thrashed and bullied, he was hated. But he was master.** [. . .] **And in school, it was power and power alone that mattered.** [. . .] That seemed to be his one

~~craving, almost his mania: to keep absolute, undisputed authority in the school, at whatever cost.~~ **reason in life, to hold, inviolable authority over the school'** (WR 229).

Whereas Ella, initially still an individual, becomes the superfluous element: 'the system, which ~~he had built up like an~~ **was his** extension of himself, which was the ~~organised growth of~~ **the machine working to** his will, was attacked and threatened at the point where ~~Ella~~ **Ursula** was included. She was the extraneous matter that he must cast forth' (WR 243).

Ella remains 'extraneous' and a threat at school until two violent encounters with her pupils split her individual self from her persona as a schoolteacher. First, after Ella's pupils have taken to shouting verbal abuse at her when they spot her outside of school in the town, they catch her walking along a deserted high road one day and hurl stones at her, which triggers 'a change' and she vows: 'never again would she give herself as individual to her class [. . .] she did not want to be a person, to be her self any more, after such humiliation' (WR 247–8). This vowed split then becomes a rupture following a second scene, in which Ella brutally canes an insubordinate boy: 'again and again, whilst he struggled making inarticulate noises, and lunging vicious kicks at her' (WR 251). After this second episode, 'something had broken in her' (WR 254).[6]

Despite serving a positive end, Lawrence's aim in writing *Women in Love*, to knock 'a loop-hole in the prison where we are all shut up', can appear destructive, and Ella's ordeal at the school indicates the collateral damage for those individuals who populate his novel. However, despite revealing an apparent split between the personal, human/e self and the abstract, modern world, the characters in *Women in Love* also demonstrate, more positively, some of the ways in which these splits can be stitched back together. Perhaps the most powerful example is in the passionate bonds which emerge between characters, often through dialogue. These bonds are evoked by each of Lawrence's primary titles, from 'The Sisters', which evokes the highly articulate bond between Ella/Ursula and Gudrun Brangwen, to 'The Wedding Ring' and 'Women in Love', which evokes the sisters' attempts to form new and more intimate romantic bonds in the world. While the first and second fragments provide evidence of these latter attempts, the remainder of the third fragment – following Ella's trials inside and outside of the schoolroom – provides evidence of a more sisterly bond between Ella and fellow schoolteacher Maggie Schofield. Like Ursula and Gudrun at the outset of *Women in Love* – as we will see in the fourth and final fragment – Ella and Maggie 'talked of love and marriage, and the position of women in marriage' (WR 266).

Finally, having hinted at the shift of trope from 'prison' to 'shell' – the latter being a more dynamic trope which can not only contain things and be 'knocked' open, but can also open itself, be cast aside, and explode – it is worth highlighting an example from the closing pages of the fragment. Just before Ella finishes her work at school following the end of term, the Brangwen family move from their old farm house at Cossethay to a new town house in Willey Green, and, as the narrator describes it, 'the old, bound shell of Cossethay was to be cast off, and [Ella] was to dance away into the blue air' (WR 274). We see then how, after the (fluid, ongoing) self has left the old (static) space, the latter becomes a closed remnant of the past, a 'shell'. Likewise, during Ella's last day at school, 'it was as if the walls of the school were going to melt away. Already they seemed shadowy and unreal. [. . .] the prison was a momentary shadow halting about them. The place stood bare and vacated. She had triumphed over it. It was a shell now' (WE 279–80).

Genesis II: 'Prologue'

Whereas the three fragments from 1913 to 1914 fit somewhere in the middle or end of their respective drafts, the fourth fragment, the so-called 'Sisters III' fragment, which dates from 1916, consists of the *opening* fifty-five pages of its respective draft. It contains a subsequently discarded 'Prologue' chapter, which provides an alternative beginning to *Women on Love* and thus allows us to consider the novel's framing more generally. The Prologue occupies pages 1–32, while pages 33–55 contain an incomplete second chapter entitled 'The Wedding', which maps directly onto the novel's first chapter in subsequent drafts (as well as the published version), including familiar dialogue between Ursula and Gudrun Brangwen followed by an excursion to view a local wedding. The direct mapping of the second, incomplete chapter indicates that Lawrence kept this particular draft to hand and followed it closely when writing the subsequent version (emphasizing the interlinked nature of each draft and the fragment's status *as* a draft).

The fragment itself is written in pencil on small, loose sheets of notepaper, taken from the kind of school exercise books used by Lawrence to complete the subsequent notebook drafts (discussed in Chapter 5); at around twenty-three lines per page, the sheets are barely half the size of the massive sheets used for the two earliest fragments. The fourth fragment is revised throughout, quite heavily in places, while the inclusion of chapter titles is itself unusual as, elsewhere in the composition of *Women in Love* (as well as *The Plumed Serpent*), Lawrence tended to add these *after* having completed a draft (though if this draft was itself based closely on the earliest versions of 'The Sisters', Lawrence may have intended it as a 'final' draft while writing).

The Prologue chapter begins with a quasi-mythic account of a meeting between Rupert Birkin and Gerald Crich, which takes place four years prior to the events of the novel and features an existential proximity between the men reminiscent of the exchange between Ella and Birkin in the 'Sisters II' fragment: 'there had been a subterranean kindling in each man ~~toward the other~~. **Each looked toward the other and knew the trembling nearness**' (SIII 1). Brought together by a common friend (Hosken), the three men spend a transformational week mountain climbing in the Tyrol, which passes 'like an intense brief lifetime' (SIII 1–2):

> The three of them had reached another state of being, they were enkindled in the upper silences into a rare, unspoken intimacy, an intimacy that took no expression, but which was between them like a transfiguration. [. . .] It was another world, another life, incorporate **transfigured**, and yet most vividly corporeal, the senses all raised till each felt his own body, and the presence of his companions, like an essential flame, they radiated to one enkindled, transcendent fire, in the upper world.
>
> Then had come the sudden falling down to earth, the sudden extinction. [. . .] On the station they shook hands, and went asunder, having spoken no word and given no sign of the transcendent intimacy, which had roused them beyond the everyday life. (SIII 2)

With a curious blend of physics ('they radiated') and metaphysics ('an essential flame'), this opening section takes place in an otherworldly Alpine setting, which the eventual narrative returns to in the latter stages (when Ursula, Birkin, Gudrun and Gerald holiday there together). Here, the violent divisions examined in the previous fragments are momentarily transcended through this quasi-mythic 'state of being', where the characters experience a 'transcendent intimacy' which is yet rooted firmly in the body ('the senses all raised till each felt his own body, and the presence of his companions, like an essential flame'). The 'unspoken' nature of this companionship also suggests a level of ambivalence in the characters, which perhaps foreshadows the later events of the novel when Gudrun and Gerald (in particular) are overcome by this transcendent 'upper world', while Ursula and Birkin escape it.

This mythic opening provides a completely different introduction to *Women in Love*. The episode occupies only a couple of pages, although the rest of the Prologue is also different, providing a brief history of Gerald, Birkin and Hermione (initially named Ethel but revised to Hermione), whose 'country house in Derbyshire' (SIII 3) – belonging to her father Sir Charles Roddice – provides the scene for Gerald and Birkin's next meeting. These pages appear more improvisational than the previous fragments. They contain a bewildering array of detail (Birkin's 'loveable eyes were, in the last instance, estranged and unsoftening like the eyes of a wolf', while Gerald 'in the last issue was wavering and lost' (SIII 4)), as well as a confusing sense of time. Aside from a shifting present tense, the chronology in these thirty pages ranges over nine years:

- We are told briefly about Birkin and Hermione's first meeting in Oxford when Birkin was 'twenty-one': he was a Fellow of Magdalen College whose 'essays on Education ~~had been very well received~~ **were thought brilliant**', while Hermione, a year Birkin's junior, had read 'political economy' and listened to his 'passionate declarations [. . .] holding forth against Nietzsche', 'loved him' and devoted herself to 'this mental and spiritual flame'; when Sir Charles troubles her with the formal question of marriage, she responds: 'How vulgar you are!' and so their relationship had 'continued' (SIII 5–6).
- Birkin and Gerald's second meeting at the Roddice house appears to take place five years later, as Hermione is then 'twenty-five'.
- When the Prologue ends, with Hermione and Birkin 'running to the end of their friendship', Birkin 'was now thirty, and she was twenty-nine' (SIII 31).

Gerald is a fleeting presence in the Prologue and ultimately journeys 'abroad to South America' (SIII 31). The majority of the chapter therefore focuses on the relationship of Birkin and Hermione.

Lawrence appears to have abandoned the Prologue chapter by July or August 1916 as it is completely absent from the first typescript. The immediate effect is that the viewpoint of the Brangwen sisters again becomes primary, with their view of the Hosken wedding serving as an introduction to the other main characters

(Birkin, Gerald and Hermione, all of whom are absent in *The Rainbow*). It also means the major characters in *Women in Love* are all somewhat enigmatic as we are introduced to their conversations with no immediate backstory, and this feature is accentuated by Lawrence's rewriting of the 'Wedding' chapter in subsequent drafts.

The fourth fragment provides greater continuity with *The Rainbow*, with its dreamlike opening mirroring the both dreamlike and nightmarish ending to the latter novel, while its more formal introductions to Gerald, Birkin, and Hermione help bridge the gap between the novels. Likewise, when Ursula and Gudrun do appear in the second chapter of the fragment, we learn they are both 'a good deal changed. Ursula was twenty-seven years old now, and Gudrun twenty-six' (SIII 34). Bearing in mind that Gudrun is a minor character in *The Rainbow*, prior to the sisters' opening conversation, we learn that she had 'been home a couple of days' (SIII 36) and had previously received a 'scholarship in Nottingham, and in London she had lived freely' as an artist, whose 'little models in clay, of animals and birds and people' were well-received (SIII 34-5). Similarly, of Gerald, we learn at the outset of the 'Wedding' chapter that 'William Crich, Gerald's father, was the principal owner of the mines that went down the valley of Beldover' and that 'the Criches were the only considerable people in the whole neighbourhood' (SIII 33). The framing of characters in the fourth fragment is much more descriptive, therefore, whereas the later versions of *Women in Love* appear elliptical. A key detail about Gerald and Birkin's relationship in the Prologue is that 'they knew ~~that~~ they loved each other', and 'all this knowledge was kept ~~in the dark, subterranean~~ **submerged in the** soul of the two men' (SIII 3). Along these lines, we might say that the later versions of the novel keep these details submerged in its own 'subterranean soul' (the *avant-texte*).[7]

As mentioned, the majority of the Prologue focuses on Birkin and Hermione. We learn that, while Birkin wanted to be 'vital and ordinary [. . .] to be common, vulgar, a little gross', Hermione feels Birkin is 'prostituting his mind' in his friendship with Gerald. This growing antagonism is mutually destructive yet neither Birkin nor Hermione appear capable of breaking off their relationship:

> He recognised that he was on the point of breaking, becoming a thing, losing his integral being, or she of becoming insane [. . .] a mere disordered set of processes without purpose or integral being [. . .] yet he could not save himself. (SIII 21)

Birkin is essentially a different character in the Prologue, with a Wildean prior life as a sensualistic, nihilistic aesthetician (much more obviously akin to Gudrun in *Women in Love*). Meeting a 'strange' type of man, Birkin 'would feel the desire spring up in him, the desire to know this man, to have him, as it were to ~~devour~~ **eat** him, to take the very substance of him' (SIII 29) (just as Gudrun, in a subsequent draft of *Women in Love*, 'looked at Gerald. He looked like a fruit made to eat. He was her apple of knowledge. She felt she could set her teeth in him and eat him ~~till nothing but a~~ **to the** core ~~was left~~' (N7 216)). We learn of Birkin's 'harsh, jarring poetry, very real and painful' and his 'shallower, gentle lyrics', while his 'records and his oracles [. . .] **would be** nothing if his worship were neglected' by Hermione, his 'priestess' (SIII 6). Given the rarity of Lawrence's protagonists figuring as writers, this artistic atheism is noteworthy. The Prologue also rehearses some of Birkin's famous monologues: 'if there *be* no great philosophic idea, if, **for the time being,** mankind, instead of going through a period of growth, is going through a corresponding process of decay and decomposition from some old, fulfilled, absolute idea, then what is the good of educating?' (SIII 12). These monologues are indeed dramatic, with Birkin's own destructive relationship with Hermione providing the key context.

Genesis II: 'The Wedding'; mapping 'A ghostly replica of the real'

Following the Prologue, as well as the opening pages of the incomplete 'Wedding' chapter, which introduce the Criches and reintroduce the Brangwen sisters, much of the remaining twenty or so pages of the fourth fragment map directly onto the subsequent typescript draft of *Women in Love*. I will provide some examples here in order to demonstrate just how closely Lawrence worked with the previous draft, while also highlighting the ways in which Lawrence revised, often by either including more reflexive passages, or by making the content more elliptical (both forms of revision which I have already highlighted).

In both the 'Sisters III' fragment (SIII 36) and the first typescript (TSI 1), 'Ursula and Gudrun sat **one morning** in the large window-bay of their father's house in Beldover'. Their conversation then begins to deviate slightly through revision:

SIII 36	TSI 1
'Ursula', she said, putting the question nearest her heart, 'don't you want to get married?'	'Ursula', said Gudrun, 'don't you ~~ever want~~ **really want** to get married?'

Lawrence cuts the parenthetical phrase 'the question nearest her heart', rendering the later version more repressed. This is a trend which continues in the following passage, where Gudrun reflects on the family home and her father:

SIII 37–8	TSI 5
'It's rather hard to be sure what a home *is*, ~~nowadays~~ **really** – whether it is the place where one is *never* oneself, and never can be oneself, or whether one is most natural there [. . .] I think father is the greatest stranger I ever set eyes on – the greatest outsider, too', she said.	'I find myself ~~a complete alien~~ **completely out of it**. [. . .] ~~The completest stranger.~~ **I haven't thought about him: I've refrained'**, she said coldly.

Here, while the initial rewrite in the first typescript is slightly more suppressed, following further revisions to the typescript itself Gudrun reveals she has completely suppressed the issue. A similar shift occurs as the sisters decide to leave the house:

SIII 38–9	TSI 5
They were aware of the room in which they sat, the familiar furniture, the burdensome, familiar atmosphere, more ~~wearying stark~~ **insistent and obtrusive** than violent change. [. . .] Under Gudrun's influence, the hatred had flashed across her consciousness like a spark struck from a flint. She had never before admitted this violent, radical loathing of all her condition, of all the old, close, familiar things that had formed her. But now she knew. [. . .] 'Let us go out', Gudrun exclaimed.	'Yes', wavered Ursula; and the conversation was really at an end. The sisters found themselves confronted by a ~~kind of~~ void, ~~a terrifying chasm,~~ as if they had looked over the edge ~~of a precipice~~. They worked on in silence for some time. Gudrun's cheek was flushed with repressed emotion. She resented its having been called into being. 'Shall we go out and look at that wedding?' she asked at length, in a voice that was too casual.

Whereas, in the earlier version, the sisters 'were aware' of this uncanny experience of 'burdensome' familiarity, with the 'old, close, familiar things' of the past hemming them in, in the later version the sisters are 'confronted' by a repressed 'void', and, interestingly, this creative suppression inflects the content, as Gudrun's cheek flushes 'with repression'. The narrative itself is therefore *more* self-conscious in revision, with Gudrun's desire to repress the conflict made explicit.

By removing the Prologue, Lawrence makes the opening to *Women in Love* much more dialogical. It replaces the inarticulate and unconscious meeting of the bodies of Gerald and Birkin with the reflexive dialogue between Ursula and Gudrun, who, gazing through their front window, articulate some of the novel's central themes – love, marriage, family and the home – and hint at what I argue is the key theme, which is how each of these concepts can become fixed things (ideas or institutions), which then hinder the flux of the real self. The sisters' dialogue continues during their excursion and Lawrence's rewritten version in the first typescript follows the same pattern in becoming increasingly reflexive:

SIII 40	**TSI 6**
'It is like a country in ~~the underworld~~ **another world**', said Gudrun; 'the people all ghosts, and everything a ghostly degraded replica of what it should be. Ursula, it's marvellous, it is like being mad.'	'It is like a country in an underworld', said Gudrun. 'The colliers bring ~~Hell~~ it above-ground with them, shovel it up. Ursula, it's marvellous, it's really marvellous – it's really wonderful, another world. The people are all ghosts, and everything is ghostly. Everything is a ghostly replica of the real world, a replica, a ghost, all ~~soiled~~, everything soiled **sordid**. It's like being mad, Ursula.'

Perhaps Lawrence's ability to envision such spectral detachment is grounded in the increasingly reflexive process of rewriting and revision. In the Prologue chapter draft, Birkin describes 'all ideas' as 'mere sounds, old repetitions, or else novel, dextrous sham permutations and combinations of old repetitions' (SIII 14). In the narrative itself, it seems to be a consequence of the sisters' self-consciousness: everything in the visual field is commented on as though a spectacle constructed for their own bemusement; elsewhere in the fragment, Gudrun describes the locals as 'worse than Goya' (SIII 44).

Lawrence's novels escape this dizzying self-consciousness by transitioning from dialogical to descriptive passages, which themselves, intriguingly, are hardly rewritten at all despite multiple draft stages. Consider the following example, which follows immediately after the previous dialogue and provides an anchorage in the landscape:

SIII 40	TSI 6–7
The two sisters were crossing a black path across a soiled, worn field. Before them was a large landscape, a valley with collieries whose white stem ~~waved an~~ **and black** smoke waved and rose in strong columns, hill-sides where rows of ~~red~~ **grimy** dwellings with slate roofs climbed in a naked contour, fields with iron fences, fields with deep clayey holes dug in them, then more brittle rows of houses. The paths on which the girls walked were of black, trodden earth, the grass of the fields was worn and padded. They passed through a stile of two posts, rubbed shiny by the transit of many colliers in moleskins, then along the end of some alleys.	The two sisters were crossing a black path through a dark, soiled field. On the left was a large landscape, a valley with collieries, and opposite hills with cornfields and woods, all blackened with distance, as if seen through a veil of crape. White and black smoke rose up in steady columns, ~~like~~ magic within the dark air. Near at hand came the long rows of dwellings, approaching curved up the hill-slope, in straight lines along the brow of the hill. They were of darkened red brick, brittle, with dark slate roofs. The path on which the sisters walked was black, trodden in by the feet of the recurrent colliers, and bounded from the ~~degraded~~ field by iron fences; the stile that led again into the road was rubbed shiny by the moleskins of the passing miners.

I will provide many more examples in this book of Lawrence switching from passages of constrained dialogue, which are themselves heavily revised or rewritten, to more restful descriptive passages, which go virtually unrevised, and have also done so elsewhere.[8] These transitions generate a rhythmic structure which I think is common to virtually all of Lawrence's fiction and provides a clue not only as to how Lawrence was able to write so rapidly but also as to how to interpret Lawrence's famous advice to Garnett, to look in his writing for 'some other rhythmic form' (see endnote 3).

Notes

1 Lawrence's allusions to his writing self as his 'demon' and his 'hard, cruel', 'second me' suggest an interesting reading of Nick Lowe and Johnny Cash's 'The Beast in Me', as a song about the creative self.

2 The insufficiency of everyday intentionality to describe creative processes is perhaps clearer in relation to other, more physical art forms like visual art and music, and it is perhaps for this reason that Lawrence made his semi-autobiographical protagonist Paul Morel a painter rather than a writer, while the protagonists of *The Trespasser* (1912), *Mr Noon* (1987) and *Aaron's Rod* (1922) – written shortly before, during or after the completion of *Women in Love* – are all musicians (the most Dionysian art

form); on Lawrence's relationship with music more generally, see Susan Reid (2010 and 2019).
3. Lawrence's famous letter to Garnett in June 1914, reflecting on the finished typescript of 'The Wedding Ring', exhorts the reader along the same lines: 'you mustn't look in my novel for the old *stable* ego of the character [. . .] don't look for the development of the novel to follow the lines of *certain* characters: the characters fall into the form of some other *rhythmic* form, like when one draws a fiddle-bow across a fine tray delicately sanded, the sand takes lines *unknown*' (my italics; ii. 183–4); 'lines' and 'characters' are also typographic features, which suggests an underlying distinction between manuscript draft and printed text.
4. Gudrun's choice is perhaps more obvious in the 'Sisters I' fragment as Gerald and Loerke propose at the same time, while her pregnancy adds a layer of depth which Lawrence initially included as an epilogue to *Women in Love* but ultimately removed from the final versions of the novel.
5. Gerald's attitude towards forgiveness in 'The Sisters I' fragment is also transgressive: 'he was glad if she made him suffer [. . .] for if she had forgiven him anything, that left him in the position of the forgiven, which he could not bear [. . .] he had such a horror of the indoor, dark atmosphere of women, who forgive a man because they know his weakness. Gudrun knew his weakness, and hated him for it, and made him suffer for it till he was level with her. And that was fair. And so he could be open with her, and himself' (SI 295).
6. Interestingly, 'feeling too upset to go home' after this second violent exchange, Ella takes shelter in a 'small tea-shop' in town, which is described as 'a mechanical action, to cover over her existence. There she sat in the dark, obscure little place, without knowing' (WR 254). In *The Plumed Serpent*, Kate takes the exact same course of action, visiting a teashop in town this exact course of action is chosen as a therapeutic response by after leaving similarly traumatic bullfight.
7. Defending this elliptical style in a letter to Carswell in November 1916, Lawrence argues that it is more realistic: 'about the Gerald-Work part: I want it to come where it does: you meet a man, you get an impression of him, you find out *afterwards* what he has done' (iii. 57). In a different context, Hannah Sullivan (2013) has argued that editorial 'subtraction' is a key mode of revision in modernist literature (alongside 'addition'), helping to generate the elliptical quality of many paradigmatic modernist texts, from Imagist poetry and Eliot's *The Waste Land* to Hemingway's 'Iceberg principle'.
8. My genetic study of 'The Shades of Spring' also focuses on this point (Morsia, 2014).

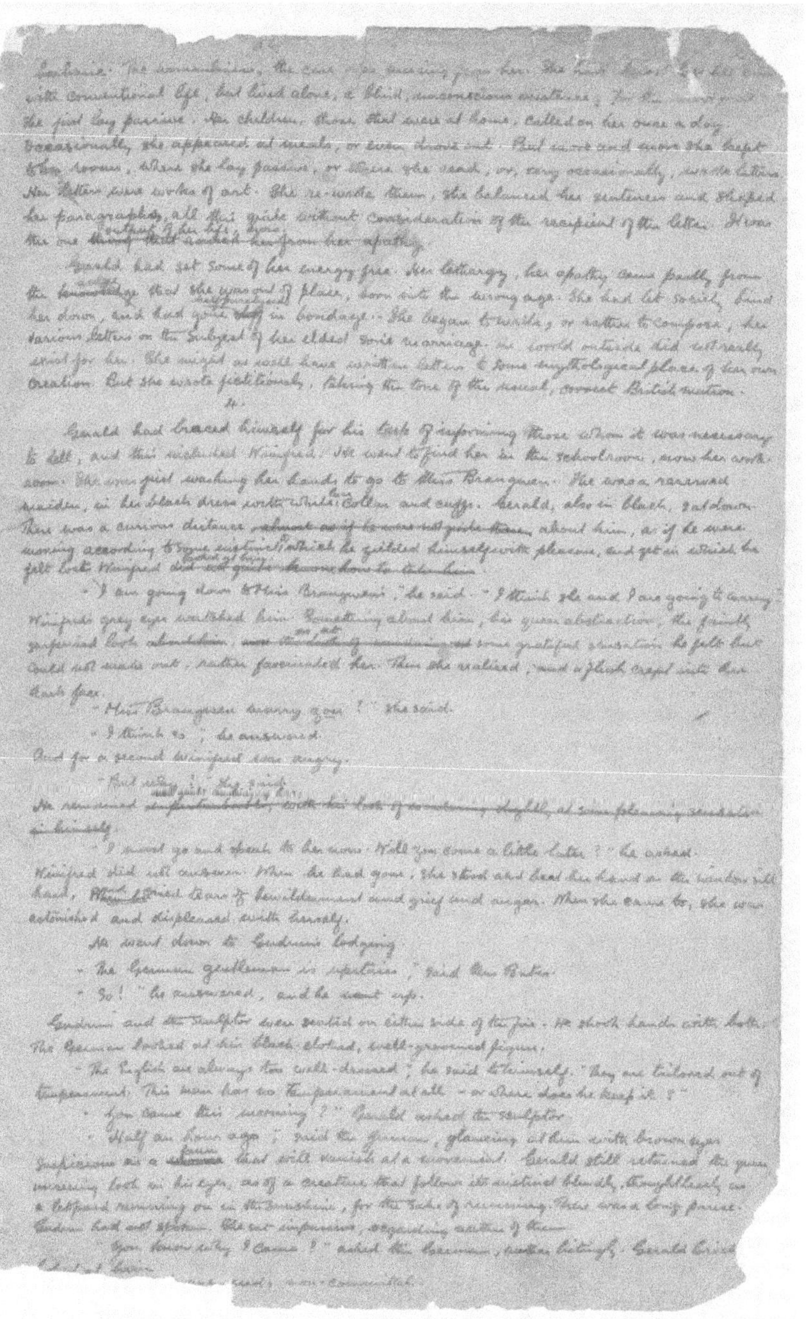

Figure 1 The first page of the earliest extant manuscript of *Women in Love* (March–June 1913), 'The Sisters I' holograph fragment (pp. 291–6), p. 291. The Harry Ransom Centre, University of Texas at Austin, D. H. Lawrence Collection, 23.5.

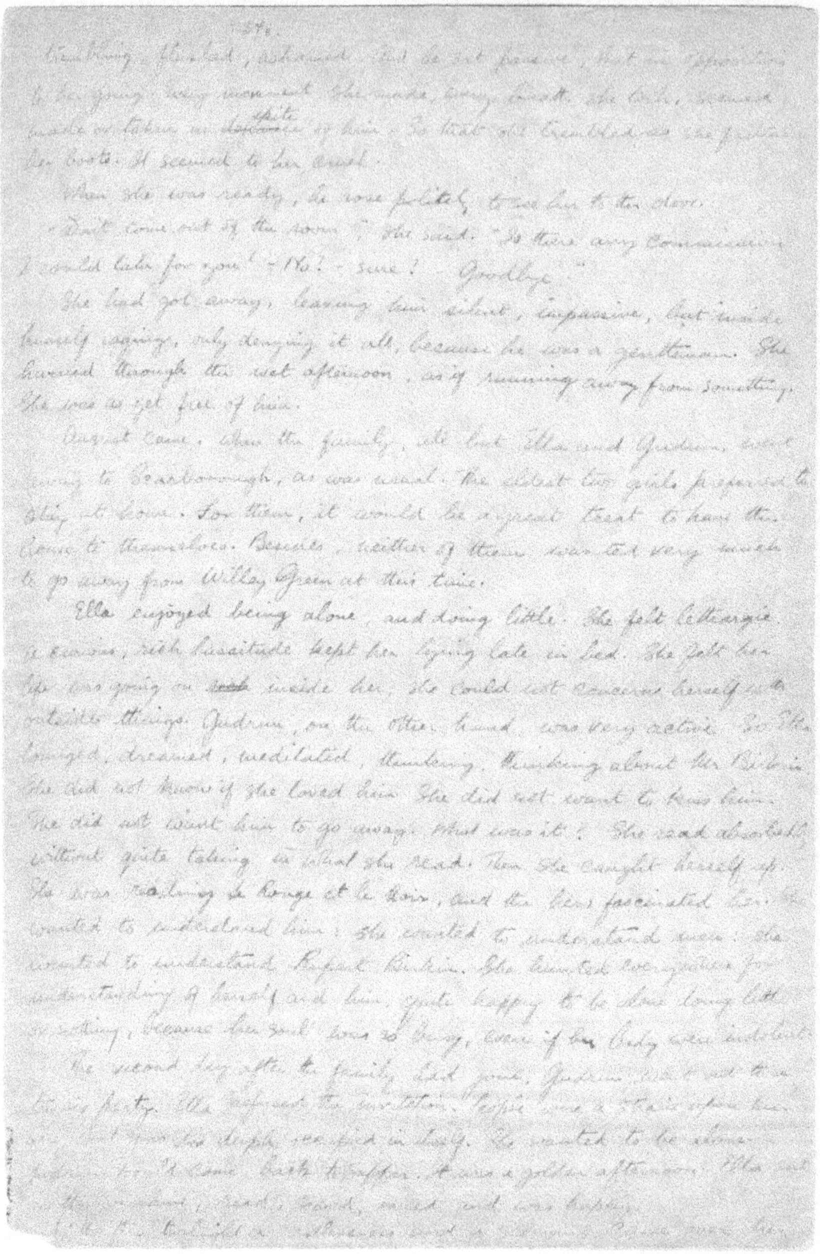

Figure 2 The first page of the second earliest extant manuscript of *Women in Love* (August 1913–January 1914), 'The Sisters II' holograph fragment (pp. 373–80), p. 373. The Harry Ransom Centre, University of Texas at Austin, D. H. Lawrence Collection, 23.5.

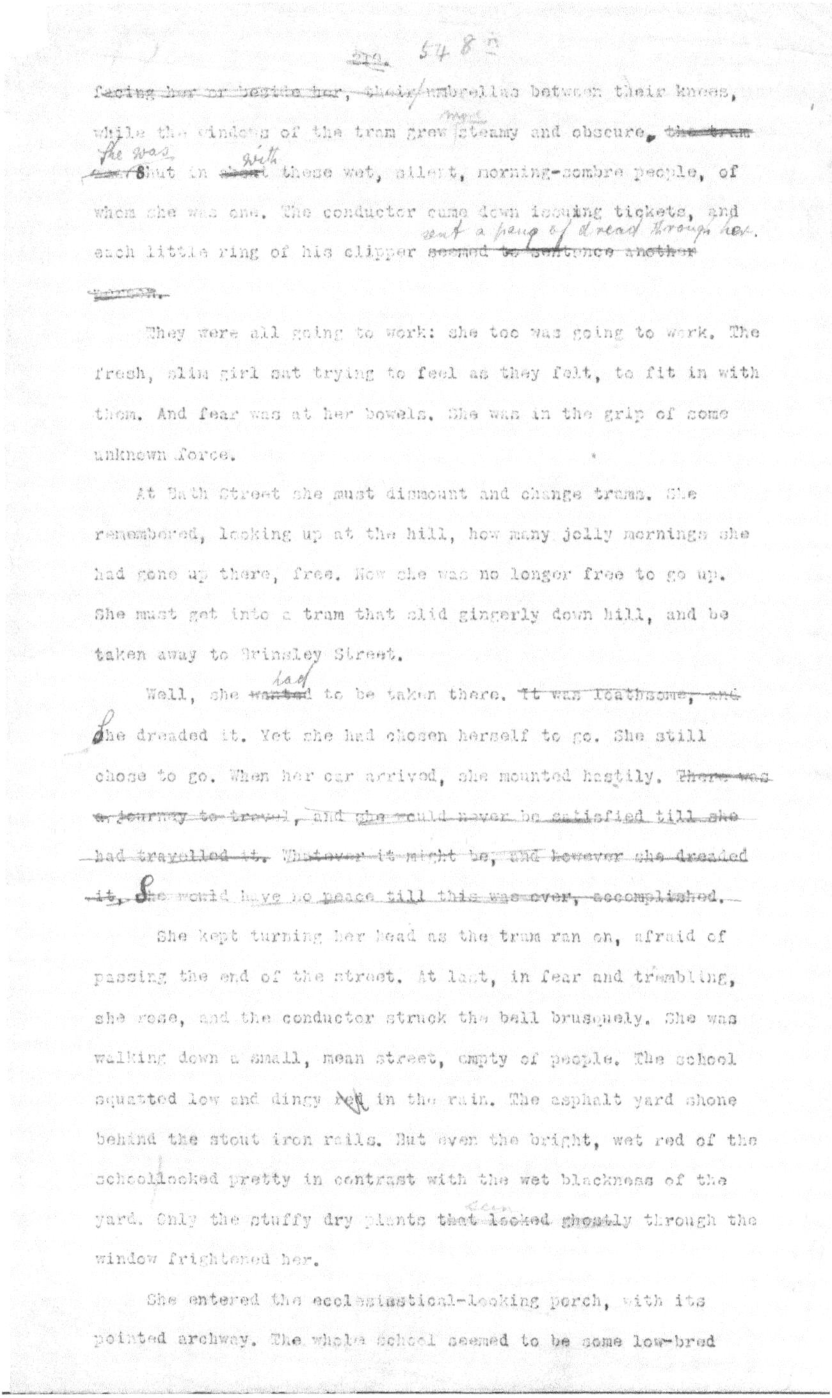

facing her or beside her, their umbrellas between their knees, while the windows of the tram grew ~~steamy~~ most and obscure. ~~the tram~~ ~~she was~~ ~~Shut in~~ Shut in with these wet, silent, morning-sombre people, of whom she was one. The conductor came down issuing tickets, and each little ring of his clipper seemed ~~to sentence another~~ sent a pang of dread through her. ~~prisoner.~~

They were all going to work: she too was going to work. The fresh, slim girl sat trying to feel as they felt, to fit in with them. And fear was at her bowels. She was in the grip of some unknown force.

At Bath Street she must dismount and change trams. She remembered, looking up at the hill, how many jolly mornings she had gone up there, free. Now she was no longer free to go up. She must get into a tram that slid gingerly down hill, and be taken away to Brinsley Street.

Well, she ~~wanted~~ had to be taken there. ~~It was loathsome, and~~ She dreaded it. Yet she had chosen herself to go. She still chose to go. When her car arrived, she mounted hastily. ~~There was a journey to travel, and she would never be satisfied till she had travelled it. Whatever it might be, and however she dreaded it,~~ She would have no peace till this was ~~over,~~ accomplished.

She kept turning her head as the tram ran on, afraid of passing the end of the street. At last, in fear and trembling, she rose, and the conductor struck the bell brusquely. She was walking down a small, mean street, empty of people. The school squatted low and dingy red in the rain. The asphalt yard shone behind the stout iron rails. But even the bright, wet red of the schoollooked pretty in contrast with the wet blackness of the yard. Only the stuffy dry plants that looked seen ghostly through the window frightened her.

She entered the ecclesiastical-looking porch, with its pointed archway. The whole school seemed to be some low-bred

Figure 3 The first page of the third earliest extant manuscript of *Women in Love* (February–May 1914), 'The Wedding Ring' typescript fragment (pp. 219–75, 279–84), later interpolated into the manuscript of *The Rainbow*, p. 219. The Harry Ransom Centre, University of Texas at Austin, D. H. Lawrence Collection, 19.3.

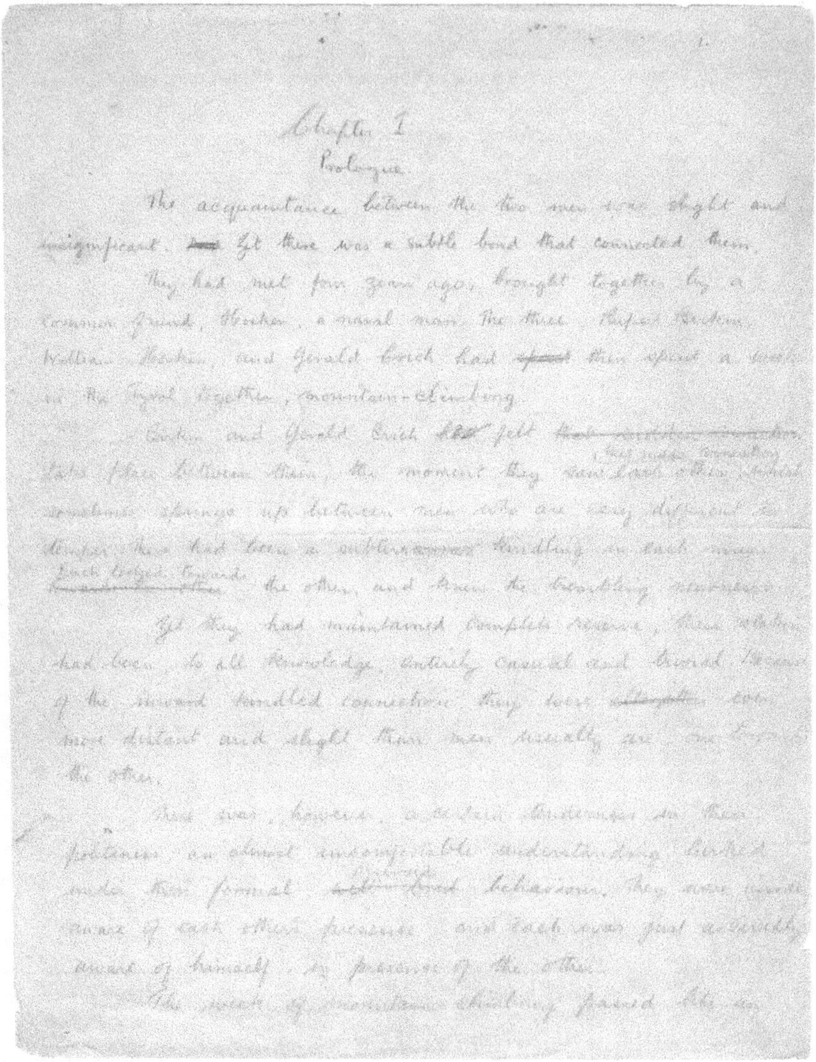

Figure 4 The first page of the fourth earliest extant manuscript of *Women in Love* (April 1916), 'The Sisters III' holograph fragment (pp. 1–55), p. 1. The Harry Ransom Centre, University of Texas at Austin, D. H. Lawrence Collection, 23.6.

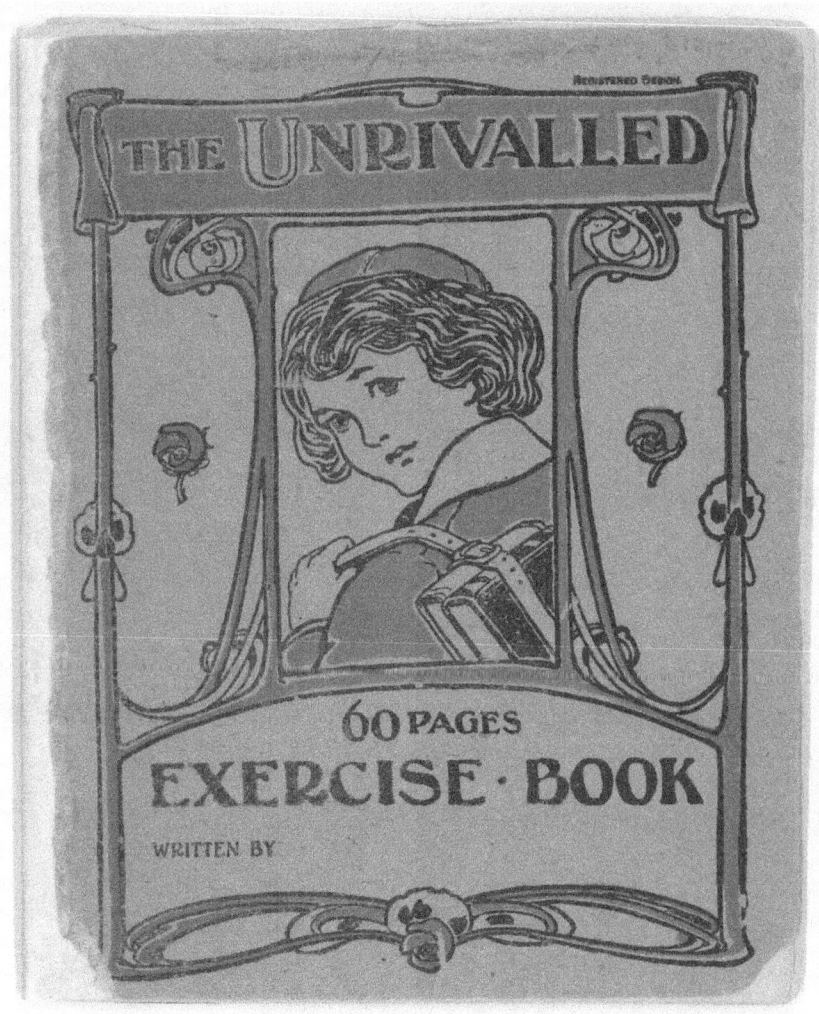

Figure 5 The front cover of one of the four notebooks containing the fifth earliest extant manuscript of *Women in Love* (April–June 1916), later interpolated into the first typescript of *Women in Love*, along with six other notebooks, 'The Sisters III' holograph fragment (pp. 650–863), notebook 9. The Harry Ransom Centre, University of Texas at Austin, D. H. Lawrence Collection, 24.

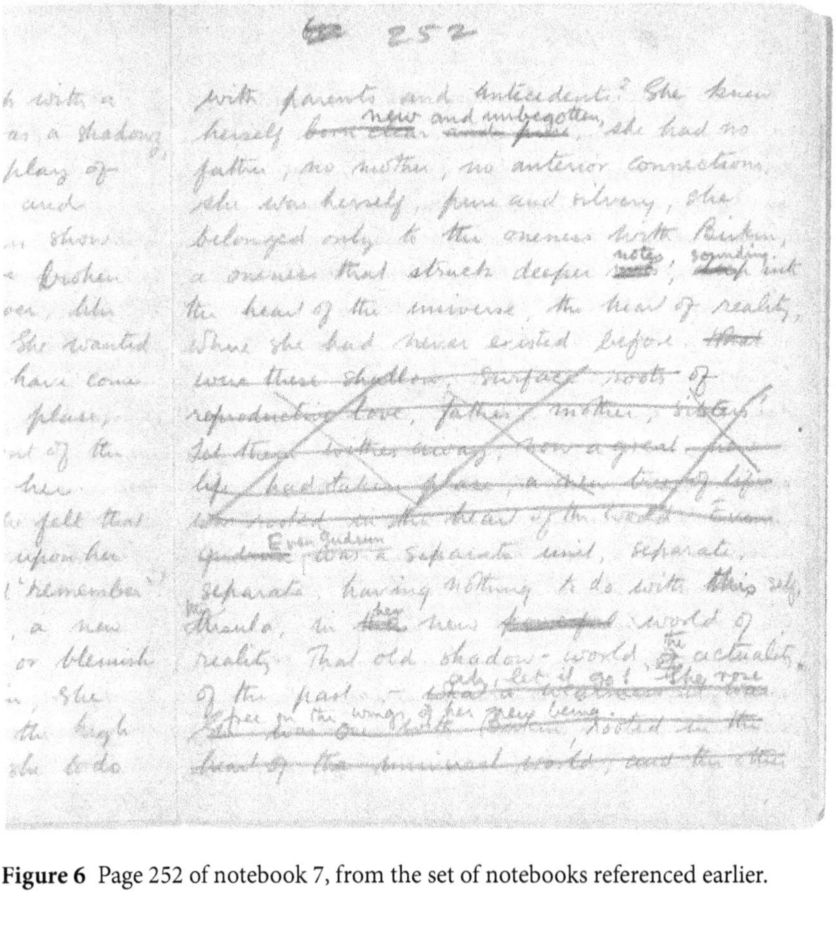

Figure 6 Page 252 of notebook 7, from the set of notebooks referenced earlier.

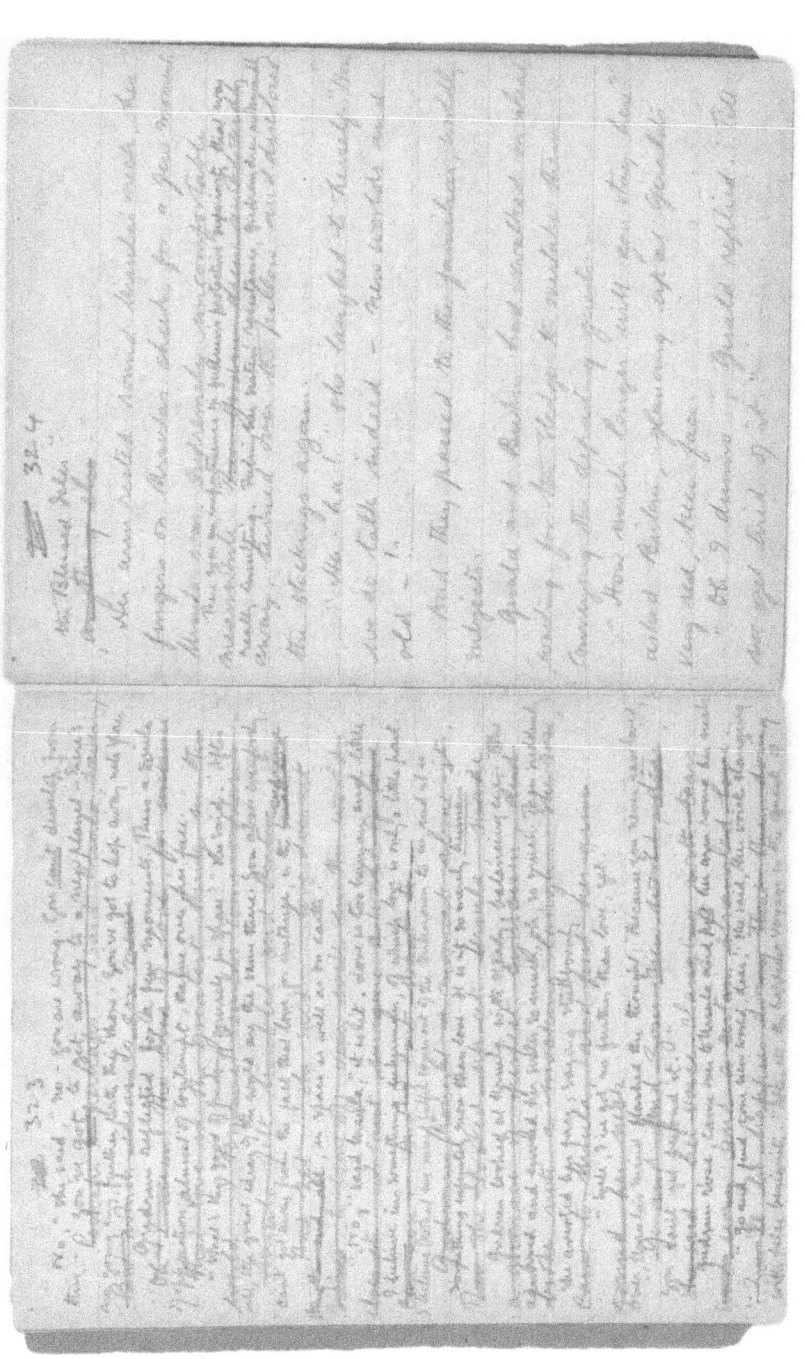

Figure 7 Pages 323–4 of notebook 9, from the set of notebooks referenced earlier.

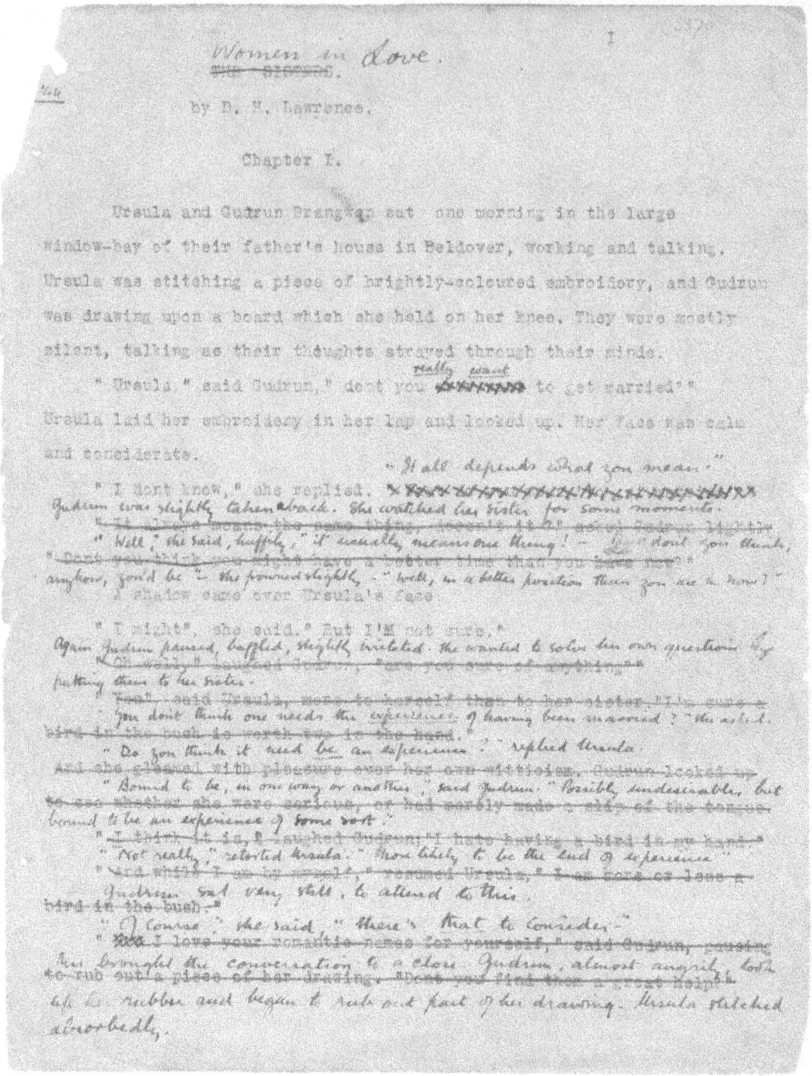

Women in Love.
~~THE SISTERS~~.

by D. H. Lawrence.

Chapter I.

Ursula and Gudrun Brangwen sat one morning in the large window-bay of their father's house in Beldover, working and talking. Ursula was stitching a piece of brightly-coloured embroidery, and Gudrun was drawing upon a board which she held on her knees. They were mostly silent, talking as their thoughts strayed through their minds.

" Ursula " said Gudrun, " dont you really want to get married? "
Ursula laid her embroidery in her lap and looked up. Her face was calm and considerate.

" I dont know," she replied. " It all depends what you mean."
Gudrun was slightly taken aback. She watched her sister for some moments.
" Well," she said, huffily, " it usually means one thing! – dont you think, anyhow, you'd be – " she frowned slightly, – " well, in a better position than you are in now? "
A shadow came over Ursula's face.

" I might", she said. " But I'M not sure."
Again Gudrun paused, baffled, slightly irritated. She wanted to solve her own questions by putting them to her sister.
" You dont think one needs the experience of having been married? " she asked.
" Do you think it need be an experience? " replied Ursula.
" Bound to be, in one way or another," said Gudrun. " Possibly undesirable, but bound to be an experience of some sort."
" Not really," retorted Ursula. " More likely to be the end of experience."
Gudrun sat very still, to attend to this.
" Of course," she said, " there's that to consider."
This brought the conversation to a close. Gudrun, almost angrily, took up her rubber and began to rub out part of her drawing. Ursula stitched absorbedly.

Figure 8 The first page of the first typescript of *Women in Love* (July–November 1916), 'TSI' (p. 666), p. 1. The Harry Ransom Centre, University of Texas at Austin, D. H. Lawrence Collection, 25.1.

"And it's failed," he murmured, in ~~an ecstasy~~ *a poignancy* of pain. "You're dead."

Then gradually the wound in his breast seemed to get quiet again.

"Never mind, Gerald," he murmured, "never mind. Perhaps it had to be like this. ~~And we will carry on the hope~~ *It means destroying that which does live* ~~just the same~~ *— why should it?*." The tears rose again. "I *did* want it to come right for us all, I did want you to be happy, I *didn't* want you to be alone, and die." The tears ran freely down Birkin's face. "But we couldn't help it – ~~it had to be.~~ *This was no helping it.* I wish it needn't have been – " The acute pain convulsed his features again. "But perhaps this was the only way ~~for you, Gerald~~ – *this nothingness.* perhaps it was. Perhaps ~~it is your fulfilment, Gerald~~ *Something must be a living nothingness —* – perhaps *perhaps it must.* ~~there was no other.~~ We won't feel bitter and frozen – perhaps your death is ~~one gift to life~~ *the same as your life.* – *Only it seems so empty, so nothing it all seems. Nothing.* ~~Notwithstanding, the tears ran out of Birkin's heart,~~ *His heart tore with anguish. It was not the death he could* ~~and it was hard to keep that inner peace, which is the reality~~ *not bear, but the nothingness of the life and death put together. It* ~~of faith.~~ *Killed the quick of one's life.*

~~"Perhaps you sleep now in fulfilment – your very~~ *"At any rate, you sleep," he said, through his tears and pain.* ~~failure is a fulfilment – and one is wrong to oppose it. Perhaps~~ *At any rate you sleep now; we need not grieve for you any more.* ~~you couldn't be happy, as I wanted.~~ We will cover you over, and ~~love~~ *love* you – and you will be warm in death. We will love you – you won't be cold."

Then again his face broke with tears.
"But it was horrible for you," he cried. "And then – nothing – nothing – never to struggle clear – never to struggle clear – Gerald."
He could not bear it. His heart seemed to be torn in his chest.
"But even then," he strove to say, "we need not all be like that. All is not lost, because many are lost. – I am not afraid or ashamed to die and to live."

Figure 9 The final page of the first typescript of *Women in Love*, referenced earlier (box/folder: 27.2), p. 666.

Figure 10 Chapter II page of the second typescript of *Women in Love* (March 1917–September 1919), 'TSII' (p. 766). The Harry Ransom Centre, University of Texas at Austin, D. H. Lawrence Collection, 28.1.

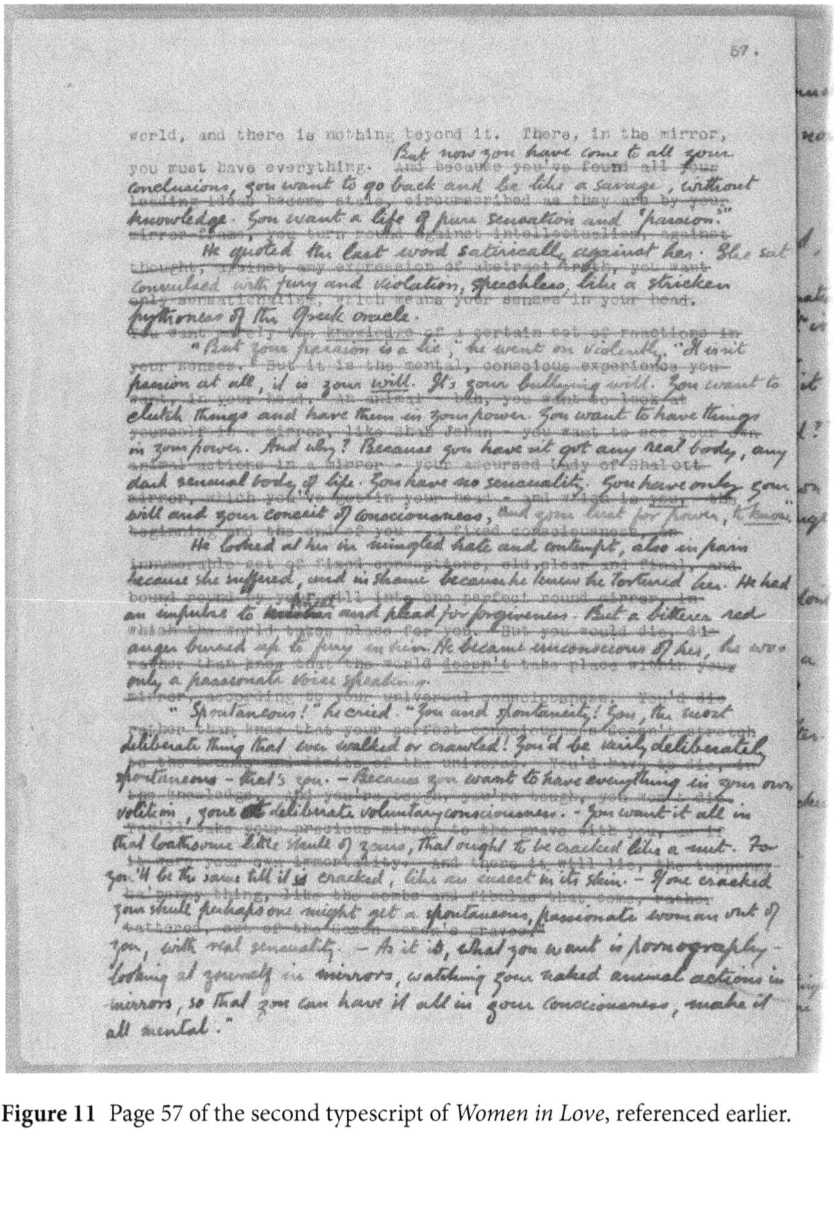
57.

world, and there is nothing beyond it. There, in the mirror, you must have everything. But now you have come to all your conclusions, you want to go back and be like a savage, without knowledge. You want a life of pure sensation and "passion."

He quoted the last word satirically against her. She sat convulsed with fury and violation, speechless, like a stricken pythoness of the Greek oracle.

"But your passion is a lie," he went on violently. "It isn't passion at all, it is your will. It's your bullying will. You want to clutch things and have them in your power. You want to have things in your power. And why? Because you haven't got any real body, any dark sensual body of life. You have no sensuality. You have only your will and your conceit of consciousness, and your lust for power, to know."

He looked at her in mingled hate and contempt, also in pain because she suffered, and in shame because he knew he tortured her. He had an impulse to kneel and plead for forgiveness. But a bitterer red anger burned up to fury in him. He became unconscious of her, he was only a passionate voice speaking.

"Spontaneous!" he cried. "You and spontaneity! You, the most deliberate thing that ever walked or crawled! You'd be verily deliberately spontaneous – that's you. – Because you want to have everything in your own volition, your deliberate voluntary consciousness. – You want it all in that loathsome little skull of yours, that ought to be cracked like a nut. For you'll be the same till it is cracked, like an insect in its skin. – If one cracked your skull perhaps one might get a spontaneous, passionate woman out of you, with real sensuality. – As it is, what you want is pornography – looking at yourself in mirrors, watching your naked animal actions in mirrors, so that you can have it all in your consciousness, make it all mental."

Figure 11 Page 57 of the second typescript of *Women in Love*, referenced earlier.

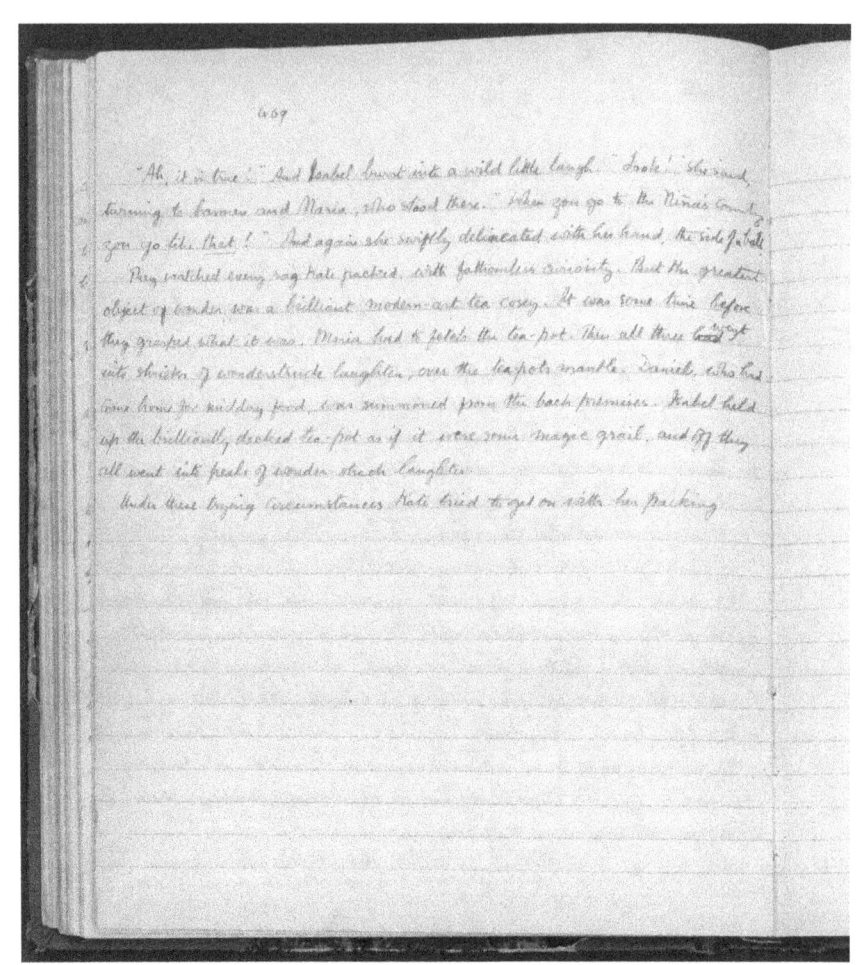

Figure 12 The final page of the first manuscript of *The Plumed Serpent* (May–June 1923), 'MSI' ('Quetzalcoatl') (p. 469), p. 469. The Harry Ransom Centre, University of Texas at Austin, D. H. Lawrence Collection, 14.1.

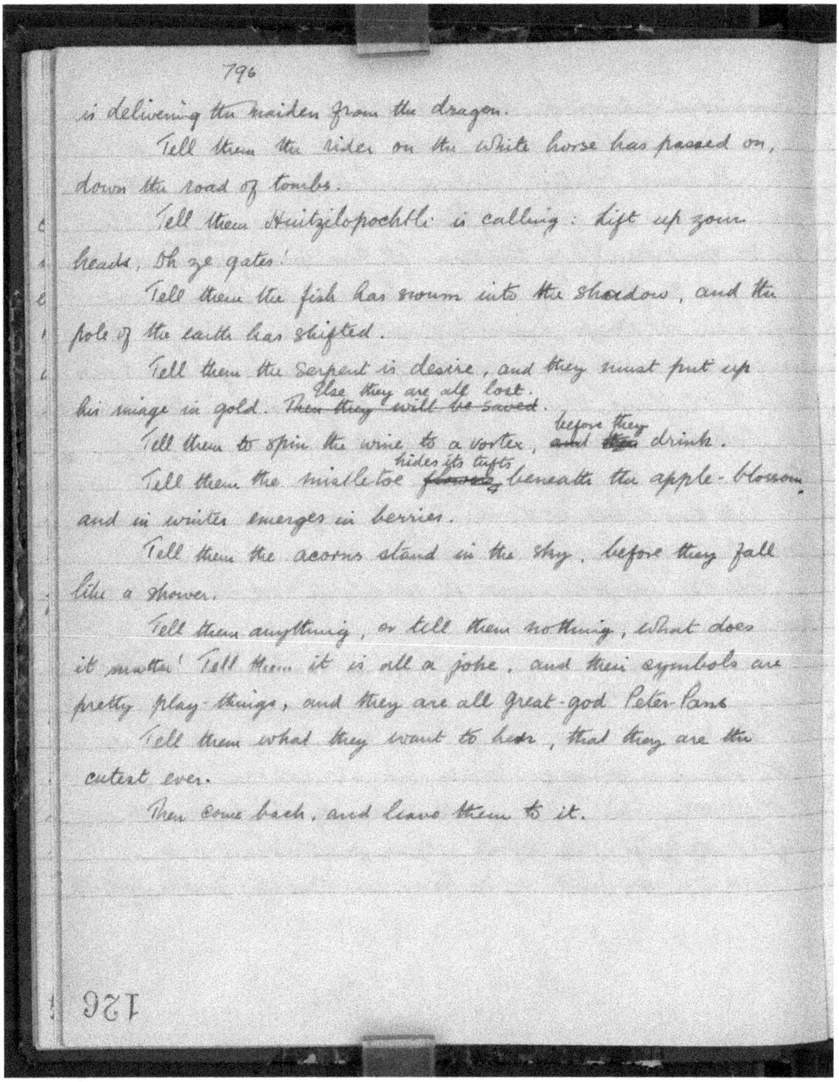

796

is delivering the maiden from the dragon.

Tell them the rider on the white horse has passed on, down the road of tombs.

Tell them Huitzilopochtli is calling: Lift up your heads, Oh ye gates!

Tell them the fish has swum into the shadow, and the pole of the earth has shifted.

Tell them the Serpent is desire, and they must put up his image in gold. Else they are all lost. Then they will be saved.

Tell them to spin the wine to a vortex, before they and they drink.

Tell them the mistletoe hides its tufts flowers beneath the apple-blossom, and in winter emerges in berries.

Tell them the acorns stand in the sky, before they fall like a shower.

Tell them anything, or tell them nothing. What does it matter? Tell them it is all a joke, and their symbols are pretty play-things, and they are all great-god Peter Pans.

Tell them what they want to hear, that they are the cutest ever.

Then come back, and leave them to it.

Figure 13 The final page of the second manuscript of *The Plumed Serpent* (November 1924–July 1925), 'MSII' ('Quetzalcoatl') (p. 796), p. 796. The Harry Ransom Centre, University of Texas at Austin, D. H. Lawrence Collection, 14.1.

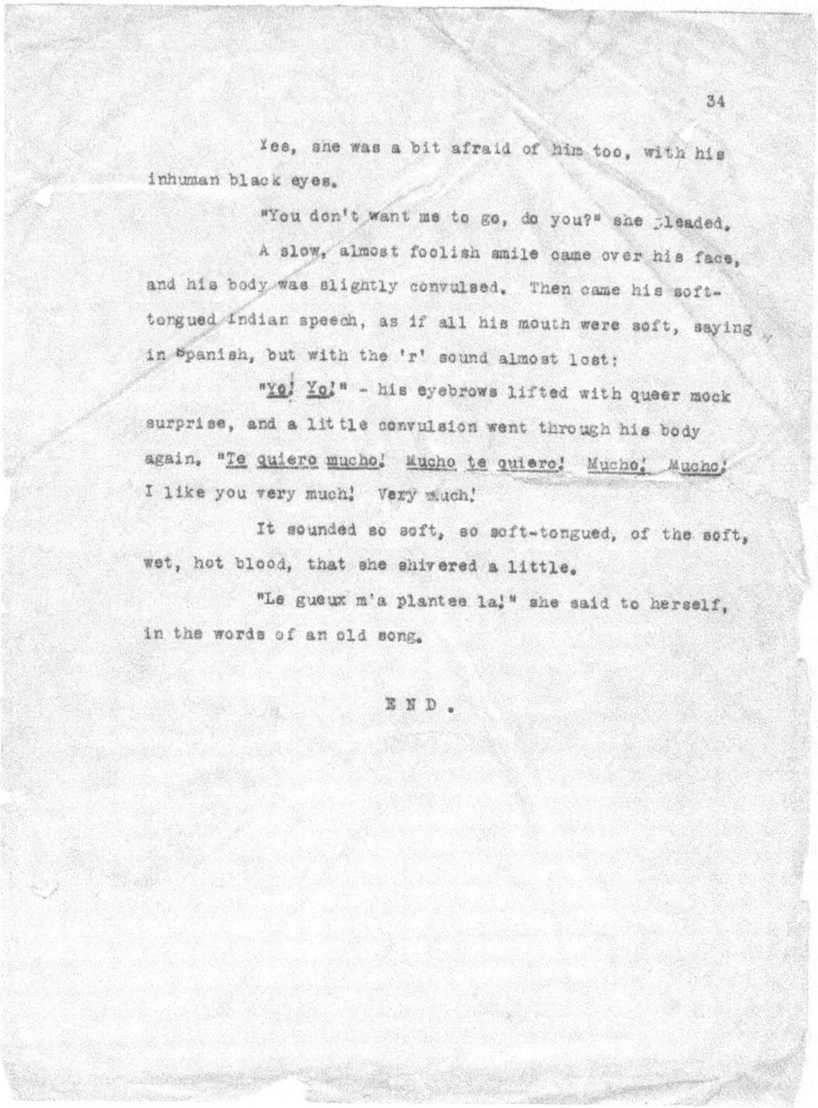

34

Yes, she was a bit afraid of him too, with his inhuman black eyes.

"You don't want me to go, do you?" she pleaded.

A slow, almost foolish smile came over his face, and his body was slightly convulsed. Then came his soft-tongued Indian speech, as if all his mouth were soft, saying in Spanish, but with the 'r' sound almost lost:

"Yo! Yo!" - his eyebrows lifted with queer mock surprise, and a little convulsion went through his body again. "Te quiero mucho! Mucho te quiero! Mucho! Mucho! I like you very much! Very much!"

It sounded so soft, so soft-tongued, of the soft, wet, hot blood, that she shivered a little.

"Le gueux m'a plantée la!" she said to herself, in the words of an old song.

END.

Figure 14 The final page of the complete typescript of *The Plumed Serpent* (November 1924–July 1925), 'TS' ('Quetzalcoatl'), each chapter is numbered separately, p. 34. The Harry Ransom Centre, University of Texas at Austin, D. H. Lawrence Collection, 15.2.

5

Genetic dialogism in the notebooks

Introducing the early 'notebooks'

This chapter takes the next surviving manuscript in chronological order: the last four of ten notebooks (N7–10), which comprise the second half of the first typescript (TSI) and equate to roughly the final third of the narrative of *Women in Love*. Another longer fragment, which, as with the 'Wedding Ring' fragment, survives because Lawrence incorporated it into a subsequent full-length typescript draft (like the 'Wedding Ring' fragment, they contain an earlier pagination (pp. 650–863), which is revised to pp. 220–436 to follow on from TSI); the four notebooks seemingly formed the concluding segment of an earlier handwritten draft and were probably composed in July 1916 (while notebooks 1–6 were probably written a few months later, as discussed in Chapter 3).

These 'notebooks' are in fact children's school exercise books (see Figure 10), which explains why all ten combined amount to just over 400 pages (for comparison, the two more concisely written manuscripts for *The Plumed Serpent* both fit into a pair of notebooks each and amount to approximately 500 and 800 pages, respectively). The earlier notebooks contain around twenty lines per page and are longer than the later notebooks (1–6, which are on average just thirty pages in length) at around sixty pages on average. They are also much more heavily revised (while just forty-three individual words are revised in the *entirety* of notebook 1, forty-one individual words are revised on the first *page* of notebook 7 alone), which makes sense if they were taken from an earlier draft, though, as we will see, some revisions were also made while writing.

As mentioned, while many of these revisions are likely to have taken place when incorporating the notebooks into the first typescript, there are also numerous examples where Lawrence's revision clearly took place *during* the initial writing process. The main indication is where a subsequent original piece of text follows on from a previously revised piece of text (or does not follow on from the unrevised text). In N8, for example, the location of a large artwork which Loerke is producing is revised from 'Dresden' to '**Cologne**' (N8 288) when first referenced, but the new location is then given *unrevised* in the next paragraph (Gudrun finds it interesting 'to think of [Loerke] making the great granite frieze for a great granite factory in Cologne' (N8 289)). To reference the new location unrevised on the second occasion, Lawrence must have revised the original location immediately (he may have opted to change the location when writing the second reference and then gone back to revise the first). Mid-compositional revision emphasizes the contingent nature of writing, and, as we have seen already and will see again, this contingency is nowhere more dramatic than in the climax to Lawrence's work. Consider the following passage, which I transcribe from the final notebook, a dozen or so pages before the end:

> [Gerald] knew he was going the ~~road~~ ᵗʳᵃᶜᵏ towards the summit of the slopes, where was the Marienhütte, ~~where one could stand over the world, on the ridge, to descend on the other side~~ and the descent on the other side. But he was not interested, it did not interest him. ᴴᵉ ᵒⁿˡʸ wanted to ~~wander~~ ᵍᵒ on, ~~then to rest; but~~ to ~~move[?] forward~~ ᵍᵒ ᵒⁿ whilst he could, to move ~~forward [?]~~ ˒ ᵗᵒ ᵏᵉᵉᵖ ᵍᵒⁱⁿᵍ, that was all, to keep going· ᵘⁿᵗⁱˡ ʰᵉ ʰᵃᵈ ᶠⁱⁿⁱˢʰᵉᵈ. He had lost all his sense of place. And yet, ~~for the sake of ease~~ ⁱⁿ ᵗʰᵉ ʳᵉᵐᵃⁱⁿⁱⁿᵍ ⁱⁿˢᵗⁱⁿᶜᵗ ᵒᶠ ˡⁱᶠᵉ, his feet sought the track where the skis had gone. (N10 421–2)

Aside from physical evidence on the page, such as irregular gaps (e.g. in the first line of the extract, the original phrase 'towards the summit' follows after a space created by the superscript inserted word '**track**', which protrudes in the following), there are also semantic incongruities (e.g. the original phrase 'wanted to wander' does not follow on from the previous, 'where was the Marienhütte') caused by mid-compositional revision. While the extract also demonstrates Lawrence's revisionary focus upon *descriptive* phrases, which I will discuss in more detail later (e.g. the more passive 'wander' and 'move forward' are both replaced with the more demanding and persistent phrase 'go'), it is worth emphasizing the paradoxical *writerly* context of these revisions. Having 'lost all sense of place', Gerald's basic desire to '**go on** [. . .] **until he had finished**' is exposed. This is a basic desire (the relief of an ending) shared by Lawrence and by any author. And yet, as with 'Odour of Chrysanthemums', this tortuously rewritten passage essentially extends and frustrates a clean ending, and Lawrence will 'go on' to do the same again in subsequent drafts.

In the aforementioned extract, as Gerald approaches 'the summit of the slopes', he, like the novel, has come full circle from the mythical 'upper world' experience as divulged in the discarded 'Prologue' chapter. This invisible layer in the novel's textual genesis provides an additional tragic dimension to Gerald's death. However, of equal significance is the sense that Gerald had 'lost all his sense of place'. As mentioned, the earlier notebooks (7–10) under discussion in this chapter comprise the concluding section of narrative in the novel. The majority of this fragment is taken up by the main characters' visit to an Alpine resort (Ursula and Birkin arrive at the hotel in Innsbruck on page 204, near the end of notebook 6, while the earlier draft begins on page 220 (in notebook 7)), where they also meet Loerke (present in the earliest *Women in Love* fragment, from 1913). Gudrun comments self-consciously on their transportation in the closing pages of notebook 6:

> 'Isn't it marvellous', said Gudrun, 'how thankful one can be, to be out of one's country. I cannot believe myself, I am so transported, the moment I set foot on a foreign shore. I say to myself, "Here steps a new creature into life."' (N6 214)

There is an intriguing parallel between the subsequent section of narrative, with the characters taken out of their familiar surroundings, and the section of manuscript itself, which is extracted from its original setting (and incorporated into the subsequent typescript, as part of a larger series of notebooks).

The book has begun to demonstrate the complex nature of Lawrence's composition, and the longer extract mentioned earlier – with words and phrases swapped on the page and other words and phrases 'constructed' around it – as well as the notebooks themselves – with an entire chunk of manuscript swapped from one location to another – suggest that Lawrence may even represent a 'constructivist' (or bricoleur) type of writer. However, the complete absence of paper planning points to a key difference between Lawrence and the many literary modernist giants who were influenced or inspired by Flaubert and the mythical quest for *'le seul mot juste'*. Respecting technical craft above all, this latter 'type' of writer, who is traditionally the most common subject for genetic criticism,[1] commits detailed and direct preparatory work to paper and likewise revises their existing work in a self-consciously 'constructivist' manner (with a particular focus on form and structure). As we progress through a series of substantial new drafts for *Women in Love*, it should become clear that there is no single 'continuous manuscript text' (as Gabler terms it in his synoptic edition of *Ulysses*). Lawrence essentially worked in a different way, producing multiple separate versions of his works. The Cambridge Edition reflects this to some extent (and its publisher Michael Black has argued this point himself (1999)), but goes to the opposite extreme by ignoring the direct, intimate connections between Lawrence's drafts and alternative versions, which 'tag' together and are *provisional* (as in the mapping and invisible layering discussed in the previous chapter); this is reflected in the Cambridge Edition's General Editor's Preface, which misleadingly claims that Lawrence 'rarely compared one stage to the next'. Rather than build upon (or with) preceding material, I argue that Lawrence's revisions represent a form of dialogue.

Adjectives, viewpoints, enchantment

Except for a few heavily rewritten passages which I will turn to later, most of Lawrence's revisions to the early notebooks consist of the deletion or substitution of single words or short phrases, which, at a glance, resemble 'pruning' (or selecting *le seul mot juste*). Lawrence's lack of prior design (or paper planning), however, emphasizes the sense in which revisions to literary texts merely represent the author's different viewpoints at different points in time (in this sense, regardless of how much time Flaubert spent fine-tuning his text, the *mot* could only ever be *juste* in Flaubert's eyes, at a particular point or set of points in time). In addition, taken as a whole, there is (as mentioned) an overwhelming focus upon adjectives in Lawrence's revisions, which, as I will discuss, adds to this sense of multiple viewpoints.

This is evident from the very first page of the segment, which begins with the following description of Gudrun and Gerald from the perspective of some 'peasant-women', who 'turned in the way to look':

> the full-breasted, laughing girl running **the soft, rhapsodic girl running** with such strange fleetness from the lithe, swift **glowing, vigorous** man, who was overtaking her so fatally **inevitably** like a greyhound a rabbit.
>
> They passed the guest-house, and a little shop **inn, with its painted shutters and balcony,** a few cottages crouching low **half buried** in the snow; then the silent saw-mill, and then they went over **by** the snow-buried bridge, and the snow-buried **which crossed the hidden** stream, **over which they ran** into the very depth of the untouched sheets of snow. It was a silence and a sheer whiteness exhilarating to madness. But the perfect silence was most terrifying, isolating the soul, surrounding the heart with frozen air.
>
> 'I'm glad we came here, Gerald **It's a marvellous place, for all that**', said Gudrun, looking into his eyes with a strange, meaning look. His soul leapt with a violent, **an** almost evil **satanic** bound. He was going to let loose now.
>
> 'So true **Good**', he said. (N7 220)

Adjectives and descriptive phrases are here replaced or added in each consecutive paragraph. In the first, the originally jumbled sentence is slightly simplified in revision, while the revised description of Gudrun as the 'rhapsodic girl running' is more alliterative. In the second, some phrases are again condensed (e.g. the 'guest house' and 'little shop' become the '**inn**'), though new descriptive features are added (the inn is equipped with '**painted shutters and balcony**'). Rather than describing herself as 'glad', in the revised third paragraph Gudrun describes the place itself as '**marvellous**'. Lawrence also revises the description of Gerald's soul from making 'a violent, an almost evil bound' to a more condensed and loaded '**satanic**' bound. While there is perhaps a subtractive theme to these revisions, which we might consider modernist (see Chapter 4, note 7), the overall impression is of an abundance of descriptive/adjectival potential.[2] In terms of genetic dialogism, and as each revision revolves around a fresh descriptor, rather than individual components within 'the' scene being modified, taken together (and despite the appearance on the page) these revisions provide a new viewpoint and therefore represent different versions of 'a' scene, which are dialogically related.[3]

Violeta Sotirova has considered Bakhtinian dialogism in relation to Lawrence by looking at some of his revisions to his third novel, *Sons and Lovers*, though she does not consider the question of adjectives. Sotirova argues that Lawrence *intentionally* integrated individual character viewpoints into the narrative viewpoint in *Sons and Lovers* through the development of *free indirect style* (which is seen as contributing towards a breakthrough moment in his career, following the traditional critical assessment of Lawrence's 'breakthrough to maturity'). Sotirova compares this to the less dialogical style of 'Quoted Thought', which is more prevalent in *The Trespasser*: 'Quoted Thought', a more theatrical style with an earlier historical provenance, where a character's thoughts or feelings are presented as an interior monologue, is less dialogical in that the overarching narrator retains control of the narrative and mediates individual character viewpoints. From a genetic perspective, though, we might also consider how the traditional, teleological approach to Lawrence's manuscripts is itself monological: focusing upon a single authorial intention, which is projected across the manuscripts. In contrast, genetic critics regard each layer of writing (the *avant-texte*) as contingent and thus attend to the internal dynamics of writing which play a role in shaping the emerging text. Whereas 'constructivist' models of composition see the text as enchanted by the author's spell of intentionality, a 'dialogist' model (featuring numerous dialogically related versions) allows us to notice the reverse: that the author is also enchanted by the text.

There is a close connection between adjectives (or descriptors), viewpoints and enchantment. The former are markers of a way of seeing, which implicate a subject (or 'viewer') in the activity of seeing. Vision is both descriptive and a kind of enchantment: it is always to some extent unique (to a particular viewpoint). To return to the revised extract mentioned earlier, it is to the 'peasant-women' that Gudrun appears to run 'with such strange fleetness'; to Gudrun that the place itself is 'marvellous'; and Gudrun's 'strange, meaning look' into the eyes of Gerald is an observation of one or both of those protagonists. In the same way, by focusing on the adjectives, the author's own revisions suggest a kind of genetic enchantment.

The section of the novel contained in notebooks 7–10 – in which the characters, having left their habitual environment in England, whose uncanny discomfort Ursula and Gudrun begin the novel by discussing, and find themselves in a new and foreign place, an 'upper world', for which Lawrence's discarded Prologue originally provided an overture – provides an extended reflection on the theme of enchantment, its sinister potential as well as its allure, and provides a core to the eventual novel itself, whose final title is, after all, *Women in Love*. Many of Lawrence's revisions highlight this theme, which may also have been influenced by Lawrence's engagement with his own seemingly 'strange' process of writing (a quality frequently remarked upon in his letters while writing). Gudrun's description at the end of notebook 6, for example: 'Isn't it marvellous [...] I cannot believe myself, I am so transported' (N6 214), was explicitly written to frame the subsequent (and chronologically earlier) segment of narrative contained in notebooks 7–10, and is later echoed by Gudrun's revised description of the place itself as '**marvellous**'; 'marvellous' is a deceptive word, which hints at the illusory nature of enchantment by anticipating or even stemming from a more detached, ironic, disenchantment.

There are numerous examples of this rapport between the theme of enchantment and Lawrence's revision of adjectives as Gudrun and Gerald settle into their new environment. Consider Gudrun's description of their room:

> "'I love it," she said. "I love the It is wonderful," she equivocated. "Look at the colour of the wooden walls and ceiling and the floor the panelling – it's wonderful, like being inside a nut." (*N7* 225)

Again, we have a repetition of a vague superlative, and again, while revising from 'love' to 'wonderful', Lawrence makes the text more self-conscious in revision, with Gudrun's equivocal feelings made explicit ('**she equivocated**'). There is also a familiar condensation of details ('the wooden walls and ceiling and the floor' into '**the panelling**'), encapsulated by the simile of the nut with its claustrophobic and imprisoning connotations.

Being 'inside a nut' is also analogous for the way in which the subject of a viewpoint is always bound up in the act of seeing, and the sinister potential for this type of enchantment becomes increasingly apparent as the narrative progresses. Consider the following passage, as Gudrun gazes at the mountains through the window of their room a couple of pages later:

> filled [...] with a strange rapture. She crouched in front of the window, ~~swinging slightly, rocking~~ **clenching her head in her hands**, in a sort of ~~rapture~~ **trance**. (N7 227)

The traditionally sublime objects of love and hate (for Gerald) and the Alpine peaks (which surround them) here induce Gudrun into a state of semi-consciousness, and it is again noteworthy that Lawrence's revision ('**trance**') is more equivocal than the original descriptor ('rapture').[4]

It is also important to note that Gudrun, like Lawrence, is an artist. It is easy to vilify Gudrun for her mutually destructive relationship with Gerald – where Gerald is essentially objectified as a sublime male body ('after all, what was the lover but fuel for the transports of art, for a female art, the art of pure, perfect ~~sensation~~ knowledge, in sensuous understanding' (N9 351)) – and to contrast this with the more healthy and positive attitudes of Ursula or Birkin, but we must remember that Lawrence is an artist himself, while the eventual novel *Women in Love* is itself a sublime aesthetic object.

It is not a coincidence that it is Gudrun who provides the framing description of the novel's transformation in the final segment of narrative ('I say to myself, "here steps a new creature into life"') and I discuss the significance of Gudrun's role as artist again in the next chapter when looking at the full-length typescript drafts of *Women in Love*. It should also be possible to draw a line between Gudrun's artistic nature and her apparent sadomasochism, but this line is ambiguous. This is apparent when Gerald reflects on Gudrun's 'strange rapture' on the next page of the current draft: 'he knew that there were tears in her eyes, her own tears, **tears of her strange religion,** that had nothing to do with him' (N7 228). Lawrence's revision is again descriptive, but the added phrase about Gudrun's '**strange religion**' could refer to either her artistic or her sadomasochistic tendencies (and perhaps both).[5] It is also interesting to note that Gerald's (powerfully repressed) sense that Gudrun's inner life has 'nothing to do with him' echoes a climactic line from the very earliest fragment, where Gerald senses 'this aloofness of hers' (SI 296).

The most eye-catching adjectival revision comes a few pages later, however, as the couples rejoin each other in the hotel and Birkin (in revision) provides a comic rejoinder to Gudrun:

> 'I like this place immensely I think the place is really wonderful, Gerald', he said. 'You are a genius for finding the right spot. It is prachtvoll and wunderbar and wunderschön and unbeschreiblich and all the other German adjectives'.
> (N7 233)

Recoiling from the past: 'Memory was a dirty trick'

Aside from the minor revisions sampled earlier, there are two heavily rewritten passages in notebooks 7–10. These appear in quick succession and both contain climactic conversations, the first between Ursula and Gudrun, and the second between Birkin and Gerald. There is an air of finality to both dialogues, as the couples are preparing to part ways, with each individual keen to have the final say on their respective partnerships. These heavier revisions therefore follow a familiar pattern, with Lawrence's most intense rewriting focusing on both dialogue and endings. We also see the overarching thematic antagonism between flux and stasis re-emerge. Before examining these passages in detail, however, it is important to set out their wider context: Birkin and Ursula's decision to depart is itself a result of an existential split between the sisters, Ursula and Gudrun, hence Gudrun describes their departure as 'spiritually' decisive (N9 320).

While Gudrun describes the transition to the Alps in superficially sublime and magical terms, which reflect perhaps her own distracted and/or repressed state of mind – as well as the fact that, for her and Gerald, the trip is merely a vacation – Ursula's journey to the Alps is a much more vivid and visceral one, and one which marks the beginning of a new phase of life. Having quit her job, and the everyday routines in which her emotional life was out of place – as detailed in those chapters of *The Rainbow* which were themselves lifted from 'The Wedding Ring' (as discussed in the previous chapter) – and having also argued with her parents and belatedly agreed to elope with Birkin, Ursula moves 'in an unreal suspense' the days before going away: 'she was not herself – she was not anything. She was something that is going to be' (N6 192); she does not 'really come to, until she was on the ship crossing from Dover to Ostend' (N6 192).

We then follow Ursula as she travels by train, through the night, disorientated, across unfamiliar and nondescript rural landscapes:

> It was all so strange, so extremely desolate, like the underworld, grey, grey, dirt-grey, desolate, forlorn, nowhere – grey, dreary nowhere. (N6 199)

These descriptions are reminiscent of the novel's opening pages, with the setting shifted from an underworld of mineshafts and trampled fields to the artillery battered fields of the Western front. At the start of the novel, however, the sisters were on a mere jaunt. Here, Ursula is travelling into a new life, 'the unknown with Birkin, an utter stranger' (N6 201). In Levinassian terms (1991), while the initial 'sojourn' with Gudrun ends with a return home, and otherness is assimilated into the 'same' of identity, here, Ursula is on a much more radical journey, becoming estranged from 'the way of the same'.[6]

Seeing 'a man with a lantern come out of a farm by the railway', Ursula thinks back to 'the Marsh, the old, intimate farm-life at Cossethay', and reflects:

> My God, how far was she projected from her childhood, how far was she still to go! In one life-time one travelled through centuries. The great chasm in memory from her childhood in the intimate country surroundings [. . .] was so great, that it seemed she had no identity, that **the** child she had been [. . .] was a little creature of imagination, not really herself. (N6 200–1)

Ursula's sudden split from the past gives her a sense of *no* identity: her past self has become a 'creature of imagination'. The passage also raises the question of *textual* memory: following Lawrence's division of what was originally a single novel, Ursula's childhood on 'the Marsh' takes place in a separate, published novel (*The Rainbow*); interestingly, in the second typescript draft, Lawrence also revises this line to 'a little creature of ~~imagination~~ **history**' (TSII 624).

Following this journey then, Ursula's self has become discontinuous, divisible into an imaginary before and a real after. The key behind this division, which is only latent so far, however, is the antagonism between *stasis* (the imaginary before, iconically represented by a fixed image) and *flux* (the real after, iconically represented by the smashing of the fixed image). Hence the importance (and dreamlike power) of the earlier episode in the eventual chapter 'Moony', which I discuss in the next chapter, and in which Birkin temporarily smashes a reflected image of the moon by throwing pebbles into a pool of water. These associations become more apparent after Ursula arrives in Innsbruck. Shortly after arriving, her and Birkin go for a walk, where Ursula spots another man exiting a farm 'with a lighted lantern'. This time on foot and close enough to smell the animals, the experience triggers a more intense stream of conscious reflection on the incongruity of the past:

> A smell of cows, hot, animal, almost like beef, came out on the ~~terribly ponderously heavily~~ **heavily** cold air. There was a glimpse of cattle in their dark stalls, then the door was shut again, and not a chink of light showed. It had reminded Ursula **again** of home, of the Marsh, of her childhood, ~~of her grandfather, of the grandmother, of Skrebensky~~ **and of the journey to Brussels, and strangely, of Anton Skrebensky**.
>
> Oh God, could one bear it, this past which was gone down the abyss? Could she bear, that it even had been! She looked round this silent, ~~motionless~~ **upper** world of snow and stars and powerful cold. There was another world, like ~~a lantern show. The~~ **views on a magic lantern: the** Marsh, Cossethay, Ilkeston, lit up with a common, unreal light. There was a shadowy, unreal Ursula, a whole shadow-play of unreal life. It was as unreal, and circumscribed, as a magic-lantern show. She wished the slides could all be broken. [. . .] She wanted to have no past. She wanted to have come down from the slopes of heaven to this place, with Birkin, not to have toiled out of the [?] muck of her childhood and her upbringing, slowly, all soiled. She felt that memory was a dirty trick played upon her. (N7 250-1)

While half of the revisions in this extract focus once again on descriptive phrases ('the ~~terribly~~ **heavily** ~~ponderously~~ **heavily** cold air'), the more intriguing insertions of '**again**' and '**of the journey to Brussels**' acknowledge that this passage repeats Ursula's previous recollection and provide a fascinating example of invisible layering through revision. It is possible that Lawrence only realized the intimate, repetitious connection between these two scenes when re-reading the earlier draft (hence the insertions). However, given the fact that the above extract is taken from notebook 7 and hence formed part of an *earlier* draft, it is also possible that Lawrence actually inserted the 'first' vision (the previous extract from notebook 6) with this second scene in mind.

In the passage itself, the association of the past and present with stasis and flux is made explicit through the iconic image of the magic-lantern show, whose slides (or memories) Ursula wishes 'could all be broken'. This wish for an immaculate conception - 'to have no past. [. . .] to have come down from the slopes of heaven' - is positive and negative. On the one hand, it is a repressive desire to disavow the past, which is figured as 'muck', while on the other, it has a liberating potential: in order to define oneself, one must be able to transcend or detach oneself from the past. We then see how memory can become a 'dirty trick' through the deceptive manner in which it haunts the present, while agency is, like an angel, able to transcend the deterministic reality of the intramundane world. That intramundane world, the world of the past, exists in a variety of forms, from genetics, habits and memories, to material documents, such as photographs, films or written materials. To put this passage in a textual-genetic context, there is both continuity and discontinuity in the development of text. Text toils in the 'muck' of numerous drafts, and yet Lawrence's agency, the invisible process of writing, traceable through specific revisions and rewritings, provides an element of contingent freedom and produces a series of different yet dialogically related versions ('all the time, there is something working away underneath, shadowy bulbs that must be beat again for another spring').

Now we come to the split with Gudrun. As Ursula continues these reflections in the pages which follow, she goes on to disavow Gudrun and her family, too, in lines which Lawrence ultimately decided to cut when revising:

> What had she to do with parents and antecedents? She knew herself born clear and pure **new and unbegotten**, she had no father, no mother, no anterior connections, she was herself, pure and silvery, she belonged only to the oneness with Birkin, a oneness that struck deeper roots, deep **notes, sounding** into the heart of the universe, the heart of reality, where she had never existed before. What were these shallow, surface roots of reproductive love, father, mother, sisters? Let them wither away, now a great new life had taken place, a new tree of life was rooted in the heart of the world. Even Gudrun **Even Gudrun** was a separate unit, separate, separate, having nothing to do with her[?] **this self, this** Ursula, in this **her** new powerful world of reality. That old shadow-world, of **the** actuality of the past – what a weariness it was. She was one with Birkin, rooted in the heart of the universal world, and the other was nothing. She forgot, she let go again. She was riding joyously on the strength of new being. **ah, let it go! She rose free on the wings of her new being.** (N7 251–3)

Ursula's reflections contain a distinctive blend of romanticism, Nietzschean Dionysianism (or Zarathustrianism), and existentialism: from 'the oneness with Birkin' at 'the heart of the universe', rising '**free on the wings of her new being**', to the sentiment that 'even Gudrun was a separate unit [. . .] having nothing to do with [. . .] **this** self, **this** Ursula'. We find echoes of this passage later, in *The Plumed Serpent*, but the sentiment was also foreshadowed in the 'Wedding Ring' fragment, which originally contained a chapter break entitled 'Ella trys [*sic*] her wings' (on p. 272, struck through in revision).

Lawrence's removal of the confusing metaphor of *roots* in the aforementioned passage, which refers first to the 'surface roots of reproductive love, father, mother, sisters' and then to 'a great new life [. . .] a new tree of life' with Birkin which is 'rooted in the heart of the world', is also significant. I suspect that Lawrence noticed the confusing double use of the word when revising the passage and removed it in order to emphasize the split between restrictive kinship networks of blood on the one hand, and Ursula's freer kinship by election with Birkin on the other. Lawrence not only struck the offending passage through in his usual tidy style but also added three large crosses for good measure (see Figure 6). That said, it is worth noting that Lawrence uses organic metaphors prominently and in a similarly antagonistic manner in *The Plumed Serpent*, although in that novel they also allude to a deeper kinship with the earth and the cosmos.

The sublime aesthetic object: 'There, in the infolded navel of it all, was her consummation'

While Ursula reflects on her new separation from the past while walking with Birkin, Gudrun, who is herself out walking with Gerald, also reflects on a growing sense of detachment from her sister, as follows:

> Gudrun [. . .] wanted to climb the wall of white finality, climb over, into the peak that sprang up like t̶h̶e̶ sharp petals in the heart of a̶ ̶f̶u̶l̶l̶ ̶b̶l̶o̶w̶n̶ ̶r̶o̶s̶e̶ **the e̶t̶e̶r̶n̶a̶l̶ frozen, mysterious navel of the world**. She felt that there, over the strange, blind, terrible wall of rocky snow, there in the navel of the mystic world, among the final cluster of peaks, there, in the infolded navel of it all, was her consummation. If she could but come there, alone, and pass into the infolded navel of eternal snow and of uprising, immortal peaks of snow and rock, she would be a oneness with i̶t̶ all, she would be herself the eternal s̶n̶o̶w̶ ̶a̶n̶d̶ **infinite** silence, the sleeping, timeless, frozen centre of the All. (N7 253–4)

Here we witness the ne plus ultra (a phrase used in *Women in Love*) of Gudrun's aestheticism. Rather than overstate the importance of the Alpine setting, we should see how the mountains merely provide a version of the aesthetic sublime for Gudrun, described in revision as the '**mysterious navel of the world**' (replacing another archetypal symbol: 'a full blown rose', though the latter figure is still alluded to in the passage by the simile of 'sharp petals' for the mountain peaks). Whereas Ursula wishes to escape the fixed images of the past (to smash the magic-lantern slides) with Birkin, Gudrun wishes to enter the 'sleeping, timeless, frozen centre of the All' alone, blurring a literal and allegorical sublime while foreshadowing Gerald's actual fate.

As a corollary to the latter point, does Gudrun's morbid aestheticism somehow lead to Gerald's death? The earlier-mentioned passage is certainly not the only place where this is hinted at. Shortly before the earlier section of notebooks begins, Gudrun regards Gerald as follows: 'she felt she could set her teeth in him and eat him ~~till nothing but a~~ to the core ~~was left~~' (N7 216), while, from Birkin's perspective, Gudrun 'stretched out her beautiful arm, with its fluff of green tulle, and touched [Gerald's] chin with her subtle, *artist's fingers*. [. . .] it was as if she had killed Gerald, with that touch' (N7 217; my italics). It is also at the hotel that Gudrun meets Loerke, who effectively radicalizes her aestheticism. Gerald and Ursula are both shut out from their abstract (modernist) aesthetic world, which only the artists Gudrun and Loerke can sustain. When Ursula criticizes Loerke's statuette of a horse with a little girl as follows: 'how stock and stupid and brutal it is. Horses are sensitive, quite delicate and sensitive, really' (N8 303), Loerke disdains her as 'an amateur and an indifferent nobody' and responds with a piece of arch-modernist aesthetic dogma: 'that horse is a certain form, part of a whole form. It is part of a work of art, a piece of form. It is not a picture of a friendly horse to which you give a lump of sugar, do you see? – it is part of a work of art, it has no relation to anything outside that work of art' (N8 303).

The antagonism between Gudrun and Loerke's abstract aestheticism and Ursula and Birkin's personal romanticism is also an antagonism between a static monologism and a fluid dialogism. Whereas Loerke suggests a work of art exists in complete isolation, actionless and absolute: 'a picture of nothing, of absolutely nothing. It has nothing to do with anything but itself, it has no relation to the everyday world of this and the other, there is no connection between them [. . .] you *must not* confuse the relative world of **action**, with the absolute ~~actionless~~ world of art' (N8 304–5), Ursula is derisive towards such an idea: 'as for your world of art and your world of reality [. . .] you have to separate the two, because you can't bear to know what you are. [. . .] The world of art is only the truth about the real world, that's all – but you are too far gone to see it' (N8 306).[7] In a passage which echoes his own actions in the aforementioned 'Moony' chapter, Birkin similarly describes Loerke as having a 'fixed will [. . .] like an iron wheel revolving in life, without any relationship to the truth [. . .]. It is Statics that triumphs then, over all organic life. And the Static power must be smashed, because it is hard and utterly fixed' (N8 299). Unlike Gudrun, then, who later demands of Gerald: 'Can't you be self-sufficient?' (N9 340), Birkin also recoils from abstract self-sufficiency. However, Gerald, sensing that Gudrun is 'virtually sufficient unto herself, closed round and completed, like a seed closed in its envelope [. . .] self-complete, without desire' (N9 340–1), reflects on his own development in the novel in terms akin to Ursula and Birkin, though more destructive:

> A strange wound had been torn in him, like a flower that opens and gives itself [. . .] so he had been torn apart and given to ~~Gudrun~~ women **Gudrun**. Why should he close again? This wound, this strange, infinitely sensitive opening of his where he was exposed [. . .] given to his complement, the other, the unknown, this wound, this disclosure, this unfolding of his own covering, leaving him incomplete, limited, unfinished [. . .] this was his deepest joy. (N9 342)

Crucially, however, Gerald's underlying feelings remain unspoken, while he, like Gudrun and Loerke, is enthralled by another sublime object, namely, Gudrun herself. Death seems to represent the only escape from his impossible desire to possess such an object. Gerald muses: 'I could kill her – I ~~could easily kill myself afterwards~~ **should be free**' (N9 333–4), while for Gudrun: 'it was so beautiful, it was a delirium, she wanted to gather the glowing, eternal peaks to her breast, and die' (N9 345).

The rewritten dialogues: 'One must turn one's face away from the old'

The first of the two heavily rewritten dialogues, which occur simultaneously within the diegesis, as all four characters walk towards the carriage awaiting Ursula and Birkin's departure, takes place between the sisters. Their conversation concerns the possibility of founding a 'new world' and Ursula's belief that, if 'one wants a new world of the soul [. . .] one must turn one's face away from the old' (N9 322), which echoes her wish to break the fixed 'slides' of memory. I transcribe both versions here in full:

> 'But', she added, 'I do think that one can't have anything new whilst one ~~accepts the old values at all. And if you stay in the world – you do accept its values.~~' **belongs to the old – do you know what I mean? – even fighting the old is belonging to it. – I know, one is tempted to stop in the world, just to fight it. – But then one goes down with it.**'
> Gudrun considered herself.
> 'Yes', she said. 'In a way,

N9 322–4: Version 1

One accepts the world's values by staying in the world. – But how do you know you are leaving the world, just because you are going to have a cottage in the Abruzzi, or wherever it may be.'

'One does one's best', said Ursula.

'And of course', said Gudrun, '*all* the world's values aren't wrong. There are plenty of ideas which are perfectly right, only they just get overlaid.'

'Perhaps – perhaps', said Ursula, wavering. 'But which ideas do you mean?'

'Oh, I mean the idea of love, for instance – that love is the greatest thing in the world. I know it sounds commonplace'.

Ursula felt troubled and beaten.

'And yet', she said, 'love doesn't seem to come off very well in the world, does it? I can't imagine a world of love – can you? – And I don't want to.'

Gudrun thought a moment about it. Then she looked up at Ursula, made a grimace of perfect cynicism, and broke into a mocking laugh. She rose, came to Ursula, and put her arm round her neck.

'Go and find your new world, dear', she said, her voice clanging with tears and irony, and a certain strangled love.

'You'll be happier doing that than doing anything else.'

N9 322–4: Version 2

One is of the world if one lives in it. But isn't it really an illusion to think you can get out of it? After all, a cottage in the Abruzzi, or wherever it may be, isn't a new world. – No, the only thing to do with the world, is to see it through.'

Ursula looked away. She was so frightened of argument.

'But there *can* be something else, can't there?' she said. 'This isn't the end?'

'This isn't the end', said Gudrun. 'But it seems to me you've got to *develop* from this to the next thing. You can't suddenly fly off on to a new planet.'

Ursula suddenly straightened herself.

'No', she said, 'no – you are wrong. You *can't* develop from this – you've got to get away to a new planet – There's no going any further with this show. You've got to hop away into space.'

Gudrun reflected for a few moments. Then a smile of opposition, almost of contempt, came over her face.

'What's the good of finding yourself in space?' she said. 'After all, the great ideas of the world are the same there. You above everybody can't get away from the fact that love, for instance, is the be-all and the end-all **supreme thing,** in space as well as on earth.'

'No', said Ursula, 'it isn't. Love is too human and little. I believe in something inhuman, of which love is only a little part. I believe what we must fulfil comes out of the unknown to us and it is something infinitely more than love. It isn't so merely *human*.'

Gudrun looked at Ursula with steady, balancing eyes. She admired and envied her sister so much, oh, so much. Then suddenly she averted her face, saying stubbornly:

'Well, I've got no further than love, yet.'

N9 322–4: Version 1

N9 322–4: Version 2

Over Ursula's mind flashed the thought: 'Because you never *have* loved, you can't get beyond it.'

Gudrun rose, came over to Ursula and put her arm round her neck.

'Go and find your new world, dear.' she said, her voice clanging with false benignity. 'After all, the happiest voyage is the quest of the Blessed Isles.'

In both versions, Ursula expresses her desire for a clean break from the past and the values currently espoused by society, whereas Gudrun insists this is impossible, that love, for example, is a ne plus ultra. The topic of conversation in the second version is vaguer, initially, as multiple references to 'values' are cut. However, the second version is ultimately more expansive than the first. In it, Gudrun expresses greater cynicism over Ursula's ability to '**hop into space**', while Ursula openly criticizes Gudrun's cynicism: '**because you never *have* loved, you can't get beyond it**'; however, in the first version, Gudrun makes a repressed 'grimace of perfect cynicism'. Ursula is also more explicit about the perceived limitations of love, with Lawrence again theorizing in revision: it is 'too human and little. I believe in something inhuman, of which love is only a little part. I believe what we must fulfil comes out of the unknown to us and it is something infinitely more than love. It isn't so merely *human*'. Interestingly, Ursula's argument echoes Lawrence's own remarks about the writerly self while completing the many drafts of *Women in Love*, with the latter seen as emerging from 'the unknown'.

The second dialogue, between Gerald and Birkin, is more one-sided, with Gerald dominating the conversation, but echoes the first as Gerald expresses his desire (or grim determination) to stay with Gudrun and 'see it through'. Birkin initially asks Gerald how long he and Gudrun intend to stay, but the dialogue quickly shifts to Gerald's monomaniacal desire for Gudrun, about whom there is 'something ~~deadly~~ **final**':

N9 325–7: Version 1

'It goes to your brain and sends you mad. [. . .] I'd stand cutting to bits, cutting to small bits, to have her', he continued. 'I couldn't not have her now – I should go mad, and begin to murder somebody.

N9 325–7: Version 2

'It goes to your brain. But what the devil's at the end of it – [. . .] I couldn't do without her – I'd rather be killed by inches. And yet –

[. . .]

[. . .] Do you know what it is to die when you are with a woman? [. . .] you're gone – you're gone – your head is like a piece of ice, smashed into nothingness. That's death. You can know death without dying. – But I've never got back myself, since that time. – But I was grateful for it – oh, I was grateful – I never knew anything like it. But I couldn't do without her now. There'd be an end of some sort. – I shan't go away from her. I couldn't – not now. We must stop on here.' Birkin looked at him, at his strange, scarcely conscious face. He seemed so far away. 'When you get more satisfied', he said, 'things will resolve out.'	Do you know what it is to die when you are with a woman? [. . .] it's nothing – your heart might have burst inside you – and' – he looked round into the air with a queer histrionic movement – 'it's nothing – you understand what I mean – it was a great experience, something final – and then – nothingness'. He walked on in silence. It seemed like bragging, but like a man bragging in extremis. 'Of course', he resumed, 'I wouldn't *not* have felt it: it's a final experience. And she's a magnificent woman. But god – I think she's deathly, I do really.' Birkin looked at him, at his strange, scarcely conscious face. Gerald seemed to wonder at his own words. 'Haven't you had enough now?' said Birkin. 'Can't you stop now?' 'Oh', said Gerald, 'it's not finished yet.'

There are some noteworthy differences between these two versions. In the first, Gerald gives more detailed analogies for his feelings, describing being cut to bits and being smashed like a piece of ice. There are also more repetitions: 'cutting [. . .] cutting', 'you're gone – you're gone' and 'grateful [. . .] grateful'. However, the second version repeats the single phrase 'nothingness' three times in quick succession. Overall though, there isn't a great shift between the two versions. Gerald is monomaniacal in both: 'I couldn't do without her now. There'd be an end of some sort' (V1) and 'I couldn't do without her [. . .] it's not finished yet' (V2). Of greater significance, genetically, is the context of both passages, as climactic, dialogical and conflicted: these traits are common to most of the heavily revised passages across the drafts of *Women in Love* (and we will see the same pattern in those of *The Plumed Serpent*). Likewise, though the second versions of both dialogues are clearly written on the basis of the first, neither represent a traditional 'revision' or obvious development of the first; rather, they represent a genetic dialogue.

Notes

1. Luca Crispi's focus on Joyce's 'construction' of characters in *Ulysses* (2016) provides a recent example.
2. Lawrence's focus on adjectives is not unique to *Women in Love*. He described his first novel, *The White Peacock*, as 'all about love – and rhapsodies of spring scattered here and there – heroines galore – no plot – *nine-tenths adjectives* – every colour in the spectrum discanted upon' (i. 144; my italics), while, when revising the proofs of his second, *The Trespasser*, Lawrence wrote that his intention was to 'wage war on my adjectives' (i. 381).
3. Even the added phrase '**over which they ran into**' in the second paragraph in this extract, which appears to represent a more conventional modification, is necessitated by the previous adjectival revision of the 'stream', from 'snow-buried' to '**hidden**'; without the added phrase, it would have meant the bridge itself 'ran into the very depth of the untouched sheets of snow' (rather than Gudrun and Gerald, as intended).
4. It is interesting to compare Gudrun in this scene to Beckett's eponymous and solipsistic protagonist in *Murphy* (1938), who induces *himself* into a trance-like state by tying himself to a chair and rocking back and forth, in order to *transcend* his body. While conceding that Beckett's Murphy is a more comic protagonist (than Lawrence's Gudrun), this comparison provides a perfect example of the difference between Beckett's cognitivist modernism and Lawrence's essentially post-cognitivist modernism; not in the sense of an 'extended mind', which suggests that the mind can incorporate external objects such as a notebook or literary manuscript (as Dirk van Hulle argues), and could therefore be termed 'extended-cognitivism', but through the more basic post-cognitivist insight that the mind is *embodied* (for a discussion of psychology after cognitivism, see Wallace et al., 2007).
5. Remember that Birkin's artistic predilections are likewise framed as a kind of religion in the discarded Prologue chapter, where Hermione is described as Birkin's 'priestess' (SIII 6).
6. We can also map the Levinassian self-other dialectic onto the writing process itself, with the unwritten as 'other', which, once written, is brought into the same of 'identity', but can be made 'other' again by rewriting.
7. Doo-Sun Ryu argues that Ursula's argument here reflects Lawrence's own views on art (2005, pp. 16–19), but I wonder if the very antagonism between Loerke and Ursula is not more reflexive of Lawrence's own beliefs.

6

Genetic dialogism in the typescripts

Introducing the typescripts

This final chapter on the manuscripts of *Women in Love* covers much more ground than the previous two combined: while the early manuscript fragments range from 6 to 214 pages in length, and are generally only lightly revised, the two typescript drafts total nearly 1,500 pages altogether, and are both extensively revised. The first (TSI) was compiled and revised between July and November 1916, while the second (TSII), initially providing a clean version of the revised TSI, was heavily revised itself between March 1917 and September 1919 (a detailed compositional history of *Women in Love* is provided in Chapter 3 of this book).

John Worthen and Lindeth Vasey provide a useful overview of Lawrence's revisions of the two typescripts in their introduction to *The First 'Women in Love'*. They too note the fact that it is often the 'particularly agonized quarrels' that are heavily revised or completely rewritten, in addition to 'a number of crucial monologues', and they also note Lawrence's propensity to rewrite chapter endings (though they don't note Lawrence's propensity to rewrite endings in general). However, they also claim much more broadly (and subjectively) that 'it is the relationship between Birkin and Ursula which changes the most', and that, in the first typescript, 'the characters are less sure of themselves and each other' (*FWL*, pp. xlix-liii). As is customary of the Cambridge Edition of Lawrence, the editors also intimate that the typescripts merely present two different versions of *Women in Love*, whereas many scenes and passages are in fact written many more times (across various drafts); it is more accurate therefore to note that the Cambridge Edition merely presents two different versions.

Having discussed the latter stages of the novel at some length in the previous chapter, the present one provides some balance by focusing mainly on the opening chapters, across the two typescript drafts. As mentioned already, I have also picked out the iconic 'Moony' chapter for discussion, which is located in the very centre of the novel and is itself heavily revised, as well as the novel's conclusion, which allows us to continue tracking Lawrence's propensity to rewrite endings. As mentioned, Lawrence tends to focus on sections of *dialogue* when revising and this focus dovetails with the contrapuntal structure and rhythm of the narrative, which shifts between constrained passages of dialogue and restful descriptive passages. Lawrence's revisions are also 'dialogical' in a more specific sense, offering multiple versions rather than linear progression, and we will see many more examples of this. A common theme which emerges across virtually all of these rewritten dialogues, as well as in Birkin's monological speeches (also revised), is the thematic opposition between flux and stasis, completion and incompletion. This theme is most explicit in monological passages which Lawrence later cut, arguably for dramatic purposes (to integrate Birkin as a character within the narrative, rather than functioning as a spokesperson for the novel's own themes). Like the latter segment of *Women in Love*, the opening section of the novel is also focalized through the two sisters, Ursula and Gudrun, whose respective ways of seeing also, again, share an antagonism between flux and stasis.

Process or product

Lawrence's vernacular language often conceals more complex ideas. Consider again his report to Garnett in January 1914 while rewriting 'The Sisters':

> I write with everything vague – plenty of fire underneath, but, like bulbs in the ground, only shadowy flowers that must be beaten and sustained for another spring. (ii. 143)

While the surface generalizations and metaphors – 'everything vague', 'plenty of fire underneath', 'bulbs in the ground', 'shadowy flowers', 'another spring' – may suggest an almost blasé fatalism (poetic truth as a transcendental bulb awaiting its inevitable expression or bloom), 'shadowy flowers' refer to existing manuscript pages and 'beating and sustaining' to the active labour of writing. In phenomenological terms, the written object is figured as a reflexive for-itself ('shadowy flowers') – a shell left behind by the process (or kernel) of writing – whereas the latter is an in-itself ('fire underneath'). Lawrence therefore reverses the norm: the physical object (the manuscript) becomes a kind of mirage (like the projection of a magic-lantern slide).

The opening scene of *Women in Love*, in TSI, toys with similar metaphors as Ursula reflects on her own self as process:

> If only she could break through the last integuments~~, to enter into a new life~~ **to get hold of something**~~.~~! She seemed to try to put her hands out, like an infant in the womb, and she could not, not yet. Still she had a strange prescience, an intimation ~~of~~ **f**~~uturity, a flowering in the unknown~~ ~~something beyond, yet to come~~ **of something yet to come**. (TSI 4)

As in the relationship between writing and the written, Ursula's present self is, like the manuscript page, rendered shadowy by a 'strange prescience' of the future. Like a series of drafts, Ursula feels she may 'break through' the 'integuments' of her current condition, while Lawrence's revisions indicate that these ideas are grounded in the process of writing. Rather than weaken her, Ursula's provisional, process-like status (echoed by Lawrence's hesitant revisions, with two lines inserted and then removed), her ability to break through existing 'integuments', sets her free.

However, set immediately opposite Ursula's vision of the self as a precocious 'infant in the womb' is Gudrun's aesthetic vision of the self as a *thing*, to be completed, or finished. Consider Gudrun's view of the wedding crowd after the sisters go for their walk near the start of the novel:

> Gudrun watched them all closely, with objective curiosity. She saw each one as a complete figure, like a character in a book, or a subject in a picture, or a marionette in a theatre**, a finished creation**. . . .] She knew them, they were finished, sealed and stamped and finished with, for her. There were none that had anything unknown, unresolved, until the Criches themselves began to appear. [. . .] Here something was not quite so preconcluded. (TSI 10)[1]

Gudrun's 'objective curiosity' stems from her (artistic) mode of vision, deploying a fixed frame and limiting or freezing her subject within it. Lawrence's minor revision also emphasizes the inherently teleological nature of Gudrun's mode of vision: targeting '**a finished creation**'. The Criches appear 'not quite so preconcluded' to Gudrun, and hence it is again suggested that her struggle with Gerald is to some extent an artistic one: to 'finish' her character sketch and render Gerald as a thing.

Women in Love is partly a novel about the ills of viewing the world in terms of finished things. Gudrun's vision is characterized as a particular *way* of seeing, contrasted with Ursula's own and later theorized by Loerke and vocally opposed by Ursula and Birkin. While Gudrun and Loerke represent forms of artistic vision (and can perhaps be identified with modernist art, specifically),[2] Gerald represents modern industry, while Ursula and Birkin detect a similar desire for fixity in a variety of spheres, from the schoolroom (as discussed in Chapter 4, in relation to the 'Wedding Ring' fragment) to Hermione's coterie at Breadalby. Completion figures in the novel as a kind of fantasy for the master, who strives for control, against the threat of uncertainty and incompletion.

Rewriting dialogues/dialogic rewriting: 'Sisters' and 'Shortlands'

If the novel is partly a critique of a particular, *modern* way of viewing the world, it is worth noting that modernity also enables radical opposition. Reflecting the novel's relativistic universe, the central antagonism between flux and stasis figures heavily in the internal dialogues, beginning with the novel's opening conversation between the sisters, who effectively deconstruct the traditional female narrative arc of the nineteenth-century English novel (from Jane Austen to Thomas Hardy) while reflecting on marriage, family and the home. As we can see, this opening dialogue was revised many times in the typescripts (ellipses and blank spaces in the right-hand column indicate unrevised text in TSII):

TSI 2–3: Version 1	TSI 2–3 and TSII 2–5: Version 2	TSII 2–5: Version 3 (further revisions)
'What do you mean "to get married"?'	'It all depends what you mean.'	'It depends how you mean.' [...]
'It always means the same thing, doesn't it?' asked Gudrun lightly. 'Don't you think you might have a better time than you ~~have~~ do now?'	Gudrun was slightly taken aback. She watched her sister for some moments. 'Well', she said, huffily, 'it usually means one thing! – But don't you think, anyhow, you'd be' – she frowned slightly – 'Well, in a better position than you are in now?'	'Well', she said, ironically, 'it usually means one thing! – But don't you think, anyhow, you'd be' – she darkened slightly – 'in a better position than you are in now?' [...]
A shadow came over Ursula's face.		
'I might', she said. 'But I'm not sure.'		
'Oh well', laughed Gudrun, 'are you sure of anything?'	A shadow came over Ursula's face.	
'Yes', said Ursula, more to herself than to her sister. 'I'm sure a bird in the bush is worth two in the hand.' [...]	'I might', she said. 'But I'm not sure.'	
	Again Gudrun paused, baffled, slightly irritated. She wanted to solve her own questions by putting them to her sister.	Again Gudrun paused, slightly irritated. She wanted to be quite definite. [...]

TSI 2–3: Version 1	TSI 2–3 and TSII 2–5: Version 2	TSII 2–5: Version 3 (further revisions)
'And while I am by myself', resumed Ursula, 'I am more or less a bird in the bush.'	'You don't think one needs the *experience* of having been married?' she asked.	
[. . .]	[. . .]	
'But would you refuse a good offer?'	'Not really', retorted Ursula. 'More likely to be the end of experience.'	
'Oh yes, inevitably!' cried Ursula. 'What a horrible **an unpleasant** thought!'	[. . .]	
[. . .]	'You wouldn't even accept a good offer?' said Gudrun.	'You wouldn't consider a good offer?' asked Gudrun.
'Yet I hate the thought of marrying, and being put into a home of my own, and having my little circle of acquaintance, and my little set of interests **and the usual man**. If you add it all up, Prune, there's damned little to be to be got by marriage. Even children – I see **hope for** so much of other people's children, that I can't see much fulfilment in having more of my own. There are so many people and so little meaning in it all.'	'I think I've rejected several', said Ursula.	[. . .]
	[. . .]	
	'Really. But weren't you fearfully tempted?'	
	'In the abstract, but not in the concrete', replied Ursula. 'When it comes to the point, one isn't even tempted. Oh, if I were tempted, I'd marry like a shot. – I'm only tempted *not* to.'	'In the abstract, but not in the concrete', replied Ursula. 'When it comes to the point, one isn't even tempted. Oh, if I were tempted, I'd marry like a shot. – I'm only tempted *not* to.'
	[. . .]	[. . .]
	'I know', she said, 'it seems like that when one thinks in the abstract. But really imagine it: a home of one's own, one's own set, oneself like a picture framed and hung up, finished! – I always feel like it is selling one's soul – if only only **except** for children – and Gudrun I don't believe in marrying for the sake of having children.'	'[. . .] But really imagine it: that imagine any man one knows, imagine him coming home to one every evening, and saying "Hello," and giving one a kiss.'
[. . .]		There was a blank pause.
'There's such a great *quantity* of human life', said Gudrun, as if she were giving the nail the final hit on the head, 'and so little quality.'	'Certainly not', said Gudrun. 'I am certainly not willing to live vicariously – which is what motherhood amounts to.'	[. . .]
		'Of course there's the children', said Ursula, doubtfully.
	[. . .]	Gudrun's face hardened.
'So little meaning', repeated Ursula.	'There's such a great *quantity* of human life', said Ursula, 'and it all seems to *mean* nothing.'	'Do you *really* want children, Ursula?' She asked coldly.
		[. . .]
		'When one thinks of other people's children' – said Ursula.

These transcriptions demonstrate the difficulty in analysing some of Lawrence's writing processes in a linear fashion. Somewhat akin to a cubist painting, new versions are effectively superimposed onto old ones, with some passages completely rewritten, some passages merely altered and others left intact, and Lawrence often repeats the process at the next manuscript stage. The typescripts present neither an increasingly well 'crafted' scene, nor do they present completely distinct 'versions'. I believe *dialogue* provides the closest analogy, however, as, besides providing variations upon a theme, each version is partly a *response* to another.

Ursula and Gudrun provide sceptical feminine viewpoints at a particular historical moment, when human life is becoming increasingly commodified and, in a sense, mass produced, while women in particular are still haunted by earlier traditions. However, while the wreckage of industrialization provides an implicit context for their scepticism – and this is made evident during their subsequent walk through the sordid rows of fields and houses in Beldover – both the dialogue and Lawrence's rewriting are orientated around the central thematic opposition between flux and stasis. Ursula's reversal of the cliché about a bird in the hand in the first version (she prefers one in the bush to two in the hand) immediately reveals her resistance to fixity, while in the second version this is more explicit and stylized, beginning with Ursula's iconic remark about 'the end of experience', which she follows by cringing over the apparent stasis of conventional, post-marital domestic life; interestingly, Ursula's comparison of 'oneself like a picture framed and hung up, finished!' foreshadows, ironically, Gudrun's subsequent view of the wedding crowd as 'finished', as well as her later image of married life at Shortlands (as a picture fit for the Royal Academy, entitled 'Home'). However, while Gudrun is in theory the more radical of the two sisters, having lived in London as an artist while Ursula stayed at home working as a schoolteacher, it is she who repeatedly questions Ursula, as though wishing to tie her down, and this latent desire for stasis in Gudrun is brought out more clearly in the third version: 'again Gudrun paused, slightly irritated. She wanted to be quite definite'.

The dialogue ends after the sisters go out for a walk and spy upon the local wedding crowd. The narrative viewpoint eventually switches to the wedding crowd itself, which includes Birkin, Gerald and Hermione. The novel's second chapter then relocates to Shortlands, home of the Criches, where the wedding reception takes place. The party quickly fall into a discussion about society, which is again heavily revised by Lawrence and again features the familiar antagonism between flux and stasis. Both typescripts begin with Hermione 'having a conversation with the bridegroom', which is about 'the building of Dreadnoughts' (TSI 28) in TSI and 'nationality' (TSII 36) in TSII, and end with Birkin defending the rights of the individual against those of the state, in opposition to Gerald.

As indicated by the original starting topic, the building of Dreadnoughts, the dialogue in TSI is both more specific and, in the context of Britain's ongoing participation in the war, controversial. Birkin suggests that the nation may be more barbaric than the individual, and questions whether it is not the nation who requires policing: 'it isn't the individual that wants watching, it is those great uncouth ~~barbarians~~ **Bill Sykeses**, the nations' (TSI 30); reminiscent of Brecht's quip from *The Threepenny Opera* (1928): 'What is robbing a bank compared with founding a bank?' In bad faith, Gerald suggests he would sooner trust his nation than 'the next individual I meet', and Birkin's response is then completely rewritten within TSI:

TSI 30: Version 1

'That's because your life is based on property that you want protected', said Birkin. 'You're not afraid of your life, only for your property. *You* don't matter, only your property. That is crude and barbaric, and is just the case of a nation.'

'I'm crude and barbaric?' asked Gerald.

'Oh very', said Birkin. 'It is such an old, worn out job, this estimating a man by his possessions, as you estimate yourself. You don't say, "I am what I am", you say, "I am what I have". And that is why you are like a nation.'

TSI 30: Version 2

'Would you really! Do you mean with your life or your property, – which?' said Birkin. 'Your property, I suppose- for your life isn't safe five minutes, in the hands of your nation.'

'Really!' laughed Gerald.

'~~Yes, quite.~~ Not two minutes', said Birkin. 'Your nation will have your life in a twinkling - but it will carefully hand on the bulk of your property to your next of kin. – Which is all you care about, I suppose. Therefore you are just like a nation yourself.'

Both versions are, again, very similar, with Birkin highlighting the nation's care for one's property over one's life in both, though the passage is perhaps more dramatic in the second version, with both Birkin and Gerald making exclamations.

Lawrence decided to rewrite this entire scene in TSII and did so by inserting several new lines at the bottom of page 36, followed by four new typescript sheets (TSII 37–40).[3] Having switched the opening topic of conversation between Hermione and the bridegroom from 'the building of Dreadnoughts' to '**nationality**', the conversation in the third version revolves around the more general question of what a nation *is*, with Hermione rejecting 'the appeal to patriotism' (TSII 36) and likening each nation to 'a house of business', while Gerald suggests that 'nationality roughly corresponds to race' (or at least 'it is *meant* to') (TSII 36) but concedes that a race 'is like a family', it '*must* make provision' and defend its possessions (TSII 37). In response to Gerald, Birkin concludes by suggesting that 'it is a question [of] which is worth more to me, my pleasant liberty of conduct, or my hat' (TSII 39), and he prefers the former.

Though the latest of the three versions is less direct and historically specific, it is perhaps more dialogical, with each speaker holding their own, whereas, in the first and second versions, Birkin's critique holds greater sway. That said, while each version pulls in a slightly different direction, the underlying tone of conversation is constant, and, as in the sisters' opening dialogue, it mixes glibness with persistence, playfulness with penetration. Another constant is the narrative context, with the dialogue taking place at a wedding reception between champagne-toting guests, as the following descriptive passage, which follows immediately after all three versions of the dialogue (though heavily revised), makes clear:

> Birkin, ~~abstractedly~~ thinking about ~~the international police,~~ **nations versus individuals,** race or national death, ~~stared into his glass, watched the champagne bubbles, and suddenly dank up all his wine.~~ **watched his glass being filled with champagne. The bubbles broke at the rim, the men withdrew, and feeling a sudden thirst at the sight of the fresh wine, Birkin drank up his glass.** (TSI 30 and TSII 40).

While the wedding is a particular setting for revelry, spontaneous play is arguably an essential constituent of any true dialogue: dialogue is always, or should be, to some extent, a group improvisation, with no fixed, central, controlling viewpoint. The narrative of *Women in Love* is spun in precisely this manner, with multiple characters providing alternative viewpoints and the reader left to take sides, hence the common perception of the novel as dialogic in the Bakhtinian sense.[4]

Unlike Bakhtinian dialogism, which concerns multiple voices, viewpoints or temporalities *within* the world of the novel, dialogical revision is *external* to the diegesis: it stems from and produces dialogue *between* alternative versions of text. Though explicit for the author during the process of writing, in order to become explicit for the reader, this type of dialogism requires a genetic reading. Bakhtinian dialogism and genetic dialogism essentially occupy different dimensions, with the former existing within a single textual level and the latter taking place across several levels. The relationship between different drafts and manuscript layers links back to the difference between 'constructivism' and 'dialogism' as metaphors for (or ways of understanding) writing. Comparing the aforementioned textual relationship to memory for a moment, consider

Sartre's point about the inadequacy of using 'possession' as an expression for one's relationship to the past:

> One cannot *have* a past as one 'has' an automobile or a racing stable. That is, the past can not be possessed by a present being which remains strictly external to it as I remain, for example, external to my fountain pen. In short, in the sense that possession ordinarily expresses an *external* relation of the possessor to the possessed, the expression of possession is inadequate. (2003, pp. 135–6)

Is an external metaphor (such as 'construction', or 'returning to a source') not similarly inadequate when expressing the relationship between alternative versions of text? A phenomenology of writing suggests that dialogism and spontaneity are basic elements, regardless of an author's method or creed.[5]

Cuts: 'As if too much was said'

Following the dialogue discussed earlier, 'several men' from the wedding reception stroll into the garden and their conversation quickly becomes another searching one, dominated by Gerald and Birkin. Revolving around the bride and groom's spontaneous race to the church prior to the wedding, the topic of conversation shifts from the nation to individual ethics, and Lawrence again rewrites heavily, beginning with the following passage:

TSI 32: Version 1	TSI 32 and TSII '41': Version 2	TSII 41: Version 3
'How do you like the race of the bride – the wedding race?' asked Birkin of Gerald, in raillery.	'But it's quite in the classic **barbaric** wedding tradition: flight of the bride, pursuit of the groom, and a show of rape,' **chase the woman, and make a show of rape**', said Birkin, in raillery.	'What about this race then – who began it?' Gerald asked.

There is an interesting transitional revision in version two where 'the classic tradition' becomes 'the barbaric tradition', echoing Birkin's earlier description of the nation as 'crude and barbaric'. However, perhaps the most noteworthy change is the fact that the question of the wedding race shifts from being posed by Birkin in versions one and two to Gerald in version three, which again renders the narrative more dramatic, less dominated by Birkin. The rest of the dialogue, predominantly between Birkin and Gerald, is then entirely rewritten, again using newly inserted sheets of typescript (TSII 43–5) which appear to have been typed manually by Lawrence. In it, the pair go on to discuss the nature of order and spontaneity:

TSI 33

"~~I think you should do everything according to a proper order,~~" **'Satan be damned! I think if you set out to do a thing,** *do* **it'**, said Gerald. 'If you're out to make a formal wedding, then you should bring it off [. . .]. Do what you're doing, and don't make confusion and chaos.'

[. . .]

'~~I am~~ **Yes**', said Gerald~~.~~, '**I** *am* **the enemy of disorder.**'

'But supposing, you see, that Laura *wanted* to run from Lupton. Supposing it was a natural impulse in her to bolt ~~up the church path~~ the moment she set eyes on him. Now the proper thing to do would be to obey that impulse, speaking in the deepest sense; otherwise she would create chaos and confusion in her own soul, her own nature.'

'How do you make that out?' Said Gerald. 'I should say, if she controlled her impulses, she would have *more* order in her soul, not less.'

'No, surely. The more she controls her natural impulses, suppresses them and diverts them, the greater chaos occurs in her ~~spontaneous~~ soul, ~~the~~ **although** greater regularity ~~is gained in~~ **may be secured for** her *material* life. Which do you choose? Which would you rather have, Lupton: Laura who ~~is spontaneous and incalculable~~ **bolts**, or Laura ~~who is regulated, going like a clock?~~" **as regular as clock-work?'**

[. . .]

'That's all very well, but you couldn't have all life like that, everybody doing just what they want', said Gerald.

TSII 43

'If you're doing a thing, do it properly and if you're not going to do it properly, leave it alone.'

[. . .]

'You don't believe in having any standard of behaviour at all, do you' he challenged Birkin, censoriously.

"~~I hate people who are good form,~~" ~~replied Birkin. "But I loathe also anybody who isn't. A man who's got any self is good form by just being himself."~~ **'Standard – no. I hate standards. But they're necessary for the common ruck. – Anybody who is anything can just be himself and do as he likes.'**

'But what do you mean by being himself?' said Gerald. "~~Who's using aphorisms now?~~" **'Is that an aphorism or a cliché?'**

'I mean just doing what you want to do. I think it was perfect good form in Laura to bolt from Lupton to the church door. It was almost a masterpiece in good form. It's the hardest thing in the world to act spontaneously on one's impulses – and it's the only really gentlemanly thing to do~~.~~ **provided you're fit to do it.'**

[. . .]

'[. . .] You think people should just do as they like?'

'I think they always do. But I should like them to like the purely individual thing in themselves, which makes them act in singleness. And they only like to do the collective thing.'

'And I', said Gerald grimly, 'shouldn't like to be in a world of people who acted individually and spontaneously, as you call it. – We should have everybody cutting everybody else's throat in five minutes.'

Both the earlier and later versions of this long segment begin with Gerald's demand for order: 'do what you're doing' (V1) and 'do it properly' (V2), and end with his rejection of Birkin's arguments in favour of liberty and spontaneity: 'you couldn't have all life like that, everybody just doing what they want' (V1) and 'you think people should just do as they like?' (V2), echoing their previous conversation about the nation. However, while these markers tag the versions together at either end, the middle content is more varied, figuring more as variations upon a theme.

Gerald is more outspoken in the first version, declaring, 'I *am* the enemy of disorder', whereas Birkin, who only implicitly falls on the side of impulse in the first, is more forthright in the second version, declaring, 'I hate standards'. In both versions though, Birkin suggests that order is complicated by impulse: 'supposing it was a natural impulse [...] the proper thing would be to obey that impulse, speaking in the deepest sense' (V1) and 'It was almost a masterpiece in good form. It's the hardest thing in the world to act spontaneously on one's impulses' (V2), the latter remark demonstrating a Gudrun-like aesthetic inflection to Birkin's thought. Birkin's linking of control to repression, suggesting that this produces negative energy, leading to 'greater chaos' in the '*soul*', initially provides the first version with greater analytic depth than the second. However, the second version compensates for this with Birkin's analysis of Gerald's repressed suggestion that 'we should have everybody cutting everybody else's throat in five minutes': 'that means *you* would like to be cutting everybody's throat' and 'you no doubt have a lurking desire to have your [own] gizzard slit' (TSII 44).

Following this passage comes a noteworthy single descriptive paragraph, which originally formed the conclusion to Chapter One in TSI but ultimately forms the conclusion to Chapter Two ('Shortlands'), following Lawrence's insertion of a chapter break halfway through Chapter One in TSII. The passage is completely rewritten on a single inserted sheet of typescript in TSII, which may seem unusual, as a descriptive (rather than dialogic) passage, but it does provide another striking example of Lawrence rewriting an *ending*. I will give both versions in turn before commenting:

TSI 35:

And the two men walked back towards the house, having come into ~~almost too close~~ **trembling nearness of** contact, in their talk. They felt tender and quivering, one towards the other. They walked in love, back to the house, there to separate in the friability of actual life~~.~~, **to escape each other.**

TSII 45:

There was a pause of strange enmity between the two men, that was very near to love. It was always the same between them; always their talk brought them into a ~~fearful~~ **deadly** nearness of contact, a strange, perilous intimacy which ~~neither of them would avow. And the tacit disavowal made almost a hatred between them.~~ **was either hate or love, or both.** They parted with apparent inconcern, as if their going apart were a trivial occurrence. And they really kept it to the level of trivial occurrence. Yet the heart of each burned ~~for~~ **from** the other. They burned ~~to love~~ **with** each other, inwardly. This they would never admit. They intended to keep their relationship a casual free and easy friendship, they were not going to be so unmanly and unnatural as to allow any heart-burning ~~or love~~ between them. They had not the faintest belief in ~~love~~ deep relationships between men and men, ~~and even the classic friendship, such as that between David and Jonathan they looked on with suspicion and contempt, as being in some way unmanly or unclean. To them the relationship of Achilles and Patroclus was moving, but womanly and suspect.~~ **and their disbelief prevented any development of their powerful but suppressed friendliness.**

The first version is much shorter but is full of tension. Love, unable to bear 'the friability of actual life', fails to keep the pair together, while, in revision, they also separate '**to escape each other**', implying that love has an overbearing quality, too. The second version loses some of this nuance, though the extended discussion of the affection between the two men is perhaps braver. In it, the 'heart of each burned' for the other, but their feelings are suppressed through a mixture of fear and disbelief, which carries a latent criticism of societal norms, about what it means to be 'manly' and 'natural'. Both versions recall the intense intimacy of the early fragments, as well as the specific closeness between Gerald and Birkin outlined in the abandoned 'Prologue' chapter.

Before moving on, it is important to note that, prior to the aforementioned chapter's conclusion, the first typescript contained an additional, long section of dialogue between Birkin and Gerald, which is heavily revised in TSI before being completely cut from TSII. In it, Birkin speaks at length about desire, God, evil, and the soul, essentially giving voice to the novel's thematic opposition between flux and stasis and the ethical and metaphysical imperatives resulting from it, in a series of playful responses to Gerald. I would suggest that Lawrence cut this section, of which I provide extracts in the following, for dramatic reasons, and the rewritten chapter ending (discussed earlier) supports this by placing far more emphasis on the dramatic tension between the two characters. In the original dialogue, Birkin responds to Gerald's suggestion that 'you couldn't have all life like that, everybody just doing what they want' as follows:

TSI 34: Version 1

'Why not?' said Birkin. 'That's the ideal. If you talk in terms of God, then God sends us our desires. The impulse from God enters into me in the shape of a desire. And that is God in me, my desire.'

'And what about the Devil, then?' asked Gerald.

'He works through my will. The evil of evils is my egoistic conceit, the great Christian sin of pride. And the agent is the will. The will is only an instrument, but it is usually the instrument of evil.'

'That's just Christianity', said Gerald. 'Be humble, and submit your will to God.'

'Quite right too – only don't have false Gods. We know nothing about God, and never shall. All you know, is that there is a desire come upon you, you don't know how, and that this desire is God.'

'Yes, but what is evil, if all desire is good?' said Gerald. 'Because if there is GOOD, there must be EVIL.'

TSI 34: Version 2

'Why not?' said Birkin. 'That's the ideal. *Fay ce que vouldras* – that is the twelfth and ultimate commandment, which swallows all the others in a [?] gulp. – If God is in me, then His voice is the still small voice of my desire – surely?'

'What about the Devil, then?' asked Gerald, smiling.

'That is he who denies my desire. He says, "I've decided what is and what isn't, and none of these irruptive desires are going to upset my scheme." – The devil, Gerald, as you need to learn, is the egoistic *will* of man – your own will is the devil in you, for example.'

'I should be humble, and submit my will to God?' laughed Gerald.

'Oh decidedly: decidedly! When a desire comes upon you, this is the Holy Ghost which is with you – submit, submit. Wilde was right, profoundly, when he said temptation was given us to succumb to.'

'What a world we should have, if anybody believed you!' cried Gerald, a wicked look of mischief on his face.

The second version is slightly longer than the first and is, for the most part, an expanded version. It repeats Birkin's first point, which equates God with desire, but adds an intriguing reference to the commandment at the Abbey of Thélème in Rabelais's *Gargantua* (1534); it also repeats the second point, which equates the Devil with the ego and the will, but adds the Devil's antithetical commandment, which clarifies the relationship between this grouping (the ego, the will, the known, and the Devil) and stasis: 'I've decided what is and what isn't, and none of these irruptive desires are going to upset my scheme'. One point which the second version does seem to lose is Birkin's caution about 'false Gods': 'we know nothing about God, and never shall', whereas the second carries a more playful note ('Oh decidedly: decidedly!') with a reference to Wilde.

The remaining segments of the dialogue in TSI are far less heavily revised. Beginning with his response to Gerald, Birkin expands on the point about evil and suggests the more fundamental opposition, in both the self and the universe, between flux and stasis:

> 'Evil is the static will', said Birkin. 'That which has come to pass ~~desires, or rather~~ *wills* to remain as it is, ~~to persist~~ **in statu quo**. And that is the root of all evil. Desire is a seed, it will bring forth the unknown. But it has against it this static entity, ~~this insect,~~ this accomplished I. And this is the devil, this me which has come to pass, and which wishes to crystallise for ever upon itself, unchangeable. Whereas in reality, this me which I am is only a point of ~~stable~~ equilibrium, unstable equilibrium at that, in the everlasting flux of ~~the universe~~ **creation**.' (TSI 34)

While there are interesting shadows of Kafka, with the ego as an 'insect', and of Deleuze and Guattari, with desire as something revolutionary, which disrupts the will to persist '**in status quo**', I believe this passage gets to the crux of Lawrence's *weltanschauung*. The universe is an 'everlasting flux', while the self is only ever a 'point' of 'unstable equilibrium', and any (wilful, egoistical) desire for greater control, for fixity (the 'accomplished I'), 'is the root of all evil'. Lawrence also revises the potentially static term 'universe' to '**creation**', which suggests a metaphysics of creativity and process, but also hints at the parallels between this thematic opposition and the novel's own process of composition, in which Lawrence himself displays relentless creativity. It is easy to see each manuscript as a 'static entity [. . .] which wishes to crystallise for ever upon itself', and the reference to desire as bringing forth 'the unknown' is reminiscent of Lawrence's own commentary (in the letters) upon the process of writing the novel.

In the final segment of this dialogue, under Gerald's questioning, Birkin hammers home this point about the illusory nature of the ego:

> 'There is no real you?' asked Gerald~~,~~ **, looking at his friend with smiling, cruel eyes. It seemed almost true – Birkin was so evanescent.**
>
> 'No. There is no *thing* contained within a certain outline, which is absolute me. [. . .] There is no absolute I, there is only a central truth, a balancing point within the flux, a point where a pure relationship is established between all the paths. This point is my soul. But you can see that a *point* isn't anything – ~~think only of~~ **even in** Euclid.'
>
> [. . .] 'My being is a centre of pure relationship between parts of the flux, a point of perfect equilibrium. But since the whole is a flux, ever-changing,

therefore this ~~relationship passes away, with time~~ **unit dissolves again, this being disappears**.' (TSI 34–5)

It is worth noting the familiar focus upon adjectives and viewpoints in Lawrence's revisions, with Birkin '**evanescent**' in Gerald's eyes. Likewise, the parallel between Birkin's argument about the universe and the self, and the concept of genetic dialogism which I am proposing for Lawrence's writing process. There is no one version 'contained within a certain outline' which is absolutely *Women in Love*: the novel, like the process of writing, exists as a 'pure relationship between parts of the flux'. I have suggested that Lawrence may have cut these passages of dialogue for dramatic reasons, as they seem to bear as much upon Lawrence's own vision of the world as they do upon the characters in the novel. However, it is worth bearing these excised passages in mind when reading the famous episode in the later chapter 'Moony', where Birkin casts stones at the moon's reflected image.

Smashing the mirror: 'Class-Room' and 'Moony'

Before moving on to the novel's heavily rewritten ending, there are two other instances where earlier versions of speeches by Birkin, in the first typescript, give more explicit voice to this central antagonism. The first of these comes at the end of the third chapter, 'Class-Room'. As with the previous chapter breaks, Lawrence inserted a new chapter break for Chapter Four when revising TSII (p. 62). Lawrence also completely rewrote the pages immediately preceding this break (i.e. the end of Chapter Three), in this case by inserting three new handwritten sheets.[6] The rewritten episode contains Birkin's harangue against Hermione, who is effectively treated as representative of the British intelligentsia (of which Birkin also counts himself, as indicated by his repeated use of the inclusive plural pronoun 'we' in the final version of the episode), with all 'your senses in your head'.[7]

Birkin's speech develops his previous dialogue with Gerald on the evil principle of stasis (discussed earlier), focusing on the same problematic 'fixed will', but developing an added element of reflexivity through the figure of a mirror: 'you've got that mirror, your own fixed will, your immortal understanding, your own tight conscious world, and there is nothing beyond it. There, in the mirror, you must have everything' (TSI 45; TSII 57–8 (see Figure 11)). Birkin's critique of the will to persist therefore develops into a criticism of self-affirmation, whereby knowledge becomes a reflector of the self. As with the previous dialogue between

Birkin and Gerald, the rewritten version in TSII places more emphasis on the internal drama between Birkin and Hermione, whereas in the earlier version Birkin pursues the point about the mirror in greater detail:

TSI 45: Version 1

'And because you've found all your ~~extant~~[?] **leading** ideas become stale, circumscribed as they are by your mirror-frame, you turn **round** against intellectualism, against thought, against any expression of **abstract** truth, you want only sensationalism, which means your senses in your head. [. . .] you want to look at yourself in a mirror, like Shah Jehan – you want to see your own animal actions in a mirror – your accursed Lady of Shallott mirror, which you've got in your head – and which is *you*, the beginning and end of you – a fixed consciousness, an innumerable set of fixed conceptions, ~~polished~~ **old** clear and final, and bound round by your will into one perfect round mirror, in which the world takes place for you. [. . .] You'd die rather than know that your perfect consciousness doesn't stretch to the bounds and limits of the universe. [. . .] You'll take your precious mirror to the grave with you, ~~like~~ **as if it were** your own immortality.'

TSII 57: Version 2

'But now you have come to all your conclusions, you want to go back and be like a savage, without knowledge. You want a life of pure sensation and "passion."'

He quoted the last word satirically against her. She sat convulsed with fury and violation, speechless, like a stricken pythoness of the Greek oracle.

'But your passion is a lie', he went on violently. 'It isn't passion at all, it is your *will*. It's your bullying will. You want to clutch things and have them in your power. [. . .] And why? Because you haven't got any real body, any dark sensual body of life. You have no sensuality. You have only your will and your conceit of consciousness, and your lust for power, to *know*.'

He looked at her in mingled hate and contempt, also in pain because she suffered, and in shame because he knew he tortured her. He had an impulse to [?] **kneel** and plead for forgiveness. But a bitter red anger burned up to fury in him.

In the second version, the characters' emotions provide a clear indication that the exchange is surfacing a repressed conflict. Birkin's 'anger burned up to fury', while Hermione feels not only 'fury' but also 'violation'. Hermione is actually likened to 'a stricken pythoness of the Greek oracle' in version two, which connects directly to the abandoned Prologue, where Ethel (i.e. Hermione) is described as the 'priestess' who sustains Birkin's 'oracles' (SIII 6). However, in the first version, Birkin's monologue is initially dominated by the figure of the mirror, with references to Shah Jahan (builder of the monumentally symmetrical Taj Mahal) and the Lady of Shallott (who, in Arthurian legend, is cursed to watch the world (or river to Camelot) go by in a mirror's reflection), attacking again the principle of stasis ('fixed consciousness', 'fixed conceptions', 'clear and final', 'bound round', 'one perfect round mirror').

This image of the mirror provides another key to *Women in Love*. Fixed or bounded images, many of which are prefigured in the early fragments, are attacked throughout the novel. The less clearly defined images, such as the home, marriage and the nation, are only vaguely dissolved into 'unreality' for certain characters, whereas the more precise (and often sublime) images, such as Gudrun and Gerald's sense of each other's bodies, Birkin's reflected view of the moon, and Ursula's images of her own childhood, come under more violent assault. During the period in which he left the early drafts of *Women in Love* to one side (1915–16), Lawrence himself describes fixed form as a constraint and as something to be smashed: 'there comes a point when the shell, the form of life, is a prison to the life' (ii. 285); 'I am bored by coherent thought. Its very coherence is a dead shell. But we must help the living impulse that is within the shell. The shell is being smashed' (ii. 426). On the surface, a mirror has the ability to capture a perfect image of the world, but, its latent ability, its 'inherent vice', is to crack and smash. This undertone is actually captured more explicitly in the second version of the aforementioned episode, where Ursula feels 'a sense of ~~horror~~ **violation** in the air, as if too much was said, the unforgivable' (TSII 58), and Birkin suggests 'that loathsome little skull of yours, that ought to be cracked like a nut. For you'll be the same till it *is* cracked, like an insect in its skin' (TSII 57). While it is of course Hermione who attempts to carry out this task in a literal sense, by striking Birkin over the head with a lapis lazuli paperweight in a later episode, Birkin carries out the true, symbolic task of smashing the 'mirror' (arch principle of stasis) in the iconic chapter 'Moony', which also contains the other instance in which Birkin gives a more explicitly thematic speech in TSI.

The episode in 'Moony' sits almost exactly halfway through the novel and is perhaps its symbolic heart. Following a pattern where one character or group of characters is spied upon by another, the scene is witnessed by Ursula, who, out walking, sees the moon 'transcendent' and 'perfect' over the water and is perturbed by its stillness: 'she wished for something else out of the night, she wanted another night, not this moon-brilliant hardness' (*WL* pp. 245–6).[8] The iconic scene itself is often alluded to as a paradigmatic modernist 'moment of being', where word and image seem epiphanically bound together. Jack Stewart describes it as follows:

> The symbolic action of 'Moony' is so powerful that the reader experiences it immediately and sensuously, as it were, rather than cognitively [. . .] visionary concentration and psychic projection transcend personal causes and unite the individual with the archetype. Lawrence penetrates the primordial with a highly conscious form of 'art-speech'. (1999, p. 84)

'Penetrating the primordial' is perhaps an unfortunate phrase, but I agree with Stewart's analysis of the episode in expressionist terms. However, as Stewart goes on to demonstrate, there is also a sexual context for the scene interpreted as a symbol. Stewart suggests that 'were it not for Birkin's curse on Cybele, the female sex-principle that enslaves men, the symbolic meaning might remain obscure', and he argues that the figure of Cybele 'is asserting a self-centered will-to-integration' on the water, whereas Birkin 'is asserting a contrary will-to-disintegration aimed at the "insistent female ego"' (p. 84). In the same spirit, Kinkead-Weekes even suggests that Birkin stones the moon 'in destructive misogyny, resentment, repudiation – but afterwards there is peace' (1996, p. 335). I find both readings a stretch. While the reference to 'Cybele' comes in a short, enigmatic monologue, which Birkin delivers just before casting the stones, a genetic analysis reveals that, in keeping with the previously discussed examples, Lawrence cut a large chunk of speech when revising TSII. As you can see in the following text, the theoretical point of Birkin's monologue is made explicit in the first version, while the edit seems to have been done for dramatic reasons, as Birkin's speech is curtailed and Ursula's response is foregrounded in the rewritten and revised second version:

TSI 302

'Artemis –Tanit – Mylitta – Aphrodite – be damned to her. She's really supreme now – if you should begrudge it her – damn her. All is two, all is not one. That's the point. ~~That's the secret of secrets. You've got to build a new world on that if you build one at all.~~ **It really is. – You can build a new world on that. Infinite One – god is a Point – what good is a Point?** All is two, all is not one. ~~In the beginning, all was two.~~ **All *was* two, with the beginning, and will be in the end.** The One is the result. That which is *created* is One. That's the ~~result~~ **resultant**, the consummation. But the beginning ~~is two~~ **and the end is two**, it is not one. ~~And creation~~ **The All** is two, the Whole is two, it is not one. There you've got it. I wonder what the Priscillianiste really made of it? – '

TSII 391

'Cybele - ~~and~~ curse her! ~~She's the one god left.~~ **The accursed Syria Dea! –** Does one begrudge it her? ~~Something else on[?] as well. The other half—what about that?~~ **What else is there – ?' Ursula wanted to laugh loudly and hysterically, hearing his isolated voice speaking out. It was so ridiculous.**

Though the passage remains obscure, with its allusions to ancient myth and an heretical Gnostic-Manichaean Christian sect (Priscillianism), the longer text does make a clear connection to Birkin's earlier discussion of the soul as a point with Gerald ('this point is my soul. But you can see that a *point* isn't anything' TSI 34–5): '**Infinite One – god is a Point – what good is a Point?**'. Likewise, the line 'the beginning **and the end is two**' echoes Birkin's harangue against Hermione, in which he suggests that a 'fixed consciousness' has become 'the beginning and the end of you'. I would also point out that Birkin's split or plural metaphysic ('the whole is two') foreshadows post-structuralist feminist theory (especially Luce Irigaray), which criticizes what Derrida labels 'phallogocentrism', or the assumption of unitary meaning through the use of singular, 'master signifiers'. Birkin's speech is more enigmatic and confused in the second version, with Ursula suggesting it was '**so ridiculous**'; hence, the subsequent casting of stones becomes a more purely expressionist activity.

In genetic terms, the scene itself, in which Birkin stones the moon's reflected image (into 'a battlefield of broken lights and shadows'), does not permit much commentary as it goes almost entirely unrevised throughout the typescripts, though this lack of revision does in itself provide a striking example of the familiar pattern in which a piece of conflicted dialogue (or monologue) is heavily rewritten and is followed by a rich descriptive passage which remains intact despite rewriting. The scene does however take on greater meaning when read in its genetic context, with Birkin's suggestions in the earlier versions that society's ills are founded on 'a fixed consciousness, an innumerable set of fixed conceptions, polished old clear and final, and bound round by your will into one perfect round mirror, in which the world takes place for you'.

That said, how much should we read into the fact that Birkin's actions cause only a temporary flux, which ultimately resolves itself into stasis and oneness? The moon is itself a reflector. Likewise, the episode in 'Moony' takes place within the reflexive world of a novel. Perhaps the episode is symbolic of the novel's own fragmentary resistance to stasis, which is yet made 'one' by its finished form. Is the novel in some sense then a failure? We must take into account the demands of publishers and the marketplace, of course. As mentioned in this book's Introduction, Lawrence did not work under the auspices of a wealthy benefactor, and, as he suggested in his letters to Garnett, he had to publish to live; in Paul Delany's view, without financial support, Joyce 'would have had to write more numerous but simpler books, as commercial novelists have always had to do' (1999, p. 291). We should also consider the novel's ultimate 'resolution', its ending.

'Exeunt'

Lawrence rewrote the ending to *Women in Love* on numerous occasions. Sidestepping the early drafts, in which the ending does not survive, we are able to track Lawrence writing an ending in the previous stage of composition through notebooks 7–10. Lawrence also heavily revised the closing lines to TSI (see Figure 9) and then revised the text again in TSII, striking the previous final lines and inserting four new handwritten sheets.

In all three extant drafts, Birkin reflects on Gerald's death while directly observing and commenting on his body: 'the carcase of a dead male' (N10 430, TSI 663 and TSII 772). While Gerald possibly 'survived' in pre-war versions of the novel (given his presence in the climactic episode of the 'Sisters I' fragment), this image of the dead male body clearly carried a significance beyond the loss of life during the First World War, given the parallel ending to 'Odour of Chrysanthemums', one of Lawrence's earliest pieces of fiction (discussed in Chapter 2). Beyond the biographical contexts for this mortal vision, the prematurely dead male body is perhaps most resonant of the tragedy of endings, of a pause in 'the everlasting flux of creation', just as the process of writing is (at least temporarily) fixed in the finished and printed text.

While there is extensively revised material across the closing pages, I will focus here on the final lines (the version numbers, 1–3, are purely for the purposes of comparison):

N10 436: Version 1

'Perhaps you sleep now in fulfillment – your very failure is a fulfillment – and one is wrong to oppose it. – Perhaps you *couldn't* be happy, as I wanted. – We will cover you over, and love you – and you will be warm in death. We will love you – you won't be cold – .'

TSI 666: Version 2

'At any rate, you sleep', he said, through his tears and pain. 'At any rate you sleep now: we needn't grieve for you any more. We will cover you over, and ~~love~~ **leave** you – and you will be warm in death. We will love you – you won't be cold.'

Then again his face broke with tears.

'But it was horrible for you', he cried. 'And then – nothing – nothing – never to struggle clear – never to struggle clear – Gerald –'

He could not bear it. His heart seemed to be torn in his chest.

'But then', he strove to say, 'we needn't all be like that. All is not lost, because many are lost. – I am not afraid or ashamed to die and be dead.'

TSII 776: Version 3

'Did you need Gerald?' she asked one evening.

[. . .]

'Having you, I can live all my life without anybody else, any other sheer intimacy. But to make it complete, really happy, I wanted eternal union with a man too: another kind of love', he said.

'I don't believe it', she said. 'It's an obstinacy, a theory, a perversity.'

'Well – ' he said.

'You can't have two kinds of love. Why should you!'

'It seems as if I can't', he said. 'Yet I wanted it.'

'You can't have it, because it's wrong, impossible', she said.

'I don't believe that', he answered.

The repetition of 'perhaps' and the many hyphens puncturing Birkin's speech in the first version indicate a struggle to accept death. The second version is similarly punctured and repetitive, although there is an added conciliatory note ('all is not lost'). Following a familiar pattern, the rewritten third version in TSII more clearly dramatizes Birkin: Ursula is reintroduced in a newly inserted scene and the novel ends with an inconclusive piece of dialogue between her and Birkin. Ursula's suggestion that 'you can't have two kinds of love' echoes Birkin's excised monologue of 'the whole' as 'two' in the 'Moony' episode, and those excised lines haunt the novel's eventual ending as Birkin enigmatically demurs: 'I don't believe that', at the same time giving voice to the author's own underlying resistance to completion and stasis.

Finally, Gerald's death at the end of *Women in Love* is perhaps symbolic of the end of a certain phase in Lawrence's writing. After *Women in Love*, the protagonists of Lawrence's novels, though still concerned with plotting a hopeful path for the future, become increasingly haunted by the past and by former lives. Jumping forward several years to pick Lawrence's writing up again in 1923, by which time he had finally departed from England and the dispiriting climate of the First World War, in the next chapter we confront an older and slightly more melancholic writer.

Notes

1 The 'Sisters III' fragment contains an earlier version of this passage: 'Ursula looked at their faces, Gudrun more at their clothes, their bearing, the whole figure they made. People had a mask, to her, of looking like dressed artificial figures, marionettes. She was not interested in characters, only in plastic form' (SIII 45).

2 Tony Pinkney, in *D. H. Lawrence and Modernism*, argues '*The Rainbow* and *Women in Love* together constitute Lawrence's most far-reaching engagement with modernist aesthetics' and that in *Women in Love* Lawrence sought 'to catalogue and challenge it across the whole range of its manifestations'; however, Pinkney also suggests the latter novel 'becomes an exemplary instance of precisely that which it set out to destroy' (pp. 96–100).
3 Lawrence probably wrote these himself on his own typewriter: the four inserted sheets use different type and average both extra words per line and extra lines per page (rising from twenty-five to twenty-eight); there are also two page '40s' in TSII, where the inserted scene overran the original.
4 See, for example, David Lodge's essay on 'Lawrence, Dostoevsky, Bakhtin: D. H. Lawrence and Dialogic Fiction', as well as Michael Bell's chapter on 'The Worlds of *Women in Love*', in *D. H. Lawrence: language and being*.
5 Bushell's 'Philosophy of Composition' supports this (2009, pp. 215–38).
6 The pages in question are TSII 57–61, which replaces and corresponds to TSI 45–9.
7 We can better understand Birkin's aggression towards Hermione in this episode having contemplated the excised 'Prologue' chapter draft.
8 The 'moon-brilliant hardness' echoes the perceived hardness of Birkin's eyes for Ella in the 'Sisters II' fragment.

Part Four

The Plumed Serpent (1923–6)

Table 2 Stemmatic table for *Quetzalcoatl* and *The Plumed Serpent*, with references to Roberts and Poplawski's bibliography (2001)

Bibliographical Notes		Version	Date
Holograph manuscript, Roberts E313a	MSI 594 pp. 'Quetzalcoatl'	One	May 10 1923 – June 27 1923
Typescript, Roberts E313b	TSI 360 pp. 'Quetzalcoatl'		
Holograph manuscript, Roberts E313c	MSII 806 pp. 'Quetzalcoatl'	Two	November 19 1924 – July 1925
Revised original and carbon typescript, Roberts E313d	TSII 743 pp. 'Q̶u̶e̶t̶z̶a̶l̶c̶o̶a̶t̶l̶ **The Plumed Serpent**'		

7

Criticism, composition and writing depression

Introducing *The Plumed Serpent*

As with the insertion of individual chapter titles into *Women in Love*, Lawrence reluctantly changed the title of his Mexican novel at the behest of his English publisher, Martin Secker, from 'Quetzalcoatl' to 'The Plumed Serpent', an English translation which Lawrence himself described as 'luscious' and 'a bit silly' (v. 250 and 263). The compositional history of *The Plumed Serpent* has been described in detail before, particularly by L. D. Clark and N. H. Reeve in their respective introductions to the Cambridge editions of the novel. However, as in my account of the compositional history of *Women in Love*, while Clark and Reeve provide a basis for my work, I provide a different interpretation of the materials and suggest there are flaws in the existing understanding. Following a summary of Lawrence's composition of the novel, I expand on the nature of Lawrence's manuscripts as *drafts* (written explicitly as part of an ongoing process of writing and directly reused at a later stage), in opposition to previous critics. I also provide a brief account of the heavy criticism which *The Plumed Serpent* has received and discuss how my own interpretation differs here too (by focusing on the novel's protagonist, Kate), before picking out some representative examples of Lawrence's revision of the novel from the various phases of writing. The most detailed genetic analysis comes in the next chapter, which focuses on the final chapter of *The Plumed Serpent* and Lawrence's many attempts to write an ending.

Lawrence completed the majority of work on *The Plumed Serpent* during two extended visits to Mexico, between 1923 and 1925. He wrote a first draft (MSI) while residing at Lake Chapala, in an incredibly productive spell which began on 10 May 1923 and was completed by 27 June of the same year. MSI, which forms the basis of the published version of the novel entitled *Quetzalcoatl* (including the Cambridge edition), runs to 479 pages (around 115,000 words) and is written in two bound notebooks. After completing MSI, there followed a break of over a year, during which time, besides reflecting on the novel, Lawrence completed a raft of other work, including the novel *The Boy in the Bush* (1924), written in collaboration with Mollie Skinner, and the novella *St. Mawr* (1925). Having left Mexico in July 1923, Lawrence also visited New York (where Frieda left for Europe), Los Angeles and Guadalajara, travelled to England (rejoining Frieda and throwing an infamous dinner party for friends at the Café Royal) before Christmas 1923 and then recrossed the Atlantic, returning to Taos in New Mexico in March 1924.[1] Lawrence began a second draft while residing in Oaxaca, writing an entirely new manuscript (MSII) in another industrious period which began 19 November 1924 and ended in late January 1925. MSII is significantly longer, running to 806 pages (around 185,000 words), and was written in a second pair of bound notebooks, except for the final thirty-eight pages, which, having exhausted the new notebooks, Lawrence completed, bewilderingly, in the *old* pair of notebooks; in almost layman's *Finnegans Wakean* style, he did this by turning over notebook two of MSI and writing the concluding segment inwards from the back.

Lawrence revised MSI fairly heavily, most likely during the original period of composition, and likewise had Willard Johnson begin typing it while he was still writing, in May 1923. Johnson completed 81 pages of the typescript (TSI), which equated to the first 108 pages of MSI (a few pages into Chapter Five). Lawrence only lightly revised TSI, mainly correcting words, although he did also insert chapter titles for chapters One to Four (MSI includes titles for Chapters Five to Seven only).[2] Lawrence's American publisher at the time, Thomas Seltzer, had TSI completed but it contains errors and non-authorial alterations, hence, it is not discussed in these chapters.[3] Lawrence only lightly revised MSII but had another friend begin typing the novel as he wrote, this time Dorothy Brett, who completed the first four chapters of the second typescript (TSII); TSII was then completed by Lawrence's agent, Curtis Brown.[4] Following a five-month break, during which Lawrence fell dangerously ill, was finally diagnosed with tuberculosis, and returned to Taos, he then heavily revised TSII from June to July 1925.[5]

Clark, Reeve and Louis Martz each support the basic idea that Lawrence produced two separate versions of his Mexican novel (as reflected in Table 2) and have thus edited two separate editions, beginning with the Cambridge edition of *The Plumed Serpent* (1987) edited by Clark, followed by Martz's edition of *Quetzalcoatl* (1995) and then, more recently, the Cambridge edition of *Quetzalcoatl* (2011) edited by Reeve. Outlining the relationship between these two versions, Clark suggests of MSI that

> It turned out to be not a text for revision but a first version eventually rejected in favour of a total rewriting. 'Quetzalcoatl' differs from *The Plumed Serpent* much as the three versions of *Lady Chatterley's Lover* differ. The *two works* represent *separate processes of creation*, even though one is preliminary to the other. Comparisons made here and in the Explanatory notes relate the two processes within the whole of Lawrence's American experience. (Lawrence, 1987, p. xxv; my italics)

While providing a working picture, this overview reflects the generalized tone of traditional studies of Lawrence's composition (as discussed in Chapter 1 of this book). Terms like 'text', 'revision', 'version', 'work' and 'process' are taken for granted, and the process of writing is not discussed in any great detail, while the argument supports the logic of publishing two completely separate editions. Martz and Reeve put forward very similar arguments in their respective introductions.

While Lawrence did of course produce two separate manuscript drafts, the idea that these stem from or represent 'separate processes of creation' is very misleading. As I will discuss in more detail further, MSII is a very closely rewritten version of MSI, and it is evident that Lawrence directly consulted the earlier manuscript while writing it. In addition, as with *Women in Love*, many passages and episodes in the novel are written and rewritten several times (rather than just twice); in the next chapter, for example, I distinguish *four* versions of the novel's final chapter. In the present chapter, I will pick out some specific examples of revision from Chapters One and Three, not only because they reflect Lawrence's heavier revision of the early chapters (with the exception of the final chapter) and provide a balance to the next chapter (which as mentioned focuses on the aforementioned last chapter) but also because they foreground the central role of the novel's protagonist, Kate, who largely focalizes the narrative but whose importance is often overlooked. While David Ellis has suggested that 'no work Lawrence ever wrote divides his admirers as sharply as *The Plumed Serpent*' (*Dying Game*, p. 219), many of its harsher critics focus almost exclusively on the credibility of the Quetzalcoatl movement and its leaders, Ramon and Cipriano. I argue that the latter represent a secondary narrative strand and one which is chiefly of interest in its relation to Kate's journey (the primary strand).[6]

Although, from the 1930s to 1960s, the likes of E. M. Forster, William York Tindall and L. D. Clark had each reckoned the novel to be one of Lawrence's finest, in his famous study *The Dark Night of the Body* (1964), Clark himself noted that '*The Plumed Serpent* is the most perplexing of D. H. Lawrence's novels', and that, 'in the forty years since its birth it has suffered the condemnation of many and enjoyed the adulation of a few' (p. v).[7] In the decades that followed Clark's major study, condemnation only intensified as critics subjected the novel (and Lawrence more generally, as discussed in this book's Introduction) to various forms of ideological criticism. Kate Millett in *Sexual Politics*, for example, suggested that, in *The Plumed Serpent*, Lawrence aimed at no less than 'inventing a religion, even a liturgy, of male supremacy' (p. 283).[8] More recent critics of this persuasion have provided more balanced accounts, with Brett Nielson suggesting that Lawrence 'fumbles for a formula that might dismantle the racial and sexual polarities of the colonial situation, and for this, his primitivism must be remembered' (1997, p. 322), while Jad Smith argues that, 'by forcing primitivism and *völkisch* organicism into a fretful dialogue, [Lawrence] brings problems associated with authoritarian leadership politics, particularly irrationalism and violence, to the foreground rather than quietly brushing them aside' (2002). However, as mentioned, I believe these readings are fundamentally mistaken in identifying the Quetzalcoatl cult as an authoritative component in the novel. Tony Pinkney makes a similar point in *D. H. Lawrence and Modernism*, suggesting that the 'thesis of "naïvety" applies more to characters within the novel than to the text itself, which is a formidably self-conscious work, preoccupied to the point of obsession with questions about the nature of reading, writing and meaning' (p. 148), though Pinkney does not point out the obvious distinction between (the primary character) Kate and the Quetzalcoatl cult, either.[9] Likewise, more positive accounts, by critics including Tindall and Clark, as well as, more recently, Virginia Hyde, have tended to focus on the novel's mythic symbolism.[10] I take a different approach to *The Plumed Serpent* by focusing on Kate and considering Mexico and the Quetzalcoatl movement chiefly in relation to Kate's journey, emphasizing the central themes of trauma, depression and memory, and placing these in a more personal context, which Lawrence's revisions and rewritings help demonstrate.[11]

Protocols and preparations

To some extent, Lawrence's composition of *The Plumed Serpent* consisted of one main phase of original writing, followed by four main phases of rewriting. As with the composition of the first draft of 'The Sisters' a decade earlier, Lawrence seems to have written the first draft in just a couple of months, without a concrete paper plan. The improvisational origin of *The Plumed Serpent* is typical for Lawrence: there is scant evidence of paper planning throughout his career.[12] However, as discussed in the previous chapters and as is evident again here, Lawrence usually produced a succession of drafts, for which the first draft provided a basis. While Lawrence may also have planned work mentally (albeit loosely), it is possible to see how (first) drafts functioned as a *kind* of plan for Lawrence, echoing Ferrer's suggestion that 'the draft is not a text, or a discourse, it is a protocol for making a text'.[13] Rather than devise 'separate processes of creation', then, these chapters examine the ways in which Lawrence made use of his own type of 'protocol for making a text'.

While this notion of a 'protocol' is useful in highlighting the provisional nature of Lawrence's draft, something which his editors tend to overlook, it is too instrumental for Lawrence and (as discussed in Chapter 1) provides an example of the tendency within genetic criticism to rely upon 'constructivist' metaphors for writing. These metaphors are germane for particular types of writer, especially those modernist giants who espoused Flaubertian tenets of technical craft, whereas, as I will discuss in this book's Conclusion, and like his British contemporary Virginia Woolf, Lawrence criticized instrumental interpretations of literature.[14] Constructivist and instrumentalist ideas about writing tend to focus too heavily upon premeditated features at the expense of more spontaneous features such as the rhythm of writing itself. The latter is something which I have touched on already with regards to the common shifts in Lawrence's writing between heavily revised dialogical scenes and unrevised descriptive scenes, and I discuss more detailed examples of this in the next chapter.

Before moving on to detail the phases of writing themselves, it is important to note that Lawrence did make indirect preparations in the form of an extensive reading list on ancient and modern Mexican history, as well as anthropological studies of Mexican mythology. Prior to this reading, as well as his journey into New Mexico in 1922 and Mexico the following year, Lawrence had expressed a desire to write an American novel as early as 1915, and had begun work on the groundbreaking *Studies in Classic American Literature* (1923) in 1916.[15] Clark and Reeve discuss these and other 'literary preparations' in more detail in their respective Cambridge introductions, which also provide lists of Lawrence's extensive reading.[16]

Writing and revision

The four main phases of *rewriting* consisted of the following: (1) the revision of MSI; (2) the rewriting of MSI as MSII; (3) the revision of MSII; and (4) the revision of TSII. While these phases complicate the traditional division of the novel into 'two versions', it is also important to recognize that original writing and rewriting often overlap. For example, as in the early notebook drafts of *Women in Love*, internal evidence indicates that at least some of the revision of MSI took place while the manuscript was being written, meaning Lawrence may have revised early chapters before writing later ones. As the complexity of Lawrence's writing processes have not been clearly communicated in the past, I have devised a few basic tables in the present chapters on *The Plumed Serpent*, beginning with the following, which provides an overview of the novel's overall composition and revision:

Table 3 Four rewriting phases for *The Plumed Serpent*

Rewriting phase		Version	Date
(0)	Composition of MSI	One	10 May - 27 June 1923
(1)	Revision of MSI		
(2)	Composition of MSII	Two	19 November 1924
(3)	Revision of MSII		January 1925
(4)	Revision of TSII		June - July 1925

(1) MSI

Chapter One: 'Now we're seeing the real thing.'

Lawrence heavily revised the first seven chapters of MSI (pp. 1–177; approximately the first 40 per cent), with the most extensive rewriting occurring in chapters three to seven, while the remaining chapters eight to nineteen (pp. 178–469) were only lightly revised.[17] Lawrence also inserted chapter titles in MSI and TSI exclusively for the first seven chapters, and this heavily revised early section equates to roughly the first thirteen chapters of *The Plumed Serpent* (Lawrence further divided and expanded the chapters in MSII and TSII to produce the novel's eventual total of twenty-seven chapters).

The revision of this segment is often extensive and includes the following sections, which are expanded and almost entirely rewritten: pages 73–6, which discuss Kate's cousin Owen and 'the vacuum of a modern individual'; pages 114–22, which discuss the local fear of bandit raids ('like curdled blood') and the servant family with whom Kate lives; pages 138–41, in which Ramon, the local historian and eventual cult leader, discusses the notion that 'each man has two spirits inside him', while Kate reflects on his body with a 'narcotic' attachment; pages 161–64, in which Ramon again discusses his beliefs regarding the soul; and pages 167–75, in which Ramon and Cipriano, Ramon's friend and follower, again discuss the soul and manhood, before Ramon 'converts' Cipriano into the living personification of the Mexican God Huitzilopochtli, following Cipriano's supplication.

As reflected by Lawrence's extensive revisions of the chapter in question (Chapter Seven is eventually entitled 'Conversion'), the aforementioned conversion scene between Ramon and Cipriano is awkward and fraught, and provides a culmination to the more intensely confrontational first half (approximately) of the novel. By contrast, the remaining chapters are only lightly revised, with no further rewritten scenes, and this comparative compositional ease likewise reflects the less intensely confrontational nature of the latter half of the novel (in general). We see here a correlation between process and product, as well as a type of genetic dialogism, with the shift from conflict to rest/resolution in both, at a general level.

While rhythmic counterpoint may be peaceable in itself, it is worth stressing that Lawrence's work is marked by *intensity*; thus, rhythmic transitions often reach extremes. *Women in Love* arranges itself into a series of increasingly conflicted viewpoints, whereby the characters seem on the brink of breaking apart, or of breaking each other apart. This is likewise a major feature in *The Plumed Serpent*, and is introduced immediately in the novel's opening chapter, where Kate attends a bullfight in Mexico City and arrives feeling 'uneasy, as if she were doing something ~~she ought not to do~~ **against her nature**' (MSI 2). Prior to witnessing the spectacle of the bullfight itself, this minor revision already alters Kate's foreboding from a more superficial, superego-type reprimand (she 'ought' not to) to something more fundamental ('**against her nature**'); perhaps the fact that Lawrence was himself revisiting the scene contributed to the increased sense of rupture between public spectacle and private sensibility, in revision.

However, once the spectacle begins, Kate's resulting shock is reminiscent of Ella's traumatic experience of school life in the 'Wedding Ring' fragment, where romantic expectations are crushed in a similarly cruel manner:

> Kate, watching, had never been so suddenly taken by surprise in her life. She had come with romantic notions of a gallant display. And before she knew where she was, she was watching a bull, with a red ~~wound~~ **place** on his shoulder, working his horns up and down in the belly of a prostrate and feebly plunging old horse.
>
> She looked aside, having almost lost control of herself. But the greatest ~~surprise~~ **shock** was surprise, ~~the am~~ amazement at the poor vulgarity of it. Then she smelt blood and the nauseous smell of bursten bowels. (MSI 10–11)

This scene takes the aforementioned theme of conflict to an immediate, visceral and transgressive point of extremity. Again, Lawrence's minor alterations are also significant. The second revision, from 'surprise' to 'shock', indicates a level of trauma: rather than something unexpected that she is nonetheless able to process in an ordinary manner, the obscene shock threatens her ordinary consciousness. The first revision also suggests this, though more subtly, as Kate's more specific and mundane vision of a 'red wound' on the bull's shoulder is replaced by a more abstract and ambiguous 'red place'.

Vision, as a theme in itself in this opening episode, highlights the paradoxical nature of obscenity and trauma by emphasizing Kate's inability to register what she is nonetheless able to *see*. While Kate notices that the horses are 'thickly blindfolded', it is repeatedly emphasized that Kate is able (and indeed feels compelled) to 'watch', 'look' and 'see' the events taking place. Nevertheless, as an attendant leads the wounded horse out of the arena, and Kate sees 'a great ball of its **own** entrails hanging reddish against the animal's legs', 'the shock of surprise almost made her lose her self-control'

(MSI 11). As in certain passages of *Women in Love* (narrating the relationship between Gudrun and Gerald), the episode explicitly suggests the existence of a transgressive, traumatic, Lacanian 'real': an obscene dimension which cannot register in ordinary symbolic or imaginative realms, and whose appearance therefore threatens to overturn ordinary consciousness. Kate looks at her companion, Owen, and finds him 'somewhat pale', 'half-scared' and 'somewhat disgusted', yet 'excited and pleased, as if to say: Now we're seeing the real thing' (MSI 11).

Lawrence's revisions in the first chapter of MSI tend to sharpen the nature of this conflict for Kate. As Kate looks away from Owen, the scene continues as follows:

> she felt ~~insulted, insulted~~ **she had had a sudden blow, an insult** to the last fibre ~~that~~ **in her, by** such a humiliating spectacle ~~should be offered her~~. Such a ~~degrading spectacle~~ **base, sordid show** ~~shameless spectacle!~~ All her womanhood and her breed rose ~~in revolt~~ **like a madness**. But the thing was going on, and she was powerless to stop it. And she was too startled to move. The thing had come on her too suddenly, too unexpectedly. (MSI 12)

The minor revisions again shift the register from a moralistic reprimand ('insulted, insulted') towards a more traumatic '**sudden blow**'. Similarly, rather than rise 'in revolt', Kate is less in control and feels resentment rise 'like a madness'; it is also interesting to note the familiar focus of Lawrence's minor revisions upon descriptors. While the passage itself suggests an element of class resentment in Kate's response to the 'sordid' popular show ('her breed rose'), the passage continues in the terms of trauma as Kate is rendered 'powerless to stop it' and 'too startled too move', for 'the thing', again an abstract and unspecified entity, had 'come on her too suddenly, too unexpectedly'.

Following this passage, a second horse is gored in front of the spectators, at which point Kate 'rose to her feet' (echoing Claudius in *Hamlet*) and departs, knowing 'if she saw any more she would go into hysterics. ~~Her control was~~ **She was getting beside herself**' (MSI 16), with Lawrence's revision again suggesting loss of agency and fragmentation of consciousness through shock. Unfortunately for Kate, who hadn't brought a coat, a sudden rainstorm prevents her from exiting the arena and she is forced to wait in the tunnel, where she 'could not get out of her eyes the last picture of the horse', and 'her face had the drawn, rather blank look of a woman who is on the verge of hysterics' (MSI 18). While the allusions to 'hysterics' suggest a possible feminine slant to Kate's response, it is worth noting Kate's own sense of male stupidity throughout the bullfight: 'she thought for the first time that a bull was a dull and stupid creature for all **in spite of** his excessive maleness and flourishing horns. He never distinguished his tormentors. He never knew what to single out among the movement' (MSI 12); her responses to Owen's willingness to be a spectator isn't dissimilar either. Kate is then forced to wait among the predominantly male crowd in the entrance to the arena until, Cipriano, a Mexican general who is stationed outside as part of a military guard, spots her and calls a taxi. 'Too much agitated' to go straight to her room, to recover Kate takes another taxi to 'Sanborn's, the tea-house, where she could have tea and feel at home without being alone' (MSI 17); as mentioned, this echoes Ella in the 'Wedding Ring' fragment, who likewise retreats to a tea shop in town after a violent confrontation with a pupil.

The opening shock of the bullfight provides a pattern for the early parts of the narrative (particularly in MSI), which are punctuated by intense conflicts. However, unlike the spectacle of the bullfight, which Kate is (eventually) able to escape by exiting the arena, the subsequent conflicts are dialogical, involving other people, who are able to question Kate. The first entirely rewritten section of MSI (pp. 73–6) comes in Chapter Three.

Chapter Three: '"What is it that oppresses, or depresses you?" asked the general.'

In MSI, Chapter Three begins with the quotation of 'a little paragraph' (MSI 50) about a man rising from the waters of Lake Chapala and declaring the return of the old Aztec god Quetzalcoatl, read by Kate in the English paper *Excelsior*; this reading inspires Kate and her companions, Owen and his friend (or partner) Villiers, who were 'straying rather aimlessly round' (MSI 52), to visit the lake.[18] Kate then recounts her flight from the bullfight with assistance from Cipriano Viedma and Owen discusses Cipriano's background: 'I hear he's quite the power behind the throne – or behind the Presidential Chair – in Mexico' (MSI 53–4). Their conversation is strung out across the day and later turns to Ramon, whom Owen describes in turn as 'the god in the Viedma machine' (MSI 60) and connects back to the man in the water at Lake Chapala, an event which is 'apparently being used by Don Ramon to influence the people to a sort of new religious revival' (MSI 60). As in *Women in Love*, then, readers gradually learn character backgrounds during the course of events in the narrative, with Owen sketching a background for Cipriano and Ramon in response to the newspaper report, even more so in the rewritten version of this chapter in MSII, which I discuss later in this chapter.[19] An account of Kate, Owen and Villiers's own journey to Mexico is related by the narrator or narrative itself, but, as I will continue to discuss, the latter is closely interwoven with Kate's viewpoint.

In contrast to the opening chapter, where the reader, like Kate, is exposed to the bullfight unprepared, the conversational prelude in the first half of Chapter Three in MSI introduces characters and provides the reader with a light counterpoint to the ensuing dialogical conflict, which follows once the group arrive at Cipriano's house in Goyoacan, for a dinner party which is also attended by Ramon.[20] Whereas Owen and Villiers place no great burden on Kate as a particular person, when, at the tea party, Kate asks Cipriano about Chapala, Cipriano responds in an intimate and searching manner by asking her why she thinks of going to Chapala and whether she thinks of returning to England to see her children; according to Kate, 'the general had full, dark Indian eyes' and 'as his eyes rested on Kate's face, she knew he wanted something of her' (MSI 65). Similarly, when Ramon asks if she wishes 'to stay a long time in Mexico' (MSI 66), Kate opens up on the topic of depression, which dogs her throughout the novel: 'I am half my time anxious to go away. I get moments of terrible depression – oppression it seems like – here. The country oppresses me sometimes – or something does – terribly' (MSI 66).

Cipriano then begins a string of persistent questions, first asking what it is that 'oppresses, or depresses' her, to which Kate concedes, 'It may be inside myself. But it seems to me something is trying to drag me down, down, down all the time', and Cipriano in turn questions, 'But mustn't one **why should one not come down to earth?**' (MSI 66) (perhaps echoing the theme of Milan Kundera's *The Unbearable Lightness of Being* (1984)). Kate again concedes, 'Yes. And I **I know.** I always wanted to', but adds that she does not wish to be '*dragged* down' (MSI 66). Cipriano continues to probe Kate, who, hailing from Anglo-Irish gentry and wearing a 'big emerald ring engraved with her family crest' (MSI 68), again hints at a residual element of class anxiety in her response to Mexico (albeit self-consciously): 'I don't know. The spirit of the place. Democracy. There seems to be such a heavy, heavy democracy here – like a snake pulling one down. And I don't want to stand up on any class distinction or anything false. But surely, in myself, I do stand a little higher than the mass of people. My husband made me believe I did' (MSI 66). Kate suggests that though she 'used to like them so much, to think they were right', 'I *don't* like workmen' and 'I don't believe in liberty [. . .] [or] socialism' because 'they want to pull one's *natural* soul down, and make it something mechanical and vulgar' (MSI 67). Despite this apparent confession, however, we learn that Kate's late husband is weighing heavily upon her conscience. She reveals he had been an Irish socialist republican, whose last words, having worked himself to death, were a Kurtz-like concession: 'perhaps I've been wrong [. . .] [and giving themselves to the working people had] been ~~an insult~~ **a wrong done** to the ~~very~~ best in us' (MSI 67). At this recollection, Kate's face pointedly becomes 'a mask of anguish' and 'bitter tears came down her cheeks' (MSI 67).

Echoing somewhat Birkin and Gerald's early conversations in TSI of *Women in Love*, Kate and Ramon then discuss the soul, with Ramon, in a similar though more authoritarian line of thought compared to Birkin, suggesting that 'there is no liberty, ~~except~~ **only** the will of ~~the living~~ **some** god. The will of ~~the living~~ **our own** gods is liberty to ~~men and women~~ **us, nothing else**' (though the revisions soften the passage) and that 'for men to have free will is the worst and cruelest of slavery' as 'they are slaves to every formula' (MSI 68b). As in the composition of *Women in Love*, where Birkin and Gerald's conversation is cut in TSII, these discussions are written out of *The Plumed Serpent* in MSII. Sticking with MSI for now, however, Ramon repeatedly questions Kate's suggestion that 'the mass of people' is the cause of her depression: 'do they also pull you down [. . .] Do they drag you down? [. . .] do they also pull you down?' (MSI 68–9). Kate initially reflects on her late husband and absent children, but, at the third attempt, having 'tried to collect herself sufficiently to answer' (MSI 69), she reflects at length on the Mexican labouring class, the peons: 'driving their strings of asses along the country roads, in the dust of Mexico's infinite dryness, past broken walls, broken houses, broken haciendas, along the endless desolation left by revolutions' (MSI 69) and, echoing Ella/Ursula's depth of feeling in all versions of *Women in Love*, she felt 'almost deeper than her consciousness, the bowels of her compassion stirred and bled' (MSI 71). Kate reflects on the apparent looks in their eyes: 'fear – and the companion of fear, mistrust – and inevitable ~~child~~ **result** of mistrust, a lurking insolence' (MSI 72). This leads Kate to reflect on the very possibility of 'belief between human beings' (MSI 72) in the modern, secular world; something which her husband's death led her to forsake but which her subsequent experience of life in America, where she suspects 'no one *does* trust anybody ~~else~~ **any more**: where no man or woman ever seems to have a final, ~~implicit~~ **resting** trust in ~~any other~~ **anything,** man or woman **or god**, but where everybody depends on the social code of behaviour, which everyone supports in order to make life possible at all', has led her to feel 'a craving for human trust, for belief' (MSI 72).[21]

In a rambling internal monologue written in free indirect speech, Kate then continues to ponder life in the United States, Mexico and Europe and the travails of belief and the soul. Following a trend in which Birkin's monologues are frequently cut or rewritten in *Women in Love*, this reflection, which runs from pages 73–8, is almost completely rewritten by Lawrence. While, as with *Women in Love*, the second version is more dramatized, beginning with questions, 'What was she doing herself? [. . .] Why? Why? What had she come for?' (MSI 73), in both versions she suggests that the Old World (Europe and the United States) has become a vacuum, drained of positive belief, whereas the new world is not yet completely 'cowed'.

While the reflections on Western and (the so-called) native peoples in this episode are clearly Kate's and are also dialogically framed, coming in response to a series of questions from Cipriano and Ramon and ending with Kate's belated answer: 'Yes [. . .] I feel that the peons do want to pull me down, too' (MSI 78–9), it is important to note that many of the novel's observations are more subtle extensions of Kate's thoughts, and I would also suggest that it is essential to note the (self-consciously) depressed nature of those thoughts. Kate and others discuss Mexico and the indigenous Mexican population, as well as 'the magnetic earth' and 'human blood' (MSI 79) in a somewhat oppressive manner. However, the sense of oppression is dramatized and resonates within the narrative itself, particularly via Kate, the central focalizer and a somewhat depressed person: recently bereaved, Kate has also left her children behind to travel largely alone in a far-flung country in turmoil (a fairly unprecedented journey for a lone woman in the 1920s), and she repeatedly feels herself being 'pulled' or 'dragged' down by something.

Though the episode is rewritten in MSII, as I discuss later in the chapter, it is worth visiting the earlier version in order to highlight the ways in which oppression is explicitly staged within the narrative. In the remainder of Chapter Three in MSI, Kate having likened the peons to 'the magnetic earth which everything must come ~~to rest in~~ **down to**', Owen suggests, 'maybe [. . . . . .] you are mistaken in ~~estimating~~ **considering** their level as lower than your own. It may only be different', and, 'maybe [. . .] the magnetic earth *is* the greatest reality: much greater than human loftiness' (MSI 79). Likewise, when Ramon contributes with a lengthy speech in which he suggests, 'we come back to earth to have roots in the earth. Life is still a tree, it is not a loose leaf in the air, or an aeroplane' (MSI 82), Owen is sceptical: 'what exactly *are* the roots?' (MSI 83). And when Ramon suggests, 'the roots are the human blood' and 'the human mind is only a flowering on the tree', Owen feels 'oppressed' and 'not convinced of anything. For him the blood was just a red fluid whose laws and properties ~~were absolutely~~ **are** known. This rather portentous ~~mysticism~~ **prognosticating**, as he ~~called~~ **felt** it, annoyed him. Yet he felt oppressed and annulled' (MSI 83). Similarly, when Cipriano chauvinistically questions whether it is 'necessary, pardon me, for a woman to know so much?' (MSI 80) and suggests Ramon can 'think it all for you – and even for me' (MSI 80), Kate replies: 'I shall *always* think my own thoughts [. . .] men can't think for women' (MSI 81).

While Chapter Four is comparatively lightly revised, the remaining chapters in the early parts of MSI (Chapters 5–7) are, as discussed, heavily revised, with a number of other sections completely rewritten (as outlined earlier). In Chapter Five, in which Kate moves into her new home at Lake Chapala/Sayula, these rewritten passages consist of Kate's lengthy reflections on the local people, while in Chapter Six, in which Cipriano and Ramon come to visit Kate, a long antagonistic dialogue between the group is entirely rewritten (pp. 138–41).[22] However, it is the last of the heavily rewritten chapters, Chapter Seven, 'Conversion', in which virtually every page is heavily revised and in which large sections are completely rewritten (pp. 155–6, 161–4 and 168–75).[23] Emphasizing the contrast in composition following this chapter, MSI then goes almost entirely unrevised for the next hundred pages, with the next noteworthy alteration coming on page 273. The remaining chapters (8–19) are only lightly revised, with no rewritten scenes, and what revision there is consists mainly of inserted details, often altering descriptions (as is customary of Lawrence in revision), particularly of the Quetzalcoatl dress, otherwise adding details to the social context (the revision on p. 273 is an example of this, as the passage in question is altered to provide a more detailed history of the local bandits).

(2) MSI to MSII: Focalization and expansion

The second phase of rewriting involved the greatest overhaul as Lawrence completely rewrote the original draft (MSI), producing a new pair of bound notebooks (MSII). While noting that Lawrence actually 'brought with him the manuscript and the typescript of "Quetzalcoatl"' on his second trip to Mexico, Clark suggests 'the extensive changes already contemplated could not be accomplished, he must have decided, without a total rewriting' and 'neither the typescript nor the manuscript of 'Quetzalcoatl' has any further place in the composition of the novel' (pp. xxxi–ii). However, as mentioned, MSII follows the narrative of MSI throughout, with numerous verbatim passages tagging the texts together at various points, and Clark's summary therefore distorts the actual process of writing. Consider the opening lines of MSI and MSII:

MSI 1

It was the Sunday after Easter, and the last ~~bullfight~~ **bullfight** of the season in Mexico City. ~~Two [?]~~ **Four special** bulls had been brought over from Spain for the occasion, since Spanish bulls are more fiery than Mexican.

MSII 1

It was the Sunday after Easter, and the last bullfight of the season in Mexico City. Four special bulls had been brought over from Spain for the occasion. ~~S,~~ **since** Spanish bulls are more fiery than Mexican.

Given these connections, it is clear that Lawrence wrote MSII with MSI beside him, and the former is essentially an extended rewrite of the latter.

Before considering the ways in which Lawrence reshaped Chapter Three as a more detailed example, I will highlight three patterns during this stage of rewriting:

(1) Lawrence separated out event strands in MSII, which is reflected in the greater number of chapter divisions (the earliest example being Chapters 4–5 in MSI, which are broken up into Chapters 4–7 in MSII), as well as the insertion of all remaining chapter titles, including newly inserted chapters.

(2) He also expanded the length of the novel, which, partly as a result, becomes denser and more tired in tone; as David Ellis points out, the increased length is partly 'accounted for by Lawrence's absorption as he re-wrote, in the costume, ritualistic gesture, dance and, above all, the hymns of his imagined Quetzalcoatl cult' (1998, p. 217).

(3) Connected to the change of tone mentioned in the second point, MSII is focalized more directly through Kate, with more events placed in direct opposition to her sensibility and some sections of the narrative more explicitly framed in relation to Kate's journey (as we will see when considering Chapter 3).

Kate's own depression manifests itself in her observations of the country: 'the country oppresses me sometimes – or something does – terribly' (MSI 66), a remark which is echoed at various points in the novel, as in her conversation with Cipriano at the start of Chapter 7: 'I don't like Mexico because it feels like a black bog where one has no foothold' (MSI 157). One of the biggest markers of this comes in the rewriting of Chapter 3, beginning with the chapter title itself. In MSI, Kate is reported to be thirty-eight years of age in an off-hand manner, while Lawrence inserted the chapter title 'Dinner With the General' in TSI. In MSII, however, Kate's age is revised to forty and the significance of this personal marker is indicated by the chapter title, which is also revised, to: 'Fortieth Birthday'.[24] Within the narrative itself, rather than begin with the local newspaper report, as in MSI, Chapter 3 in MSII begins with a new, introspective passage:

> Kate woke up one morning, aged forty. She did not hide the fact from herself, but she kept it dark from the others.
> It was a blow, really. To be forty! One had to cross a dividing line. On this side was youth and spontaneity and 'happiness'. On the other side was something different: reserve, responsibility, a certain standing back from 'fun'.
> She was a widow, and a lonely woman now. (MSII 74)

While the quotation from the newspaper in MSI is read by Kate, like the revised chapter title in MSII, this new opening to the chapter places more significance on Kate's inner life. As a result, it is easier to see how Kate focalizes the novel, with her oppressed viewpoint affecting the depiction of place in the narrative. Following the aforementioned extract, Kate goes to the rooftop of her hotel and the mountainous landscape is described as follows:

> Alien, ponderous, the white-hung monsters seemed to emit a deep purring sound, too deep for the ear to hear, and yet audible on the blood, a sound of dread. There was no soaring or uplift or exaltation, as there is in the snowy mountains of Europe. Rather a ponderous white-shouldered weight, pressing terribly on the earth, and murmuring like two watchful lions.
> Superficially, Mexico might be all right . . . Until you were alone with it . . . There was a ponderous, down pressing weight upon the spirit: the great folds of the dragon of the Aztecs . . . (MSII 75)

The spirit of place as a 'weight, pressing terribly' downwards is a manifestation of Kate's inner life. Kate's perception of the landscape echoes the origin of the god Quetzalcoatl, who ascends the volcano as a bird, and helps us connect the symbol to Kate herself. This blurring of narrative viewpoint with Kate's psyche is made evident by the subsequent, explicit and bleak shift back to Kate:

> But still this heavy continent of dark-souled death was more than she could bear.
> She was forty: the first half of her life was over. The bright page, with its flowers and its love and its Stations of the Cross ended with a grave. Now she must turn over, and the page was black, black and empty. (MSII 77)

Reading lines like this (and others quoted earlier), it is difficult to understand why critics have not made more of this central theme of depression before, focusing too much on a literal interpretation of Quetzalcoatl, and perhaps on Lawrence as a writer of *positive* emotions.

While I discuss some of the other major alterations to Chapter Three in MSII below, it is important to note that Lawrence also isolates Kate in MSII by curtailing the stay of her companions, Owen and Villiers. Whereas in MSI, which has significantly less chapters, the pair had continued to feature as late as Chapter Eight, almost halfway through the draft, in MSII they last feature in Chapter Four, only around a fifth of the way through the draft. Before they depart, Kate is also made to feel more antagonistic towards the pair in MSII. Compare the following passages in Chapter Two, after Villiers returns to the hotel and Kate has scolded him for his excitement at the bullfight:

MSI 26	**MSII 36**
'Well, I don't know-w', he said with an American drawl, as he disappeared.	Villiers disappeared with a wicked little laugh.
Kate felt rather angry with them both. But poor O. was really so remorseful, and rather bewildered by his confusion of emotions, that she had to relent towards him. He was really awfully kind.	And as she sat her hands trembled with outrage and passion. A-moral! How *could* one be a-moral, or non-moral, when one's soul was revolted! How could one be like these Americans, picking over the garbage of sensations, and gobbling it up like carrion birds. At that moment, both Owen and Villiers seemed to her like carrion birds, repulsive.

Whereas Kate relents in MSI and concedes that Owen is 'remorseful' and 'really awfully kind', in MSII she is unrelenting, casting Villiers as 'wicked', the pair as 'a-moral, or non-moral' and likening them both to 'carrion birds, repulsive'.

(3) MSII: Light revision

MSII is only lightly revised, which is unsurprising given that it is itself a major rewriting of MSI. What minor revisions there are tend to focus (again) on adjectives and descriptors, particularly to clothing. Lawrence also lightly revised many of the Quetzalcoatl hymns, which emerge in the second half of the novel; these alterations, though minor, often produce a more impersonal tone to the hymns and will be of interest for readers and students of Lawrence's verse.

(4) TSII: Overview and recap

Although TSII is heavily revised in places, these are mostly restricted to the opening segment of the novel (as in MSI), in this case Chapters One to Six (approximately the first fifth of the novel). The major exception to this rule however is the final chapter, which Lawrence completely reworked and which forms the focus of the next chapter of this book. I will round off the present overview by briefly surveying Lawrence's revisions to the opening segment of TSII. There are two rewritten passages, from pages 76–7 and 86–7, the latter of which involves the insertion of a new handwritten sheet, while a lengthy section from pages 90–4 is cut completely. Each of these sections comes in what was originally Chapter Three in MSI, though, as Lawrence inserted a new chapter division in MSII, the latter two passages occur in what ultimately becomes Chapter Four.

Prior to these sections, Lawrence had already made several important alterations to Chapter Three in MSII: before reading the newspaper report of the man in the lake and attending Cipriano and Ramon's dinner party, Lawrence inserted a new section in which Kate goes to see frescoes in Mexico City and then has tea with her guide, the young professor Garcia. The subsequent dinner party is also relocated to Ramon's suburban house in Tlalpam (he and his wife also own a hacienda at Lake Sayula) and three new guests are included: Garcia, 'another pale young man' called Mirabel, and 'an elderly man in a black cravat' called Toussaint, who is also described (accurately as it transpires) as a 'didactic crank'.[25] The additional guests mean that the subsequent dialogue is spread across more speakers in MSII and TSII, while the tail end of a bizarre speech by Toussaint on the importance of 'the moment of coition' for the spirit of a people (pp. 76–7) is cut in TSII and replaced with a more condensed exchange.

Owen's anticipatory character précis of Cipriano and Ramon is also removed from MSII, while, at the dinner party itself, Kate no longer reflects on her husband's last words during the discussion at dinner. Instead, following

Toussaint's speech, Kate goes to smoke outside with Cipriano and it is during their more private conversation that Kate tells Cipriano of her husband's death and last words, in MSII. Cipriano also relates the story of his own upbringing in his own words during the exchange, while the events are also made less fantastical.[26] Following a new chapter break in MSII, Lawrence then reinserts and reframes as a recollected dialogue the intense exchange between Ramon and Kate, during which Ramon repeatedly questions whether it is the peons who drag her down.[27] This exchange contains the heavily revised passage from pages 86-7, in which Lawrence inserted a new sheet of manuscript in TSII. Kate's subsequent reflections on Mexico, the United States and Europe, which were expanded and comprise the newly framed Chapter Four in MSII, then contain a long section which Lawrence cut completely while revising TSII (pp. 90-4).

Coda

This chapter provided an overview of Lawrence's complex composition and revision of *The Plumed Serpent*, excluding the extensively rewritten final chapter, which I discuss in the next chapter. I have picked out examples from the early chapters to help describe the way in which Kate focalizes the novel, with descriptions of both people and place often a veiled manifestation of her own inner life, and the subsequent reason why depression is a major theme. I have indicated a number of avenues which could be pursued in greater detail, such as the fraught and heavily rewritten 'conversion' scene between Ramon and Cipriano, in what eventually becomes Chapter Seven, and which represents a tipping point in the novel's compositional economy. In the next chapter, besides concluding the present survey by providing the most detailed examples of rewriting (including revision in TSII), I will consider the dilemma of writing an ending for Lawrence, concluding the foregoing discussion of Kate's journey by considering its end.

Notes

1 For a full account of Lawrence's typically frenetic activity during this break in composition from July 1923 to November 1924, see Ellis, 1998, pp. 118-212; for a list of works completed during this time, see pp. 547-51 and p. 568.
2 For a list of these revisions, see the textual apparatus in Q, pp. 363-406.

3 Seltzer went bankrupt later the same year, hence the eventual American publication of *The Plumed Serpent* (1926) by Alfred Knopf.
4 Chapters I–V of TSII are paginated continuously, while Chapters VI–XXVII each begin a new pagination.
5 For an account of this second break, see Ellis, *Dying Game*, pp. 234–52.
6 Charles Burack (2005) has provided a survey of criticism on the novel, suggesting that 'the current critical response to the novel is still quite divided' (p. 180).
7 See Forster (2008) and Tindall (1952).
8 More recently, Marianna Torgovnick has suggested that we should 'modify the anger in Millett's critique to a new understanding of, and even sympathy with Lawrence' (1990, p. 167).
9 Joyce Wexler has also suggested '*The Plumed Serpent* anticipates postmodernism's extremity by representing sensational scenes of violence and erotic domination' (1997–8, p. 47).
10 See Hyde, 1992, pp. 173–206; Hyde's chapter on the novel also compares *Quetzalcoatl* and *The Plumed Serpent*, considering some of the differences between 'early' and 'late' published versions of the novel.
11 David Ellis has similarly suggested that 'Kate's struggle to decide what she feels about the Quetzalcoatl cult and its organisers' is 'the psychological drama which is, or perhaps more accurately, should be, at the centre of *The Plumed Serpent*' (*Dying Game*, p. 216), but the large qualification here is telling.
12 The main exceptions are a skeleton plan for the closing chapters of Lawrence's first novel, *The White Peacock*, and a loose chapter outline of his third, 'Paul Morel' (or *Sons and Lovers*). Both of these are very short, written on a couple of notebook sheets in one of Lawrence's early Nottingham University College notebooks (1910); the 'outline' of 'Paul Morel' occupies a single page and is a kind of memo, providing only a dozen or so words (often less) for fifteen chapters (see *Paul Morel*, 2003, Volume Two, pp. xxv–ix and Appendix II). One later example, which suggests that Lawrence may have continued to produce such miniature paper plans, is contained in a notebook dated 26 August 1924 (thus produced during the break between the two main periods of work on *The Plumed Serpent*), in which, besides miscellaneous short writings, Lawrence wrote some 'Suggestions for Stories'. These 'suggestions' run to just over a page in length and consist of four single-paragraph outlines for stories entitled 'The Weather-Vane/The Flying Fish', 'The Wedding Ring', 'The Dog' and 'The Woman out of the Water'. Although Lawrence added the proviso 'never carried out!' in pencil, he did in fact begin a work entitled 'The Flying Fish', which is based on the aforementioned outline, in March 1925, and completed forty manuscript pages; the first nine of which were, unusually, dictated by Lawrence and written by his wife, Frieda (see *St Mawr and Other Stories*, 1983, pp. xxiv–xxxvi and Appendix I).

13 Ferrer, 1998, p. 261. Lawrence's own descriptions of MSI, in June 1923, likewise emphasize the provisionality of the first draft: 'Hope to have finished it, in rough, before I leave here' (iv. 454). 'It only depends now, on my finishing the first draft of this novel here' (iv. 455). 'Hope to finish the first rough draft by the end of this month' (iv. 457).
14 See Lawrence, 'German Books' and Woolf, 'Craftsmanship' (1942, pp. 126–31). Intriguingly, in her posthumously published 'Notes on D. H. Lawrence', Woolf suggests, 'Comparing him again with Proust [. . .] one feels that not a single word has been chosen for its beauty, or for its effect upon the architecture of the sentence' (1941, p. 98).
15 According to Sandra M. Gilbert, 'as several recent scholars have observed, not only was Lawrence perhaps *the* most influential "founding fathe[r] of modern American literary theory," he also defined what is still the central canon of American literature and pioneered many of the key approaches to this canon' (2007, p. 5).
16 See Clark, 'Introduction', *PS*, p. xxv, and Reeve, 'Introduction', *Q*, pp. xxiii–vii.
17 N. B. Lawrence's pagination of the manuscripts is often erroneous.
18 Lawrence originally used real names for both Lake Chapala and the family residing in Kate's house, which Lawrence adopted from the family staying at his own house at Lake Chapala, on Calle Zaragoza; there is a note inside the cover of MSI for Seltzer when typing to 'change the word Chapala to Sayula', as well as each of the family names.
19 Echoing somewhat the dialogue between Ursula and Gudrun in *Women in Love*, the characters actually debate the pros and cons of knowing character backgrounds in advance within the narrative itself: Kate tells Owen, 'if I've got to know him, I'd rather not start by knowing things about him', while Owen replies, 'Well there I differ from you. It seems to me I get a much fuller picture of the man when I know these important facts' (MSI 62).
20 This type of structure – chatter as a contrapuntal prelude to a more intimate and intense type of dialogue – is echoed in Lawrence's subsequent novel *Lady Chatterley's Lover*, as discussed by Michael Bell in *D. H. Lawrence: Language and Being*, pp. 208–25 (Chapter 7, "'Love' and 'chatter' in *Lady Chatterley's Lover*). For an example of the tone of conversation, Owen concludes his précis of Cipriano by quipping about his having handed his cloak to Kate as follows: 'Anyhow it's awfully interesting that he engineered Mrs Norris into that tea-party. Ha-ha! – The Knights of the Cloak. A second Walter Raleigh. – Better! Walter Raleigh didn't have an automobile at hand for the Lady – who was it – yes, Queen Elizabeth. Ha-ha-ha!' (MSI 54).
21 The original version of this passage is transcribed in Appendix I of Q.
22 The earlier version of this section is transcribed in Appendix II in Q.
23 The earlier versions of these passages make up the remaining appendices, III and IV, in Q.

24 Lawrence's own age trailed just behind Kate's: he was thirty-seven while writing MSI and celebrated his own fortieth birthday a few months after completing the revision of TSII.

25 Ramón's aunt Doña Isabel is also present, but does not participate in the conversations.

26 Whereas, in MSI, Cipriano had been a peon's son and had been sent to Oxford by an Englishwoman with a coffee plantation near Jalapa, after saving her life following a poisonous snakebite, in MSII, his benefactor becomes Bishop Severn of Oaxaca. Lawrence also changed Kate's late husband's name from Desmond to James Joachim Leslie; she was also given a previous husband, a lawyer, whom she divorced to marry Leslie.

27 In MSII, Kate's reflections on the Mexican peons are also reframed by the question of whether or not to return with Owen to the United States, rather than by Ramón's persistent and explicit questioning, as in MSI.

8

Writing an ending

The dilemma of writing an ending

The apparent ease with which Lawrence could begin a work of fiction is evidenced by the number of drafts produced, with minimal planning, during the compositional histories of *Women in Love* and *The Plumed Serpent*. By contrast, the many rewritten endings to 'Odour of Chrysanthemums' and *Women in Love*, and the frequency of heavy revision at the ending to individual chapters in the two novels, suggest that writing an ending was a much tougher task. The most detailed case study comes in the present chapter, which looks at the final chapter of *The Plumed Serpent*, the most heavily rewritten section of the novel. Having already produced three substantive versions across MSI, MSII and TSII, Lawrence revised the final chapter once again at a late stage (most likely while checking the proofs), producing a fourth and final version for publication (these late changes included rewriting the final line itself and inserting a chapter title).

Narrative beginnings generally involve opening up possibilities and throwing out narrative strands in many directions, whereas endings involve closing down possibilities and tying the different narrative strands together (or cutting off loose ends). While writer's block involves a failure to begin writing, where the writer may be said to suffer precisely from the weight of narrative potential and fail to make a choice, given the antagonism between flux and stasis which I see as central to Lawrence's writing, where flux falls on the side of universal creation and stasis on the side of egotistical imaginings, it makes sense that Lawrence might 'suffer' from the opposite problem: a failure to *stop* writing ('flow' or even hypergraphia). Beginnings are where flux is most keenly felt, where all possibilities are open and everything is undecided and ongoing, whereas endings are where flux runs into stasis, where process is resolved into product, and things no longer go on.

In a practical sense, Lawrence's method of writing drafts without a concrete plan meant the author was unusually open-minded about 'where' a narrative would end. Describing a new draft of *Women in Love* in May 1916, for example, Lawrence reported: 'I have begun a new novel: a thing that is a stranger to me even as I write it. I don't know what the end will be' (ii. 604). However, this suggestion can be tempered by Lawrence's equal commitment to 'always write my books twice'. Of *Women in Love*, for example, we know that Lawrence's 'new novel' was in fact a rewritten version of a thoroughly sketched draft dating back to 1913 and 1914; the 'Sisters I' fragment already contains a draft of the (at least partly) climactic conflict between Gudrun, Gerald and Loerke.

Of greater significance, I would argue, is the problematic nature of an 'ending' in itself. In the two published versions of Lawrence's Mexican novel, *Quetzalcoatl* and *The Plumed Serpent*, Cipriano alludes to this problem when discussing Navajo women, who, when weaving a patterned blanket, always leave 'some loose threads' at the end, so that their work is never completely 'finished off' and thus their 'souls' may escape (*Q* 156). It is easy to spot the interest of such a custom for Lawrence. When, in *Quetzalcoatl*, Cipriano contrasts the Navajo practice with his experience of England, his description of the latter echoes many of Lawrence's own observations in his late articles:

> All, all the intricate ways of life, so many, like the pavements of a city. Even your country, very beautiful, your woods and your fields and hills, but like a beautiful park around a city. All made. All made and finished. [...] So all the soul is in the goods, in the books, and in the roads and ways of life, and the people are finished like finished serapes, that have no faults and nothing beyond. [...] Their pattern is finished and they are complete. (*Q* 156–7)[1]

Lawrence here presents a vital problem that most readers would recognize: if everything we make is finished, don't we ourselves feel shut-off, 'finished'? And isn't this something we ultimately wish to avoid (by always starting a new project, making a new thing or leaving something incomplete)? Is this part of the reason why desire (or Schopenhauer's universal 'Will') is always fleeting, never ultimately satisfied? However, in classic Lawrentian style, Cipriano's use of the term 'soul' is almost calculated to disturb modern, secular readers. The term is effectively used as a vanishing mediator in the above-mentioned description, as much a reflection *of* as it is reflected *in* the products and processes of labour. If this seems to over-reach the text, Cipriano explicitly suggests that the soul is formed in this way in the rewritten version of the dialogue in *The Plumed Serpent*: 'The soul is also a thing you make, like a pattern in a blanket' (*PS* 234). That said, the term 'soul' undoubtedly has a different bearing to the more modern term 'self' and is not therefore exchangeable. While the term 'self' is favoured by modern Western readers, representing an anti-essentialist equivalent, ridding an individualistic concept of its historical spiritual baggage, the term 'soul' not only implies a more fundamental and impersonal (i.e. cosmological) principle of animation (particularly in a pre-Christian, pagan context, as in ancient Mexico) but also implies a weight of judgement and hence of responsibility (particularly in a Catholic context, as in modern Mexico). It is unsurprising, therefore, that Cipriano uses the term 'soul' while scolding modern European culture: if the products of labour are 'finished' and ready-made, the people too become trapped in fixed 'habits and conventions and ways of life', and hence 'are like excellent fabrics [. . .] all made and finished off' (Q 156).² The responsibility of the 'soul' is therefore to avoid being 'finished'. The paradoxical challenge for Lawrence, then, was how to end his novel without rendering it 'finished' and 'complete' (Q 157). His was a quest for the imperfect ending.

'Here!': Four versions

Aside from being the most heavily rewritten section of the book, the composition of the final chapter of *The Plumed Serpent* is also more generally representative of Lawrence's fiction writing both in terms of his predilection for rewriting endings, as well as the role of counterpoint and structural rhythm. As mentioned, it is possible to describe four different versions of the chapter:

Table 4 Four different versions of the final chapter of *The Plumed Serpent*

Version:	Documentation:
1	MSI, Chapter XIX, pp. 303–8 (6pp. = around 2,500 words)
2	MSII, Chapter XXVII, pp. 775–96 (22pp. = around 4,500 words)
3	TSII, Chapter XXVII, pp. 1–34 (34pp. = around 7,500 words)
4	*PS*, Chapter XXVII, 'Here!', pp. 426–44 (19pp. = around 6,500 words)

Like the first draft of the novel as a whole, **version one** serves as a kind of 'protocol' for the subsequent completion of the text in versions two to four, and the majority of its six manuscript pages are transferred into the subsequent versions. In it, Kate returns home along Lake Sayula, having visited Ramon's hacienda in the preceding chapters, and then begins to pack her bags, having made up her mind to leave Mexico. In **version two**, besides altering the beginning, three new scenes are inserted, which roughly double the chapter in length and completely alter the ending: the third newly inserted scene provides the basis for the chapter's new ending in versions two to four. In **version three**, large sections of the inserted scenes are entirely rewritten, while in **version four** smaller sections within the same scenes are rewritten once again.[3] While this level of revision may, once again, suggest a constructivist style of writing, it is important to note that despite multiple rewritings only a minute amount of revision is actually carried out *within* specific versions. The rewriting is therefore at a more macro-level, with 'revision' taking place between the different, segmented versions; the resulting passages are themselves in a sense 'unrevised'. Lawrence rewrites these larger chunks in a dialogical manner as discussed in the chapters on *Women in Love*. Before diving into Lawrence's insertions and rewritings in versions two to four, we'll need to survey the ground laid out beforehand in the much shorter version one.

Version one: Life by the lake

Version one opens with two long paragraphs. The first of these, after informing us that 'Kate went home that day' as 'she didn't want to stay longer' at Teresa and Ramon's hacienda, Las Yemas, goes on to reveal Kate's apparently final thoughts on the couple, both of whom 'she almost hated', Ramon in particular for his 'abstraction', his 'excessive maleness' (echoing her feelings towards the bulls in Chapter One), his influence over Cipriano and his apparent jealousy of her and Cipriano's relationship (Q 303). Although the second paragraph begins the chapter's subsequent extended and positive depiction of life by the lake at Sayula, with Kate 'forced to admit the lake had a real beauty' (MSI 462) as she makes her way home alongside it, Kate is clearly preparing to leave Mexico and the chapter ends underwhelmingly, with Kate packing her bags while the servants look on. The final line reads as follows: 'Under these trying circumstances Kate tried to get on with her packing' (MSI 469 (see Figure 12)).

While the opening and closing segments described earlier are each removed in subsequent versions of the final chapter, the rest of the first version survives and goes virtually unrevised. Beginning at the tail end of the second paragraph, this long unrevised section of text contains a sequence of descriptive scenes. Following immediately after the more fraught dialogical chapter preceding it – during which Kate clashes with Ramon and Teresa (finding their intimacy overbearing), participates in a second and similarly strained conversion scene with Ramon and Cipriano (the first is alluded to in the previous chapter and again later in this chapter), has an ambiguous final conversation with Cipriano and is then confronted by a wild snake – the final chapter provides a soothing counterpoint for both protagonist and reader. Kate's journey along the lake is essentially therapeutic, as hinted in the text:

> There was something soothing and, curiously enough, paradisal about it, even the pale, dove-brown water. (MSI 462)

I would also suggest that this 'something soothing' extends to Lawrence's overall writing process, provoked by and contributing towards the rhythmic structure of the text. Contrapuntal movement between dialogue and description (the social and the natural; interiority and exteriority; conflict and rest) provides an intuitive formal structure to much of Lawrence's fiction and seems to have underpinned his relatively spontaneous composition of drafts. The general compositional economy of MSI reflects this, as the first two-fifths or so is increasingly heavily revised, culminating in the highly fraught conversion scene between Ramon and Cipriano, after which both the narrative and the writing process become less intensely confrontational, as indicated by the much lighter level of revision, culminating in the final, therapeutic chapter (which is virtually unrevised in MSI itself).

These descriptive sequences contain seven, gemlike, therapeutic miniature episodes where fluid water and soft, dove-like colours feature prominently, beginning with the following depiction of a passing boat at the end of the second paragraph **(1)**:

> A boat was coming over with its sail hollowing out like a shell, pearly white, and its sharp black canoe-beak slipping past the water. It looked like the boat of Dionysos crossing the seas and bringing the sprouting of the vine. (MSI 462–3)

In the second, Kate watches on as a group of men load a cow and a bull onto a boat **(2)**:

> she saw such an amusing group perched in silhouette on the low breakwater wall – not much more than a foot high – against the dove-pale background of the lake. It was a black boat with her tall mast and red-painted roof, pulled stern-up almost to the wall [. . .] on the wall, four-square in silhouette against the lake, a black-and-white cow, with a man in dove-brown tights and dove-brown little jacket, and huge, silver-embroidered hat, standing at her head [. . .].
>
> Behind the block of a cow, three white peons, and two on the ground, looking up at a huge black-and-white bull, a colossus of a bull standing perched motionless on the wall, broadside, a passive monster spangled with black, low-aloft. Just behind him, one white peon with a red sash determinedly tied. (MSI 463)

In a perfect therapeutic progression, this reappearance of a bull in the final chapter recalls the traumatic violence of the bullfight in opening chapter. Here, the formerly transgressive, unhinged violence of the four bulls is converted into a single 'colossus of a bull standing perched motionless on the wall', placated and at ease, and, as Kate watches on, the peons load this 'passive monster' into the hull of their boat, alongside the cow, and then sail away, 'getting small on the surface of the water' (MSI 466).[4] The language within this passage is also immanently peaceful and carries a number of internal repetitions (dove, black, white, black and white) and paratactic clauses, which, rather than piling up in a Joycean manner, follow each other like waves breaking on and rolling through the commas. Unlike the many conflict-orientated dialogical scenes within the novel, in which individual passages and speeches respond to and probe each other, these descriptive scenes are virtually self-sufficient.

While the previous scene is reasonably long and charged with symbolic significance, the remaining scenes are more miniature and are almost entirely contingent. Self-sufficiency becomes a theme in itself in the third, as Kate observes a man at work **(3)**:

> A man was stripping ~~reeds~~ **palm-stalks**, squatting in silence in his white cotton pants, under a tree, his black head bent forward. (MSI 466)

This passage again displays Lawrence's wavelike parataxis, while there are no significant external references (as to 'Dionysos' in the first or the bullfight in the second).[5] In the next passage, the above-mentioned scene is interrupted by a passing horse **(4)**:

> A roan horse, speckled with white, was racing prancing along the shore, and neighing frantically. (MSI 466)

Alongside paratactic flow, another feature of Lawrence's descriptive poetic which this passage highlights is the frequent use of present participles and gerunds ('racing prancing along the shore, and neighing frantically'). These features create a sense of flow, and, aside from the staid vision of the bull in the second, each of the previous passages contains multiple examples of this (hollowing, slipping, bringing, sprouting, stripping, squatting). In the next passage, Kate spots the source of commotion which seems to have startled the 'roan horse' **(5)**:

> A peon had driven a high-wheeled wagon drawn by four mules, into the lake. It was deep in the lake above the axle, ~~deep~~ up to the bed of the cart, so that it looked like a ~~queer~~ **dark** square boat drawn by four soft, ~~slow~~ **dark** sea-horses ... (MSI 466)

Like the second passage with the bull, here the action is more static as the wagon has wheeled into the lake. The lack of present participles or gerunds reflects this, though there is again the use of parataxis and intricate repetition (Lawrence's minor revisions, which again focus on adjectives, remove an initial repetition ('~~deep~~') but insert a very similar one shortly afterwards ('**dark**')). It is also worth noting that this passage floats dreamlike between pure contingency and pure symbolism: on one level, a peon has accidentally driven his wagon into the lake, but, given that Kate first learns of the Quetzalcoatl movement after reading a newspaper report about the prophet or proponent of the god itself who rose from these waters, the lake may also represent the old Mexican gods and the wagon a mythical boat crossing its waters; the number of mules (or '**dark** sea-horses') also holds a strange symbolism (there were four large imported bulls at the bullfight).

There are two more miniature scenes before Kate arrives home, and these are purely positive, regenerative. First, she spots some young calves, as well as a donkey and her infant **(6)**:

> New white-and-yellow calves, white and silky, were skipping, butting up their rear ends, lifting their tails, and trotting side by side to the water to drink. A mother-ass was tethered to a tree, and in the shadow lay her foal, a little thing as black as ink. (MSI 466)

The passage repeats the stylistic features already highlighted, flowing and yet almost piling up with present participles, which produce a playful rhythm, while the (again) self-sufficient activities depicted are an ultimate form of therapy: watching baby animals play. After a brief interval of dialogue, in which Kate participates in the action for the first time, by asking a peon how many days old the foal is, Kate then watches the infant **(7)**:

> It rocked on its four loose legs, and helplessly wondered. Then it hobbled a few steps forward, to smell some growing green maize. It smelled and smelled and smelled, as if all the t[?] aeons of green juice of memory were striving to awake. Then it turned round, looked straight towards Kate with its bushy-velvet face, and put out a pink tongue at her. (MSI 467)

While, coming in the novel's final chapter, as Kate's current journey ends, the foal may be taken to represent new beginnings and perhaps her own new, nascent self, the 'aeons of green juice of memory' that the foal can almost *smell* 'striving to awake' is a fantastic example of Lawrence's non-brain-centric perception of the universe. The foal's movements are also rhythmic (move-pause-move-pause) and the passage demonstrates Lawrence's peculiarly repetitive use of language as well; the foal 'smelled and smelled and smelled' is virtually transgressive in terms of conventional literary grammar and style but might also be compared to a nursery rhyme.

In his otherwise negative appraisal of *The Plumed Serpent*, Michael Bell singles out the second miniature scene in the foregoing sequence (the vision of the cow and the bull) for singular praise in *D. H. Lawrence: Language and Being*.[6] Bell suggests that the passage forms one of only a handful in the novel where Lawrence's writing becomes unselfconscious, and it is precisely this type of writing which Bell suggests is Lawrence's greatest achievement: where language enacts its own ontology and reveals something fundamental about the relationship between language and being. The fact that Lawrence retained *all* of these miniature episodes (as well as the surrounding text which stitches them together), despite subsequent heavy rewritings, suggests that the author was himself content and felt perhaps he had got something 'right', unlike the subsequently inserted dialogical scenes, which were interpolated in MSII, rewritten in TSII and revised again in the proofs. However, Lawrence's general pattern of heavily revising or rewriting dialogue and leaving descriptive sections intact suggests there are deeper reasons for the particular compositional economy of the chapter. Furthermore, beyond getting something 'right' in a particular passage or text, I believe Lawrence's struggle with the finished and the formulaic is interesting and worthy of study in itself. It makes his work innately challenging as particular styles, viewpoints and ontologies are met with opposition and otherness. By analysing the rewritten sections of this chapter next, then, we can consider the ways in which Lawrence pushed beyond the spontaneous and self-sufficient nature of life by the lake as depicted in the chapter's core scenes outlined above.

Version two: 'Tell them it is all a joke, and their symbols are pretty play-things, and they are all great-god Peter-Pans.'

In short, by rewriting the ending, Lawrence opened up Kate's ultimately evasive final thoughts in version one, which had paved the way for her departure to Europe by laying aside the various questions opened up by the novel. These questions concern not only the Quetzalcoatl movement but also, and more integrally, Kate's depression and her attempts to reconcile past, present and future selves.

In version two, the original six-page chapter is expanded to twenty-two pages as Lawrence inserted three new scenes as follows:

Table 5 Three scenes added to the final chapter of *The Plumed Serpent*

New scenes:	Pages (MSII):	Events:
1	776–82[3](8pp.)	Ramon and Teresa arrive; Kate discusses her forthcoming departure with Ramon
2	786[7]–8[9](3pp.)	While walking between the village and the lake, Kate and Teresa discuss their differences vis-à-vis their potential roles in the Quetzalcoatl movement
3	793–6(4pp.)	Kate and Teresa rejoin Ramon on his boat; Kate and Ramon briefly discuss nobility; there is a recollected discussion between Kate and Cipriano regarding her forthcoming departure

These new scenes open up the closed self-sufficiency of version one by returning Ramon, Teresa and Cipriano to the narrative, in a series of dialogic exchanges between each of them and Kate. The scenes (and ensuing dialogues) also reopen the question of the Quetzalcoatl cult: its meaning and credibility. There is also a similar sense of finality to these conversations, which, as in the latter stages of *Women in Love* (when Birkin and Ursula prepare to depart from Gudrun and Gerald, as discussed in Chapter 5), are in a sense definitive.

Lawrence also amends the start of the chapter in version two, along the general lines of revision in MSII (as discussed in the previous chapter), by organizing it into more distinct episodes and aligning the narrative viewpoint more clearly with Kate (the novel's focalizer). Version two begins with the following short paragraph:

> She and Teresa visited one another along the lake. There was a kinship and a gentleness between them, especially now Kate was going away for a while. (MSII 775)

Besides setting the chapter up to include the (new) visit of Teresa and Ramon, this passage reflects Kate's greater effort to reconcile herself with Mexico in MSII: she feels a new 'kinship and a gentleness' for Teresa. The narrative's alignment with Kate's perspective is also indicated by the peculiar use of the personal pronoun 'she' (in tacit reference to Kate) as the very first word and opening frame of the chapter.

The long, descriptive second paragraph in version one is then broken up into four short paragraphs in version two, which also contain some new passages, such as the following:

> And always the day seemed to be pausing and unfolding again to the greater mystery. The universe seemed to have opened vast and soft and delicate with life. (MSII 775)

When we note the way in which Lawrence reopens the novel through its rewritten endings, this new sense of the universe unfolding for Kate reflects the novel's own attempt to 'break into the beyond' (as Cipriano says of the open-ended Navajo blankets). The third of the four short paragraphs contains the first mini-scene **(1)**, which likens a passing boat to the ship of Dionysos.

There then follows the first newly inserted scene, as Ramon and Teresa appear in a 'boat along the lake'. After landing, Kate falls into conversation with Ramon and their conversation dominates the first new scene. Ramon asks Kate whether she really *must* go away and then, quickly accepting her wish, shifts into a lengthy, semi-comic speech on the philosophy behind the Quetzalcoatl movement:

> 'Tell them in your Ireland to do as we have done here.'
> 'But how?'
> 'Let them find themselves again, and their own universe, and their own gods. Let them substantiate their own mysteries. The Irish have been so wordy about their far-off heroes and greedy days of the heroic gods. Now tell them to substantiate them, as we have tried to substantiate Quetzalcoatl and Huitzilopochtli.'
> 'I will tell them', she said. 'If there is anybody to listen.' (MSII 776–7)

There is a meta-textual irony in Ramon, a written character, scolding the Irish for having been 'so wordy about their far-off heroes' (unlike his own Quetzalcoatl movement, which is enacting Mexican mythology in practice). However, Ramon's speech is playful – his suggestion that Kate become an ambassador for Quetzalcoatl in Europe is not sincere – and the repeated use of 'Tell them. . .' to begin each new passage is rhetorical. The imagined speaker who is supposed to repeat Ramon's metaphysical musings to 'Europe' is reminiscent of Nietzsche's Zarathustra, who proclaims the death of God to a mocking audience in an atheistic marketplace:

> 'Tell them', he said, 'the centre of the cosmos is alive, and terribly alive. But not with any personal god . . .
> Tell them the only gods are men. That terrible being of the Innermost casts out rays and circles of creation, and creation casts back an answer [. . .]. The One

casts us out like a question, and we, at the far end of the ray, have to cast back the answer. If we cannot give the answer, the answer *I am*, to the One at the centre, then the One curves his rays round us and drags us back out of creation into oblivion. (MSII 777–8)

We see how isolated elements of this passage might support the reading of William York Tindall, who reckoned *The Plumed Serpent* to be a great novel, but took it to be a sincere expression by Lawrence of a diverse theory of revelation, drawing from a mixture of theosophy, Kundalini, pre-Aztec Mexican mythology, the book of Revelation and pre-Socratic philosophy (1937 and 1948). While Tindall's account of Lawrence's research is an excellent piece of early scholarship on *The Plumed Serpent*, isolating the Quetzalcoatl movement and the character of Ramon and elevating them as representative of the novel or its author is very limiting. As in *Women in Love*, the characters in *The Plumed Serpent* offer conflicting viewpoints, while the narrative itself is heavily inflected by Kate's perspective, and Kate feels herself being 'dragged' by a 'terrible' force at various points in the novel, owing largely to her personal context and history.

Kate, who 'trembled a little when Ramon became passionate in his earnestness' (MSII 780), immediately frames Ramon by noting his apparent 'earnestness'. She then attempts to fathom Ramon's meaning through her own internal musings:

> The great First Cause was like a dragon coiled at the very centre of all the cosmos, and peeping out, like her snake. Utterly incomprehensible and non-human [. . .].
> The sense of doom, the vision into the beyond, the sense of responsibility to the inner dragon, stayed with Kate all the time. So that the scenes of the day were like a mirage through the wavering of which she could see the terrible hinterland, to the cosmic centre, where the dragon is. (MSII 781–2)

While Kate's thoughts here appear to echo Ramon's speech, we shouldn't overlook the continuity between Kate's vision of the world here ('the sense of doom') and her previous dour visions, which predate her first meeting with Ramon, as in her vision from the hotel rooftop in Chapter Three (as discussed in the previous chapter). If we did wish to take these passages seriously, we should also appreciate the way in which Lawrence reshapes his religious and mythological sources to fashion an essentially existential view of human life: if a person ceases to experience an authentic sense of being or self (if one 'cannot give the answer, the answer *I am*'), they feel the universe dragging them into a kind of oblivion ('so that the scenes of the day were like a mirage').

Following the first newly inserted scene comes the second mini-scene (**2**) (reinserted into MSII), which is then followed by the second new scene, shorter than the first and third. In it, Kate asks Teresa (again somewhat comically) whether she will sit beside Ramon 'in the church as the bride of Quetzalcoatl – with some strange name' (MSII 786), and the pair discuss their differences. Teresa concedes that she is 'afraid', but will do so in order to accept 'the greater responsibility of one's existence' (MSII 786–7). She then suggests that it would be 'different' for Kate, as she has a 'fighting soul' (MSII 787), but Kate counters by conceding that she is 'as frightened, really, as you' (MSII 788). The pair are walking together by the lake and it is at this point in version two that Lawrence reinserts the remaining mini-scenes (**3–7**) from the first version.

Following the latter sequence, Lawrence then inserts the third and final new scene, which forms the newly written ending to the novel. Like the first two new scenes, the third is also dominated by dialogue. Ramon having returned with the boat to pick up Teresa and Kate, it begins with a short exchange between Kate and Ramon on the topic of nobility:

> 'It is wonderful, really', said Kate, as they rowed over the water, 'how – how *noble* it makes one feel.'
> He laughed.
> 'No nobler than one is', he said.
> 'But the people are so wonderful. They make us feel noble, like the growing maize: as if they watered my roots.'
> 'If you can give man his reverence back, he will be more grateful for that than for everything. It is the flow of life [. . .]. And ~~those who~~ **if man ~~and~~ or woman can** restore the ~~great~~ life-flow, to the people from whom it has been cut off, ~~will be~~ **then that man or woman will be** the gods and aristocrats of that people.'
> 'I was born an aristocrat, and I always *felt* an aristocrat', said Kate. 'But I never knew till now what it was like to feel it move in me like life.'
> 'Ah Señora, aristocracy is not a static thing. Aristocracy also is a flow, a living flow. If we can bring back the Living Breath to the earth, then the people will ~~back~~ **give us** glory again.' (MSII 793–4)

Like Birkin in *Women in Love* (especially the early drafts), Ramon here gives voice to the fundamental Lawrentian theme of flux and stasis, flux being associated with life ('living flow') and stasis, by implication, with death ('a static thing'). There is also a typically intriguing balance to the dialogue, with Kate ostensibly on the wrong side of the divide, claiming 'I was born an aristocrat, and I always *felt* an aristocrat', yet her intrinsic resistance to the Quetzalcoatl cult intimates how Ramon's apparent desire for 'living flow' would paradoxically resolve itself into a fixed doctrine. Although the scene quickly and rather awkwardly shifts after this exchange to a final, recollected conversation between

Kate and Cipriano (discussed later in the chapter), the above-mentioned passage is also significant in that it implicitly attempts to define the perfect self-sufficiency of life by the lake as captured in the preceding descriptive sequence, which dominates version one.

The subsequent recollected conversation between Kate and Cipriano virtually repeats Kate's conversation with Ramon in the first interpolated scene. Initially concerning Kate's imminent departure, Cipriano soon shifts into a wide-ranging speech on the philosophy of Quetzalcoatl and even echoes Ramon's rhetorical style by repeatedly telling Kate to report back to Europe with the same refrain ('tell them'):

> No, Caterina, go to your Europe. Tell them their Day of Salvation is over: the Via Crucis is travelled and finished . . . Go! Tell them the Cross is a Tree again, and they may eat the fruit if they can reach the branches. [. . .] The fruit of knowledge is digested. Now we can plant the core. [. . .] Tell them man's ~~greatest~~ **supreme** mystery is being in the flesh. (MSII 794–5)

Echoing passages from *Women in Love* (especially Gudrun's 'knowledge in sensation' and her sense of Gerald as an apple to be 'eaten to the core'), the reference to 'being in the flesh' as a great mystery, with allusions to the biblical 'fruit of knowledge' and the 'Via Crucis', refers to the limited birth of human consciousness in the mind. Cipriano suggests Europe must now conceive a deeper consciousness, which incorporates the body and hints at a redemption of waste, feculence and excretion ('they may eat the fruit [. . .] the fruit of knowledge is digested [. . .] we can plant the core'); 'flux' is itself an archaic term for organic waste and discharge.

However, as with Ramon's earlier speech, aside from being placed within the dialogical frame of the narrative, Cipriano's words are not entirely sincere. His suggestion that Kate perform an ambassadorial role is again playful and the refrain 'tell them' is again rhetorical; even his reference to Kate as 'Catarina' (in otherwise perfect English) is somewhat farcical. Kate responds in a similar tone, pointing out an obvious flaw: '"But I shall never remember", she laughed' (MSII 795), and Cipriano then concludes with the novel's final lines in MSII in farcical style:

> It doesn't matter . . . Tell them anything, or tell them nothing, what does it matter! Tell them it is all a joke, and their symbols are pretty play-things, and they are all great-god Peter-Pans.
>
> Tell them what they want to hear, that they are the cutest ever.
>
> Then come back, and leave them to it. (MSII 795–6 (see Figure 13))

These lines are almost remarkable given the ultra-serious tone of so many previous critical readings of *The Plumed Serpent*, with self-confessed Quetzalcoatl follower Cipriano concluding the entire novel by suggesting Kate tell Europe 'that they are the cutest ever' and 'then come back, and leave them to it'. I would suggest that the ending descends into farce in version two precisely because of Ramon and Cipriano's grandstanding efforts. While their ramblings contain many pithy passages, which I addressed earlier and will again later, they tackle vast stretches of history and culture and are addressed to vast swathes of geography and demography (an apostrophized Europe). These long, repetitive speeches take the narrative focus away from Kate's personal journey, and it is this personal journey which is at the heart of the novel and which Lawrence takes more seriously as a novelist.

On the latter note, Cipriano's allusion to Peter Pan is apt, not only in its (somewhat bitter) critical edge towards the role of myth in the West – where, in infantile and solipsistic fashion, symbols are 'pretty play-things' and everyone is a 'great-god Peter-Pan' – but also in its allusion to J. M. Barrie's specific story, with its child protagonists, its idealization of childhood and its fantasy of never growing old.[7] While, like Barrie's story, *The Plumed Serpent* features an exotic cult and one could even suggest that the Quetzalcoatl movement stages an *adult* fantasy of primitivism and animism, it is worth considering the more fundamental and personal connection to the story of Peter Pan and the myth of eternal youth. Kate has left her own children behind in Europe (while Ramon virtually disowns his children) and feels her own years advancing with a tragic sensitivity. These factors contribute towards her depression, which, as emphasized, inflect her (and the novel's) visions of Mexico. However, rather than cut herself off from the ongoing flux of reality, with an idealized vision of the past, these issues represent challenges and questions which Kate tarries with throughout the novel. Rewriting the ending again in versions three and four, Lawrence eventually turns our attention back to these more fundamental issues.

Versions three and four: 'It was as if she had two selves'

As mentioned, Lawrence's rewriting in version three (the typescript version) focuses entirely on the three new scenes. In the first of these, following the opening exchange between Kate and Ramon, in which Ramon encourages the Irish to 'substantiate' their myths, Lawrence cuts both Ramon and Kate's lengthy external and internal monologues and inserts a new version of the scene using new sheets of typescript. In the rewritten version, Ramon and Kate pursue their initial conversation in a far more personal manner:

> 'But why do you go away?' he asked her, after a silence.
> 'You don't care, do you?' she said.
> There was a dead pause.
> 'Yes, I care', he said.
> 'But why?'
> Again it was some time before he answered.
> 'You are a help, after all', he said.
> 'Even when I don't do anything? – and when I get a bit bored with [the] living Quetzalcoatl and the rest, and wish for a simple Don Ramon?' she replied.
> He laughed suddenly. (TSII 3)

Kate's light mockery of the 'living Quetzalcoatl and the rest' and her wish for 'a simple Don Ramon' – which even hints at Don Quixote as another, more comical context for Ramon and the Quetzalcoatl movement – elicits laughter from Ramon himself. As indicated by the number of direct questions in the short extract before, the new passage is much more inquisitive, shifting the focus from an impersonal and uncontested vision of the cosmos (in version two) to a more contested exchange of personal visions in version three.[8] We can see this as reflecting the novel's own, ultimate concern with personal questions (rather than with the meaning or fate of the Quetzalcoatl movement itself).

Whereas the characters' precise location is unspecified in previous versions, in version three we then discover that the pair 'were sitting on a bench under a red-flowering poinsettia whose huge scarlet petal-leaves spread out like sharp plumes' (TSII 3). While this added detail will prove significant later, the poinsettia reminding Kate of Christmas at home in Europe, the rewritten scene initially continues with Kate and Ramon's probing questions:

> 'And if you're not sure of yourself, what are you sure of?' she challenged.
> [. . .]
> 'I am sure – sure – ' his voice tailed off into vagueness, his face seemed to go grey and peaked, as a dead man's, only his eyes watched her blackly, like a ghost's. Again she was confronted with the suffering ghost of the man. And she was a woman, powerless before this suffering ghost which was still in the flesh. (TSII 4–5)

Ramon finally breaks down under Kate's scrutiny, although the description of Ramon as 'the suffering ghost of the man' again hints at the close interweaving of the narrative and Kate's viewpoint. Following a pause, Kate and Ramon then continue to probe, and, fuelled as mentioned by the potential finality of the exchange, with Kate's departure imminent, they ultimately question each other's 'real' self. I will quote a lengthy extract as the passage probes to the core, while the section is also rewritten by Lawrence again at a later stage (thus producing version four):

TSII 6–9: Version Three
'If you want to be so – so abstract and Quetzalcoatlian, and then bury your head in the lap of a Teresa, like an ostrich in the sand when he has brought his enemies upon him, then of course it is your affair!'

'So!' he said, smiling. 'So! Am I abstract?'

'What else? Life, just living, is not good enough for you. You want to parade something from your own will. And it is not enough for you to be a man, a real man. [. . .] I am more than all your Malintzis and Quetzalcoatls, when I am just myself.'

'So! So! Another declaration of Independence! But what is it that you are, when you are *just yourself*?'

'[. . .] Do you think that I, Kate Forrester, am not ten times as real and important as any Malintzi, or any living Quetzalcoatl either?'

'No! Frankly, I don't. Kate Forrester without any Malintzi, and with no Quetzalcoatl, or Huitzilopochtli in her life seems to me – I won't say just like anybody else – but with just a common destiny, a vulgar destiny; embedded in the rest of vulgar people.'

[. . .]

'It may *seem* to you so, But it isn't so. Of course, if you refuse to recognise in me what I am, and the real Lord that is behind me, of course it will seem to you that I am embedded in the vulgar destiny. But my destiny is my own, for all that. And it is no smaller than your destiny. And in my opinion it is more real – more alive. Because I am a woman. [. . .] I have the greatest respect for you when you are just Ramon. But when you are the Living Quetzalcoatl you seem to me a – a conceited boy, like a vain, self-conscious, posing boy of nineteen.'

[. . .]

'And I don't care what words you put on me . . . I know what I *feel* – and that is enough for me.'

'You have felt many things, contradictory things, too, in the course of your life. You have even "felt" Huitzilopochtli and Quetzalcoatl . . .'

'[. . .] Not deeply. It has been an experience – but not very deep. I know something better, really.'

'What is it?'

'Just life! And being oneself.'

[. . .]

'But which self? The one that came trailing over from England to America? – and trailing down to Mexico with your cousin Owen? – and becoming hysterical at a bull-fight, and being driven to Sanborn's for tea and strawberry shortcake?'

PS 428–30: Version Four
'If you want to be so – so abstract and Quetzalcoatlian, and then bury your head sometimes, like an ostrich in the sand, and forget.'
'So!' he said, smiling. 'You are angry again!'
'It's not so simple', she said. 'There is a conflict in me. And you won't let me go away for a time.'
'We can't prevent you', he said.
'Yes, but you are against my going – you don't let me go in peace.'
'Why must you go?' he said.
'I must', she said. 'I must go back to my children, and my mother.'
'It is a necessity in you?' he said.
'Yes!'

The moment she had admitted the necessity, she realized it was a certain duplicity in herself. It was as if she had two selves: one, a new one, which belonged to Cipriano and to Ramon, and which was her sensitive, desirous self: the other hard and finished, accomplished, belonging to her mother, her children, England, her whole past. This old accomplished self was curiously invulnerable and insentient, curiously hard and 'free'. In it, she was an individual and her own mistress. The other self was vulnerable, and organically connected with Cipriano, even with Ramon and Teresa, and so was not 'free' at all.

She was aware of a duality in herself, and she suffered from it. She could not definitely commit herself, either to the old way of life or to the new. She reacted from both . . .

[. . .]

'Yes! You put a weight on me, and paralyse me, to prevent me from going', she said.

[. . .]

'[. . .] I don't believe in your going. It is a turning back: there is something renegade in it – But we are all complicated. And if you *feel* you must go back for a time, go! It isn't terribly important. You have chosen, really. I am not afraid for you.'

[. . .] She could never be sure, never be *whole* in her connection with Cipriano and Ramon. [. . .]

'Aren't you sometimes afraid for yourself?' he asked.
'Never!' she said. 'I'm absolutely sure about myself.'

Just as the descriptive, unreflexive self-sufficiency and wholeness of the original version of this chapter is broken open by Lawrence's dialogic insertions, so it is through dialogue that Kate and Ramon reflect upon their own conflicted natures. Kate is perhaps more condescending in the earlier version, likening Ramon as 'the living Quetzalcoatl' to 'a conceited boy [. . .] a vain, self-conscious, posing boy of nineteen', while Ramon hints at Kate's own, more mundane multiplicity ('But which self?'). In the later version, Kate herself acknowledges 'a conflict' and becomes 'aware of a duality in herself' ('as if she had two selves'). In both versions, though, Kate and Ramon attack each other's respective mythologies: Ramon for his exotic (almost drag queen like) 'living Quetzalcoatl', including the memorable mocking-phrase 'Quetzalcoatlian', which can again be likened to 'Quixotic', and Kate for her conventional sense of an essential self (which is best represented by the tautologous formula 'I am what I am'). Representing opposite poles of mundane and exotic, the clash of these respective senses of self blurs the distinction between reality and myth. Reminiscent of Birkin and Gerald's discussion of the soul and selfhood in TSI of *Women in Love* (discussed in Chapter 6), through intense dialogical questioning the characters come up against an apparent limitation in language itself (or the ordinary symbolic register): it is almost impossible to define or describe 'the real' as the characters come up against the reality of multiple contingent selves.

In the later version, Kate's reflections on herself are more probing: 'it was as if she had two selves: one, a new one, which belonged to Cipriano and to Ramon, and which was her sensitive, desirous self: the other hard and finished, accomplished, belonging to her mother, her children, England, her whole past.' Through a subtle yet fantastic narrative, in which Kate only steadily comes to terms with her dramatic transplantation, from family life in England and Ireland, journeying alone in Mexico, to the almost camp heart of the Quetzalcoatl movement, Lawrence is able to capture constitutive divisions within human experience: between the self as something located in the past, accomplished and whole, and the self as divided, present and ongoing, not only open to the future, but 'organically connected' to the world (as one's imagined self is not). A dawning awareness of this illiberal 'organic' connection enables Kate to become aware of her conflicted nature and leads her to suggest to Ramon, 'you won't let me go away for a time', which foreshadows the novel's eventual final line.

Unlike the novel or its readers, Ramon cannot plummet into the layers of Kate's psyche, and thus his remarks in the earlier version reflect on her more extraneous experiences: the self that came trailing down to Mexico or the self that became hysterical at the bullfight. However, the narrative itself explores further into Kate's inner life, and, immediately after the above extracts, memories of Christmas come flooding back to Kate:

> Christmas was coming! The poinsettia reminded Kate of it.
> Christmas! Holly-berries! England! Presents! Food! [. . .] It felt so safe, so familiar, so normal, the thought of Christmas at home, in England, with her mother. (*PS* 431)

As Lawrence continues to rewrite the final chapter, the novel's underlying dilemmas come to the fore, steadily displacing the exterior journey along the lake (the focus of version one) and the urgings of Ramon and Cipriano regarding the Quetzalcoatl movement (in version two).

When rewriting the second interpolated scene in version three, Lawrence introduced the following passage in which Teresa rationalizes her participation in the Quetzalcoatl ceremonies as follows:

> So when I have to wear the green dress [. . .] I shall look away to the heart of all the world, and try to be my sacred self, not the more trivial selves that I am as well. It is right. I would not do it if I thought it was not right. (TSII 14)

Teresa reaffirms the notion of multiple selves, the relativity of which enables her to be sacred and trivial at different times, though Lawrence alters the lines in version four to place more emphasis on her more soul-orientated sense of responsibility: 'my sacred self, ~~not the more trivial selves that I am as well~~ **because it is necessary, and the right thing to do**'. The rest of the second new scene is rewritten in versions three and four along the same lines as the first, with the exchange between Teresa and Kate becoming more intense and confrontational: Kate suggests that Ramon 'would always be too didactic and overbearing for me' and 'needs far too much submission from a woman, to please me' (TSII 15) – again staging the critique of the Quetzalcoatl movement as oppressive within the narrative itself – while Teresa questions Kate in turn, placing more emphasis upon dialogical probing than (monological) ideological critique: 'How do you know that Ramon needs submission from a woman? [. . .] He has not asked any submission from you [. . .] and he does not ask submission from me' (TSII 15–15a and 15).

Endings: 'You won't let me go!'

Perhaps the most significant rewritings of all come in the much longer third and final newly interpolated scene, which contains the ending itself. The opening exchange between Ramon and Kate, in which they discuss nobility as stasis or flow, is altered so that Ramon cuts to the point with almost comic (yet brutal) rapidity, remarking that, although Kate may now feel 'splendid' among the peons at Sayula, 'as if one were still genuinely of the nobility', later on 'they will murder you and violate you, for having worshipped you' (TSII 20). In version two, following this brief exchange, the scene had shifted rather awkwardly, mentioning a brief stay at Jamiltepec (Teresa and Ramon's hacienda) by Kate, 'before Cipriano returned and she departed, for go she must' (MSII 794), which served as a prelude to Kate's final conversation with Cipriano. In TSII, however, which contains versions three and four, on hearing Ramon's warning, Kate apparently 'made up her mind still more definitely, to go away' and 'engaged a berth from Vera Cruz to Southampton: she would sail on the last day of November' (TSII 20–1). Cipriano then returns 'on the Seventeenth', Kate 'told him what she had done', and the two begin the conversation, which, in version two, had served as the novel's conclusion. However, their exchange is cut short in versions three and four, with Cipriano initially (and disturbingly) contemplating using the law 'to have her prevented from leaving the country' (something Lawrence had experienced himself, in England), but, in the end, accepting her departure with apparent 'indifference' (TSI 21–2).

TSII then contains an entirely new, thirteen-page concluding section (TSII 22–34), which extends the transition across each version from exteriority and self-sufficiency in version one, to interiority, conflict and interdependency in the later versions. Cipriano takes a boat down to Jamiltepec, leaving Kate alone, 'as usual' (TSII 22), and, as in the rewritten versions of the first newly interpolated scene, Kate once again reflects upon her own dilemma as she ponders her future either in Europe or Mexico:

> It occurred to her, that she herself willed this aloneness. She could not relax and be with these people. She could not relax and be with anybody. She always had to recoil upon her own individuality, as a cat does.
>
> [. . .]
>
> And then what! To sit in a London drawing-room, and add another to all the grimalkins? [. . .] Even the horrid old tom-cat men of the civilised roof gutters, did not fill her with such sickly dread.
>
> 'No!' she said to herself.
>
> [. . .]
>
> After all, when Cipriano touched her caressively, all her body flowered. And when she spread the wings of her own ego, and set forth her own spirit, the world could look very wonderful to her, when she was alone. But after a while, the wonder faded, and a sort of jealous emptiness set in.

'I must have both', she said to herself. 'I must not recoil against Cipriano and Ramon [...]. I say they are limited. But then one must be limited. If one tries to be unlimited, one becomes horrible.' (TSII 22-5)

Kate here contemplates her chief dilemma in the novel: whether to reconcile herself with her new and ongoing self, which is anchored in the present and the future, or to recoil instinctively 'upon her own individuality', her 'accomplished' self, which is anchored in the past, though it is this attachment to the past which fuels her depressed sense of herself as old and cut adrift from a younger, more spontaneous self (as discussed in the previous chapter). Kate has attempted to navigate this 'black page' through the course of the novel and now, keen to avoid the 'emptiness' of 'unlimited' egoism, and appearing to change the course of the novel, she decides to set off 'down the lake in a row-boat' for Jamiltepec, 'to make a sort of submission: to say she didn't want to go away' (TSII 31). There remains a strong sense of ambivalence, however: Kate is almost pleading with herself ('I must [...] I must not'), and she still insists that Ramon and Cipriano 'are limited'. It is also interesting to note the parallels to *Women in Love* in this passage: not only does the use of the wings metaphor ('when she spread the wings of her own ego') echo Ella/Ursula's coming of age (as discussed in Chapters 4 and 5), but Kate's commitment to the seemingly impossible ('I must have both') also echoes Birkin's final desire (for 'two kinds of love').

This ambivalence continues when Kate arrives at the hacienda, where she finds Ramon and Cipriano 'in the thick of their Quetzalcoatl mood' and is 'not very eager to begin' for 'they made her feel like an intruder' ('she did not pause to realise that she *was* one') (TSI 31-2). While the novel approaches a resolution, then, with Kate striving to reconcile her conflicted sense of self, the issue of Quetzalcoatl and broader social realities threaten to derail it. In the end, like Ursula in *Women in Love*, Kate zones in on the question of Cipriano's love, almost in desperation:

'I don't really want to go away from you.'
[...]
'You don't really want me.'
'Yes, I want you! – *Verdad*! *Verdad*!' exclaimed Cipriano...
And even amid her tears, Kate was thinking to herself; *What a fraud am I! I know all the time it is I, who don't altogether want them*...
[...]
'You don't want me to go, do you?' she pleaded.

> [...]
> 'Yo! Yo!' [...] 'Te quiero mucho! Much te quiero! Mucho! Mucho! I like you very much! Very much!'
>   It sounded so soft, soft-tongued, of the soft, wet, hot blood, that she shivered a little.
>   'Le gueux m'a plantee la!' she said to herself, in the words of an old song.
>   END.
> (TSII 32–4 (see Figure 14))

Rather than merely escape to Europe, a more positive resolution to the narrative is both approached and resisted. However, given Kate's oscillations throughout the novel, between recoil and reconciliation, and the manner in which the narrative itself oscillates between self-sufficiency in the descriptive passages and interdependency in the dialogic confrontations, as is best evidenced in the eventual structure of the final chapter, this oscillatory ending seems fitting.

Kate's obscure quotation from an 'old song' in French renders the final line itself somewhat baffling in this version. As John Beer suggests, the words appear to come 'from a French military marching song, concerning the plight of a young woman seduced by a man who has left her in the lurch' (2014, p. 177). Beer also notes that the song, which is collected in the *Oeuvres* (1799) of Jean-Joseph Vadé, an obscure eighteenth-century French chansonnier and playwright, laments the loss of a 'jeune, beau, vigoureux' male lover, a phrase which is also referenced by Lady Chatterley in the 'first version' of *Lady Chatterley's Lover*.[9] The quotation resonates with a more sensual dilemma for Kate in version three, as she shivers listening to Cipriano voicing his desire for her ('*Te quiero mucho!*'). Quoting 'to herself' in a foreign language suggests that Kate recoils into herself at the very climax, but Lawrence rewrites the final line in the fourth and final version. In doing so, the novel ultimately concludes with a near-perfect moment of oscillatory poise:

> 'La gueux m'a plantee la!' she said to herself, in the words of an old song.
> **'You won't let me go!' she said to him.**
>   END.

Like the poised title for the chapter itself – 'Here!' – Lawrence altered this line at a late stage in the transmission process and both phrases evoke the self as trapped (or bouncing) between a closed past and an open future. Finally, the line also captures both Kate and Lawrence's hesitation in the face of an impending ending (consider Kate's preceding remarks: 'I don't really want to go away from you'; 'You don't want me to go, do you?').

Following a protracted process of drafting and redrafting, the final chapter of *The Plumed Serpent* is ultimately dominated by the novel's central, personal dilemma. From an initial, therapeutic journey alone beside the lake, which primes Kate for a departure from Mexico in version one and concludes rather tamely with Kate packing her bags, Teresa, Ramon and Cipriano each return in the subsequent versions and, in version two, the two men provide Kate and the novel with portentous yet farcical final messages. In versions three and four, Kate's initial exchanges with Ramon and Cipriano become more dialogical and inquisitive. Kate is left alone afterwards to reflect upon her potential isolation and finally returns to the hacienda, where the novel concludes with an unfinished piece of dialogue between Kate and Cipriano. While the Quetzalcoatl movement re-emerges in each rewritten version of the ending, the question of Kate's potential departure for Europe and her struggles to overcome depression and to reconcile herself with the 'real' take centre stage in versions three and four. In the end, recognizing the reality of the struggle itself, Lawrence dispenses with Ramon and Cipriano's external messages and shifts attention back to Kate and the novel's implicit dilemma of the self, trapped between past and future states, between completion and incompletion. The writer's struggle is perhaps more determinate. Lawrence was able to resolve the process of writing by setting aside his work (the process ultimately resolving itself into the published text). Whether writers or readers ever really 'let go' of a text, though, is a more open question.

Notes

1. *The Plumed Serpent*, and Cipriano's contrast of European and non-European cultures, therefore provides another context for Amit Chaudhuri's critique of finishedness and his discussion of 'difference' in *D. H. Lawrence and 'Difference'*.
2. I use the term 'European' as Kate, Cipriano's interlocutor, is Irish, while Cipriano's 'your' also suggests the plural pronoun. Cipriano's words also echo Birkin's denunciation of the 'evil' principle of 'stasis' and 'the will to persist' in TSI of *Women in Love* (as discussed in Chapter 6).
3. As the page proofs are missing, Lawrence's final alterations are recorded in the published version of *The Plumed Serpent*.
4. There is a further complementarity between the first and final chapters in the two respective settings, the arena and the lake: one is a constructed site used to stage violent spectacles involving animals, while ordinary domestic work and life takes place alongside them in the latter, which is also a more natural site.

5 The peon's absorption in his work is of course resonant with Lawrence's own general belief in the self-rewarding nature of work, which forms a kind of theology of process (I discuss this topic in the Introduction).
6 Bell argues that Lawrence's 'conscious primitivism in this book is a sentimental falsity because it has got its mythopoeic religion "in the head"' and that 'the dramatic unreality of its primitivism arises from the self-consciousness of its rhetoric rather than the underlying metaphysic' (p. 206).
7 Lawrence was acquainted with J. M. Barrie and was friends for a time with Gilbert Cannan, who eventually married Barrie's wife.
8 Version four contains the following minor revision to this extract: '"~~You are a help, after all~~ **You are one of us, we need you**," he said,' which intensifies Ramon's loose initial remark.
9 Beer argues, 'this alternative ending [. . .] makes the novel's eventual ending seem less a gesture of submission than a mingling of reluctant recognition and desperation. [. . .] Kate seems less submissive victim than a woman who, even as she accepts the power of her own and her lover's physical desires and acknowledges the need to propitiate them, is devising a strategy to ensure her survival as an independent, free woman. This recognition of complexity seems closer to the common human condition' (p. 177). See *The First and Second Lady Chatterley Novels* (1999, p. 116).

Conclusion

I laid out the critical frameworks for this book in Chapter 1 by examining the relationship between genetic criticism and traditional Anglo-American literary and textual criticism. I tracked the gradual (and still ongoing) breakdown of the boundary between literary and textual criticism via the influential work of critics such as Hans Zeller, Hans Walter Gabler (who edited a genetic-inspired synoptic edition of *Ulysses* in 1984), Jerome McGann, Peter Shillingsburg and D. C. Greetham. I discussed how genetic criticism remained a more marginalized field within English-language literary studies, with Joyce representing something of an island for genetic critics, until, following the turn of the twenty-first century, critics such as Dirk van Hulle, Sally Bushell, Finn Fordham and Hannah Sullivan began to expand existing horizons by including a more diverse array of literature, from Wordsworth to Foster Wallace.

However, while I champion the ideas, methodology and development of genetic criticism, and suggest that it offers an innovative and unbiased route into Lawrence's manuscripts – and put this into practice in my own chapters on the manuscripts of 'Odour of Chrysanthemums', *Women in Love* and *The Plumed Serpent* – I have also looked to open genetic criticism itself by challenging what I see as its overly instrumentalist, 'constructivist' approach to writing. At the most general level, this means the text is viewed as a constructed object and the process of writing as a construction project. It places most emphasis on the relationship between subject and object: literature as an objective reproduction or manifestation of a subjective perception or feeling (or series of). By contrast, I wish to emphasize the relationship between self and other: literature as a dialogue (or series of) between different selves.

In their introduction to *Genetic Criticism: Texts and Avant-Textes*, Ferrer and Groden champion Edgar Allan Poe's 'Philosophy of Composition' as a foundational text for genetic criticism, though Poe's philosophy is a polemical modernist rejoinder to a traditional romantic myth of writing, in which the origin of literature is vaguely understood as ushering forth from the unknown, following an invisible hand or Muse. Poe therefore describes his own composition (of 'The Raven') with no Muse and a heavy, highly visible authorial hand, claiming to have written the poem in an intensely contrived manner, choosing a theme and a concluding line at the outset. Regardless of how accurate (or exaggerated) Poe's retrospective account is, his 'Philosophy of Composition' clearly says something about the empirical focus of French genetic criticism, which, as mentioned, was founded as a scientific practice based at the National Centre for Scientific Research in Paris. This legacy remains, from Pierre-Marc de Biasi's rigorous typologies for the *avant-texte* to Daniel Ferrer's notion of the draft as a 'protocol' for the completion of a text, as well as, more recently, Jean-Louis Lebrave and Denis Alamargot's joint contribution from genetic criticism and cognitive psychology ('The Study of Professional Writing') and the work of Dirk van Hulle, who draws from Jakob von Uexküll's biological notion of *umwelt* (characterizing literary manuscripts as a kind of 'GPS' system within a writer's *umwelt*) as well as Chalmers's and Clark's post-cognitivist notion of the 'extended mind'.

Another founding father for genetic criticism, though not explicitly discussed in the introduction to *Genetic Criticism*, is the supremely influential nineteenth-century French realist novelist Gustave Flaubert. Flaubert, like Poe, is a professional writer, whose general philosophy of composition is similarly self-conscious, again figuring writing as a contrived process (using deliberate skill or artifice). As mentioned, Flaubert is a big influence for modernist literature, with outspoken proponents including Henry James, Conrad, Pound, Joyce, Mann and many others. In addition to its scientific origins, then, another explanation for the 'constructivist' approach to writing in genetic criticism is the very fact that genetic critics have tended to study a particular (i.e. Flaubertian) *type* of writer. To take one important area as an example, in the work of leading contemporary genetic critic van Hulle, the pre-compositional phase (or 'exogenesis'), involving the writer's preparatory reading and research, has become increasingly prominent, with detailed work on the content and methods of research and reading. Aside from the obvious fact that this type of preparation, though part of a text's overall genesis, is not part of a process of writing (supposedly the focus of genetic criticism), this focus only makes sense for certain types of author, who, like Joyce or Becket, produce detailed reading notes and a body of preparatory work in its own right (both of whom are studied by van Hulle). In contrast, while Lawrence read prodigiously and at times conducted extensive research, he produced little by way of reading notes (discounting his published studies), neither did he develop a great personal library nor (frequently) annotate his own copies of books. In fact, Lawrence often passed books on or borrowed them in the first place, which better suited his itinerant lifestyle.

Important in their own right, these practical differences between writers also connect to broader philosophical questions, as indicated by opposing attitudes towards Flaubert and the aesthetic creed with which Flaubert is commonly identified. Besides sporadic comments in early letters to Edward Garnett and others, Lawrence expressed his own critical attitude towards Flaubert in an early review of Thomas Mann ('German Books: Thomas Mann'), which, as Lawrence's most explicit and wide-ranging critique of Flaubertian aesthetics, I have alluded to on a number of occasions.[1] Although Lawrence also identifies a Flaubertian desire for aesthetic mastery with a wider social and cultural desire for mastery in contemporary Germany (on the eve of the First World War), the essential suggestion in this review is that the human mind cannot absolutely set the lines of a book, any more than it can the 'lines' of a living being. As we have seen at various times in this book, Lawrence's texts frequently reject an egotistical desire to know or fix a thing absolutely, associating the latter process with completion, stasis and death, while flux, incompletion and the unknown are associated with life.

Despite Lawrence's notion of the universe as an infinite flux, and of the self as potentially (and creatively) open towards this flux, hence the dilemma of writing an ending, Lawrence's notion of creativity is also, like that of Poe and Flaubert, *empirical*. A classic example of this can be found in the opening lines of 'Corasmin and the Parrots', the opening essay in Lawrence's Mexican travel book, *Mornings in Mexico* (1927):

> We talk so grandly in capital letters, about Morning in Mexico. All it amounts to is one little individual looking at a bit of sky and trees, then looking down at the page of his exercise book.
> It is a pity we don't always remember this. When books come out with grand titles, like *The Future of America*, or *The European Situation*, it's a pity we don't immediately visualise a thin or a fat person, in a chair or in a bed, dictating to a bob-haired stenographer or making little marks on paper with a fountain pen. (2009, p. 9)

While Poe and Flaubert may be praised for exposing the romantic myth of the author as a peaceful receptacle, passively tuning in as though the invisible Muse were a distant radio tower, Lawrence's humble account of the writer as 'one little individual' may also be praised for exposing the *modernist* myth of the author as a godlike authority, a figure both everywhere and nowhere, as in Flaubert's famous description (which Stephen Dedalus silently lifts in Joyce's *A Portrait of the Artist as a Young Man* (1916)) and as implied by Poe's intensely intentional account of composition.

In terms of possible partners within modernism for Lawrence's anti-orthodox position, Virginia Woolf was similarly vocal in her criticism of the more general Flaubertian concept of 'craftsmanship'. Enlisted to speak on 'the craft of words' and 'the craftsmanship of the writer' for BBC radio in 1937, Woolf immediately suggested that 'there is something incongruous, unfitting, about the term "craftsmanship" when applied to words', and she distances writing from both meanings of the word 'craft' (the making of useful objects out of solid matter, as well as cajolery, cunning and deceit) (1942, p. 126). Despite being *inutile*, Woolf suggests that 'since words survive the chops and changes of time longer than any other substance' they are also 'the truest' (p. 127). While there is a playful tone to this little-known piece, it is worth extracting Woolf's central argument about the *mobility* of words as it is both powerful and carries strong echoes of Lawrence (deceased by the time of Woolf's broadcast):

> In short, [words] hate anything that stamps them with one meaning or confines them to one attitude, for it is their nature to change. Perhaps that is their most striking peculiarity: their need of change. It is because the truth they try to catch is many-sided, and they convey it by being many-sided, flashing first this way, then that. Thus they mean one thing to one person, another thing to another person; they are unintelligible to one generation, plain as a pikestaff to the next. And it is because of this complexity, this power to mean different things to different people, that they survive. Perhaps then one reason why we have no great poet, novelist or critic writing today is that we refuse to allow words their liberty. We pin them down to one meaning, their useful meaning, the meaning which makes us catch the train, the meaning which makes us pass the examination. And when words are pinned down they fold their wings and die. (pp. 130–1)

These words are just as pertinent in the twenty-first century, with phenomena like 'fake news' and 'fact-checking' both reliant upon a simple, unitary notion of words (as having single, fixed meanings). If we allow words their 'liberty' and view them as existing within a dialogical universe, we might suggest that the real myths are 'un-fake news' and 'facts' (implying as they do an authoritative, unified, universal perspective), and perhaps our appetite for a 'great poet, novelist or critic' would return, too.

In terms of more recent genetic criticism, Sally Bushell and Finn Fordham have already expressed some dissatisfaction with a perceived bias towards metaphors of 'construction'. Fordham emphasizes how writers often 'express an experience of their own conscious agency being replaced by the agency of writing and genetic criticism needs to account for this' (pp. 24–5), while Bushell, in her own 'Philosophy of Composition', describes writing as 'a movement *between* a "spontaneous" (unwilled) engagement with language and a conscious return to that engagement' (p. 227). This interplay between spontaneous and non-spontaneous states of being offsets a one-sided focus on intentional craft. I would also suggest that the notion of writing as involving an ongoing relationship between different states of being is ultimately *dialogical*, and that a notion of genetic dialogism is also helpful in enabling a more balanced and realistic understanding of writing and reading processes. Centred on the interplay between self and other, dialogue is something which both constructivist and organicist metaphors place little emphasis upon.

While analysing the genesis of Lawrence's texts in this book, I have tried to develop a notion of genetic dialogism relevant to Lawrence's particular writing processes. Lawrence demonstrates both spontaneity and artifice: producing entire drafts with very little (if any) concrete planning, yet these drafts are themselves written with a prior intention to rewrite, as the main epigraph to this book suggests. Lawrence also reuses his drafts as copy-texts and guides while writing subsequent versions. I have essentially identified two different types of dialogical writing, which are micro and macro: (1) specific rewritings, where Lawrence produces multiple versions of a passage as variations upon a theme, most commonly evident in the rewriting of *Women in Love*, particularly the typescripts (discussed in Chapter 6); (2) and general rewriting, where Lawrence steadily produces a more dialogical text by rewriting or inserting segments of dialogue, which become increasingly conflicted and yet provide a counterpoint with the (increasingly) restful descriptive segments, as is most evident in the composition of *The Plumed Serpent* (for which a far more complete manuscript record survives than it does for *Women in Love*), particularly the final chapter (discussed in Chapter 8). While a key feature of dialogue is the interplay between self and other, 'genetic dialogism' is not a rigid or absolute concept. Rather, it is a composite and flexible metaphor for writing. Unlike existing, popular metaphors, foremost among which are construction ('constructivism') and organic growth ('organicism'), there is less risk of dialogism being mistaken for a literal description of writing.

I began the primary chapters of this book in Chapter 2 by reassessing the genesis of Lawrence's iconic early story, 'Odour of Chrysanthemums'. There I began by highlighting how previous critics have marginalized early versions of the story, which contain more detailed accounts of the family at home awaiting the absent father's return, as 'immature'. I suggest that the dramatic heart of the story is in fact contained in this anticipatory dilemma by pointing to the complex web of connections which Lawrence weaves into the early narrative, and argue that the critical focus on 'maturity', and on Lawrence's heavily revised ending, is merely a preference for Lawrence's contemporaneous novel *The Rainbow* (written at the same time as the final version of the story). I also reassessed the story's heavily rewritten ending, placing it in a writerly context, rather than focusing exclusively on the theme of otherness, which Lawrence takes up in the final version and which I suggest was essentially syphoned from *The Rainbow*.

I then reassessed the compositional history of *Women in Love* in Chapter 3, pointing to gaps and uncertainties which previous critics have overlooked, including evidence that Lawrence completed more drafts than previously accounted for, which also explain the confusing and comic drama of the broken typewriter in August 1916. I also discuss the impact of the First World War, on, for example, the temporal rupture experienced by characters in the novel, as well as Lawrence's decision to split the work into two separate novels. In Chapter 4, I provided a detailed account of the early surviving fragments of *Women in Love* (from 1913 to 1916), treating them (as with 'Odour of Chrysanthemums') as valid literary documents in their own right (rather than immature off-cuts), discussing the presence of important narrative and thematic dynamics for *Women in Love*, while also considering their role as rough drafts. In Chapter 5, I provided a detailed account of the incomplete notebook draft of *Women in Love* (from 1916), focusing on the relationship between the genetic status of this section (a foreign, interpolated segment within the subsequent typescript draft) and its narrative content (where the characters travel into foreign territory and reflect upon their sense of self-transformation), as well as revision of the notebooks themselves, which focus on adjectives or descriptors, are dialogical, and in which the ending is again the most heavily revised section. I then looked at a selection of heavily revised sections from the typescript drafts of *Women in Love* in Chapter 6, most of which involve dialogue, concluding with the novel's final lines.

I began the final part of the book, in Chapter 7, with a brief account of the compositional and reception histories of *The Plumed Serpent*, before examining in more detail a few heavily revised episodes from the early chapters of the novel. I discuss Kate's role as the novel's chief protagonist and focalizer, whose consciousness is interwoven with the narrative voice and whose journey provides the central drama. Finally, in Chapter 8, I considered the end of Kate's journey, as well as Lawrence's central compositional dilemma of writing an ending, by examining the heavily rewritten final chapter of *The Plumed Serpent*.

Conclusion 217

I introduced the problem of endings for Lawrence when discussing 'Odour of Chrysanthemums', which, like the early versions of *Women in Love*, ends with one protagonist reflecting on the corpse of another. I go so far as to liken this experience to a writer reflecting on a completed draft or published book. In a sense, Lawrence's rewriting of entire works ('I must always write my books twice') is itself a kind of rejection of endings: as soon as a work is complete, Lawrence starts again/goes back to the beginning. While I emphasize that endings are also a source of relief (providing a culmination for, and putting an end to, anticipation), Lawrence's pattern of heavily revising endings is the most dramatic evidence that endings were problematic.

Revising the typescripts of *Women in Love* from 1916 to 1919, Lawrence cut an explicit suggestion by Birkin, in an early dialogue with Gerald, that the universe is an everlasting flux of creation. I suggested that Lawrence may have rewritten this (and other, similarly overt passages) in order to further dramatize Birkin as a character within, and in opposition to other characters within, the diegetic 'world' of *Women in Love* (rather than function as a commentator on the universe at large). Another instance of this type of revision comes at the end of the novel, where another speech by Birkin is rewritten so that, rather than have the novel conclude with Birkin's reflections on Gerald's dead body, Lawrence inserts a new and somewhat enigmatic dialogical scene in which Birkin denies Ursula's claim that two kinds of love are impossible.

Lawrence heavily revised the ending to *The Plumed Serpent* (more than once) in a similar manner. While the novel originally concludes in MSI with a short, self-sufficient episode on the waters of Lake Sayula as Kate returns home and prepares to depart the country, Lawrence cut the original closing lines and inserted three new, dialogical episodes throughout the chapter in MSII, and proceeded to heavily revise the new scenes in the typescript and page proofs. 'Version two' contains a grandstanding speech on the philosophy of the Quetzalcoatl movement by Ramon and concludes with a similar speech on the spiritual state of affairs in the West by Cipriano. Lawrence subsequently cut or rewrote these speeches to create more genuine dialogues and eventually settled on an extremely similar ending to *Women in Love*, with Kate delivering another unanswered rejoinder, which again provides the novel with an inconclusive moment of dramatic poise: Kate's final cry ('You won't let me go!') can be read as both an accusation and a plea.

Having emphasized the dilemma of writing an ending in this book, I would like to conclude by pointing out that genetic studies of Lawrence have only just begun. Lawrence's archive is immensely rich, and the recently completed Cambridge Edition of Lawrence provides an easy point of entry.

Note

1 In June 1912, for example, prior to Garnett's extensive cuts to 'Paul Morel' when editing *Sons and Lovers*, Lawrence wrote to Garnett as follows: 'I sent that novel "Paul Morel" off to William Heinemann yesterday. Now I know it's a good thing, even a bit great. It's different from your stuff [. . .]. It's not so strongly concentric as the fashionable folk under French influence – you see I suffered badly from Hueffer [Ford Maddox Ford] re Flaubert and perfection – want it. It may seem loose – and I may cut the childhood part – if you think better so – and perhaps you'll want me to spoil some of the good stuff. But it is rather great' (*i.*, pp. 416–17).

Epilogue

Being of mixed English and European heritage while writing a book which mixes English and European traditions, I have sometimes wondered: What would Lawrence have made of the current, epochal political predicament involving England and Europe?

Though by no means a 'little Englander', Lawrence was essentially a man of 'little England'. He grew up in small regional villages and towns in Nottinghamshire and writes of London at times as of some hellish place (though he chose to live in London several times and got married and met many of his friends there). And yet, Lawrence left the country of his youth as a young adult and rarely returned, living first in South London as a teacher, then travelling around Europe before living in various parts of southern England as a writer during the First World War, then ultimately travelling and living all around the world until his death. Why?

Towards the end of his life, Lawrence wrote a fable-like short story entitled 'The Man Who Loved Islands'. In it, a wealthy man who desires *control* above all else goes to live on a series of increasingly small, increasingly remote islands. It begins: 'There was a man who loved islands. He was born on one, but it didn't suit him, as there were too many other people on it, besides himself. He wanted an island all of his own: not necessarily to be alone on it, but to make it a world of his own.' Lawrence himself began life in an incredibly tight-knit community, before moving away to live in many different places throughout his life. He was always partly in search of another tight-knit community, similar to the one he originally left. However, perhaps above all else, he also valued *difference*, hence his constant desire to move and rarely to return.

Lawrence was persecuted by England during and after the First World War. He and his German wife had their passports removed and were prohibited from leaving the island, while many of his books – and later his paintings, too – were seized, destroyed and banned in England. And yet, he always loved the country and would return there for the setting of his final novel, *Lady Chatterley's Lover*. In 1928, the year *Lady Chatterley* was first privately printed and two years before his death, in a letter to David Chambers, a childhood friend and the brother of his childhood sweetheart, Jessie Chambers, Lawrence wrote of the Chambers' home Haggs Farm: 'whatever I forget, I shall never forget the Haggs – I loved it so. [. . .] Tell your mother I never forget, no matter where life carries us' (viii. 618). Like Lawrence, James Joyce also left his home country as a young adult, though he always set his fiction there (in Dublin), virtually exclusively, whereas Lawrence frequently wrote about England but many individual places and never exclusively. Perhaps Lawrence is not as well celebrated in England today as Joyce is in Ireland (though he is certainly celebrated in Nottingham). Perhaps Joyce, in many ways a European author, who did not campaign for Irish nationalism, will be knocked down a few pegs in Ireland one day. Or perhaps England should return to D. H. Lawrence.

As with most grand subjects, Lawrence's thoughts were not a huge secret, and, like Joyce, he was not a political campaigner. He spells out his disdain for (or transvaluation of) modern political life in his rambling essay 'Democracy': 'When men are no longer obsessed with the desire to possess property [. . .] only then shall we be glad to turn it over to the State. [. . .] The Prime Minister of the future will be no more than a sort of steward, the Minister of Commerce will be the great housekeeper, the Minister of Transport the head coachman: all just chief servants, no more: servants' (1925; 1988, p. 82). As you were.

Bibliography

Armstrong, Tim, *Modernism: A Cultural History* (Cambridge: Polity, 2005).
Asher, Kenneth, 'T. S. Eliot and Charles Maurras', *ANQ*, 11, no. 3 (1998): 20–9.
Balbert, Peter, *D. H. Lawrence and the Phallic Imagination: Essays on Feminist Misreadings* (New York: St Martin's, 1989).
Barthes, Roland, 'The Death of the Author', *Aspen*, 5–6 (1967), http://www.ubu.com/aspen/aspen5and6/threeEssays.html.
Beer, John, *D. H. Lawrence: Nature, Narrative, Art, Identity* (London: Palgrave Macmillan, 2014).
Bell, Michael, *D. H. Lawrence: Language and Being* (Oxford: Oxford UP, 1992).
Bell, Michael, *Literature, Modernism and Myth: Belief and Responsibility in the Twentieth Century* (Cambridge: Cambridge UP, 1997).
Bellemin-Noël, Jean, 'Psychoanalytic Reading and the Avant-texte', in *Genetic Criticism: Texts and Avant-Texts*, trans. Jed Deppman, ed. Jed Deppman, Daniel Ferrer and Michael Groden (Pennsylvania: Pennsylvania UP, 2004), pp. 28–35.
Black, Michael, 'Revision and Spontaneity as Aesthetic', *The Cambridge Quarterly*, 28, no. 2 (1999): 150–66.
Black, Michael, 'Text and Context: The Cambridge Edition of Lawrence Reconsidered', in *Editing D. H. Lawrence: New Versions of a Modern Author*, ed. Charles L. Ross and Dennis Jackson (Ann Arbor: Michigan UP, 1995), pp. 7–27.
Blanchard, Lydia, 'D. H. Lawrence', *English Literature in Transition, 1880–1920*, 33, no. 3 (1990a): 387–91.
Blanchard, Lydia, 'Review of *D. H. Lawrence and the Phallic Imagination*', *Modern Fiction Studies*, 36, no. 4 (1990b): 608–11.
Booth, Howard J. (ed.), *New D. H. Lawrence* (Manchester: Manchester UP, 2009).
Booth, Howard J., 'Same-Sex Desire, Cross-Gender Identification and Asexuality in D. H. Lawrence's Early Short Fiction', *Études Lawrenciennes*, 42 (2011): 36–57.
Bornstein, George, *Material Modernism: The Politics of the Page* (Cambridge: Cambridge UP, 2001).
Bornstein, George (ed.), *Representing Modernist Texts: Editing as Interpretation* (Ann Arbor: University of Michigan Press, 1991).
Bornstein, George, Gillian Borland Pierce and Hans Walter Gabler (eds.), *Contemporary German Editorial Theory* (Ann Arbor: Michigan UP, 1991).
Bornstein, George and Ralph G. Williams (eds.), *Palimpsest: Editorial Theory in the Humanities* (Ann Arbor: Michigan UP, 1993).
Boulton, James T., 'D. H. Lawrence's *Odour of Chrysanthemums*: An Early Version', *Renaissance and Modern Studies*, 13, no. 1 (1969): 4–48.

Bowers, Fredson, 'Some Principles for Scholarly Editions of Nineteenth-Century American Authors', *Studies in Bibliography*, 17 (1964): 223–8.

Brown, Keith (ed.), *Rethinking Lawrence* (Philadelphia: Open UP, 1990).

Burack, Charles, *D. H. Lawrence's Language of Sacred Experience: The Transfiguration of the Reader* (London: Palgrave Macmillan, 2005).

Burden, Robert, *Radicalizing Lawrence* (Amsterdam: Rodopi, 2000).

Bush, Ronald L., *The Genesis of Ezra Pound's Cantos* (Princeton: Princeton UP, 1974).

Bushell, Sally, 'Intention Revisited: Towards an Anglo-American "genetic criticism"', *Text*, 17 (2005): 55–91.

Bushell, Sally, *Text as Process: Creative Composition in Wordsworth, Tennyson and Dickinson* (London: Virginia UP, 2009).

Bushell, Sally, 'Textual Process and the Denial of Origins', *Textual Cultures*, 2, no. 2 (2007): 100–17.

Byatt, A. S., 'The One Bright Book of Life', *New Statesman*, 16 December 2002, www.newstatesman.com/node/156844, accessed 29 December 2015.

Callu, Florence, 'La Transmission des manuscrits', in *Les Manuscrits des écrivains*, ed. Anne Cadiot and Christel Haffner (Paris: CNRS Editions/Hachette, 1993), pp. 54–67.

Chaudhuri, Amit, *D. H. Lawrence and 'Difference'* (Oxford: Oxford UP, 2003).

Cislaru, Georgeta (ed.), *Writing(s) at the Crossroads: Process-product Interface* (Amsterdam/Philadelphia: John Benjamins, 2015).

Clark, Andy and David J. Chalmers, 'The Extended Mind', *Analysis*, 58 (1998): 10–23.

Clark, L. D., 'Introduction', in *The Plumed Serpent*, ed. L. D. Clark (Cambridge: Cambridge UP, 1987), pp. xvii–xlvii.

Clark, L. D., *The Dark Night of the Body: D. H. Lawrence's The Plumed Serpent* (Austin: Texas UP, 1964).

Cohen, Philip and David H. Jackson (eds.), 'Notes on Emerging Paradigms in Editorial Theory', in *Devils and Angels: Textual Editing and Literary Theory*, ed. Phillip Cohen (London: Virginia UP, 1991), pp. 103–23.

Coombes, Henry (ed.), *D. H. Lawrence: A Critical Anthology* (Harmondsworth: Penguin, 1973).

Coroneos, Con and Trudi Tate, 'Lawrence's Tales', in *The Cambridge Companion to D. H. Lawrence*, ed. Anne Fernihough (Cambridge: Cambridge UP, 2001), pp. 103–18.

Crick, Brian and Michael DiSanto, 'D. H. Lawrence, "An opportunity and a test": The Leavis-Eliot Controversy Revisited', *Cambridge Quarterly*, 38, no. 2 (2009): 130–46.

Crispi, Luca, *Joyce's Creative Process and the Construction of Characters in Ulysses: Becoming the Blooms* (Oxford: Oxford UP, 2016).

Cushman, Keith, *D. H. Lawrence at Work: The Emergence of the Prussian Officer Stories* (Sussex: Harvester Press, 1978).

Cushman, Keith, 'D. H. Lawrence at Work: The Making of "Odour of Chrysanthemums"', *Journal of Modern Literature*, 2, no. 3 (1971–1972): 367–92.

Davies, Alexandra Mary, 'Poetry in Process: The Compositional Practices of D. H. Lawrence, Dylan Thomas and Philip Larkin', PhD Thesis, University of Hull (2008).
Davis, Oliver, 'The Author at Work in Genetic Criticism', *Paragraph*, 25, no. 1 (2002): 92-106.
De Biaisi, Pierre-Marc, 'Towards a Science of Literature: Manuscript Analysis and the Genesis of the Work', *Genetic Criticism: Texts and Avant-Texts*, trans. Jed Deppman, ed. Jed Deppman, Daniel Ferrer and Michael Groden (Pennsylvania: Pennsylvania UP, 2004), pp. 36-69.
De Biaisi, Pierre-Marc, 'What Is a Literary Draft? Toward a Functional Typology of Genetic Documentation', *Yale French Studies*, 89 (1996): 26-58.
Delany, Paul, 'Who Paid for Modernism?', in *The New Economic Criticism*, ed. Martha Woodmansee and Mark Osten (London: Routledge, 1999), pp. 286-99.
Deleuze, Gilles and Féliz Guattari, *Anti-Oedipus: Capitalism and Schizophrenia* (Paris: Les Éditions des Minuits, 1972).
Deppman, Jed, Daniel Ferrer and Michael Groden (eds.), *Genetic Criticism: Texts and Avant-Texts*, trans. Jed Deppman (Pennsylvania: Pennsylvania UP, 2004).
Dix, Carol, *D. H. Lawrence and Women* (London: Macmillan, 1980).
Dyer, Geoff, *Out of Sheer Rage: Wrestling with D. H. Lawrence* (London: Little, Brown and Co., 1997).
Eagleton, Terry, *After Theory* (London: Allen Lane, 2003).
Eagleton, Terry, *Criticism and Ideology: A Study in Marxist Literary Theory* (London: New Left Books, 1976).
Edwards, Bruce L., 'Introduction', in *The Personal Heresy*, ed. Joel D. Heck (Austin: Concordia UP, 2008).
Eggert, Paul, 'Introduction', in *Lawrence and Comedy*, ed. Paul Eggert and John Worthen (Cambridge: Cambridge UP, 1996), pp. 1-18.
Eggert, Paul, 'Reading a Critical Edition With the Grain and Against: The Cambridge D. H. Lawrence', in *Editing D. H. Lawrence: New Versions of a Modern Author*, ed. Charles L. Ross and Dennis Jackson (Ann Arbor: Michigan UP, 1995), pp. 27-40.
Eggert, Paul, 'Textual Product or Textual Process: Procedures and Assumptions of Critical Editing', in *Devils and Angels: Textual Editing and Literary Theory*, ed. Phillip Cohen (London: Virginia UP, 1991), pp. 57-77.
Eliot, T. S., 'Le Romain Anglais Contemporain', *La Nouvelle Revue Française*, 28 (1927): 671.
Eliot, Valery (ed.), *The Waste Land Facsimile* (London: Faber & Faber, 1971).
Ellis, David, *D. H. Lawrence: Dying Game, 1922-1930* (Cambridge: Cambridge UP, 1998).
Fernihough, Anne, *D. H. Lawrence: Aesthetics and Ideology* (Oxford: Oxford UP, 1993).
Fernihough, Anne (ed.), *The Cambridge Companion to D. H. Lawrence* (Cambridge: Cambridge UP, 2001).
Ferrer, Daniel, 'Clementis's Cap: Retroaction and Persistence in the Genetic Process', *Yale French Studies*, 89 (1996): 223-36.

Ferrer, Daniel, 'The Open Space of the Draft Page: James Joyce and Modern Manuscripts', in *The Iconic Page in Manuscript, Print, and Digital Culture*, ed. George Bornstein and Theresa Tinkle (Ann Arbor: Michigan UP, 1998), pp. 249–67.

Ferrer, Daniel, 'Variant and Variation: Toward a Freudo-bathmologico-Bakhtino-Goodmanian Genetic Model?', *Genetic Criticism and the Creative Process: Essays from Music, Literature and Theatre*, ed. William Kindermann and Joseph E. Jones (Rochester: Rochester UP, 2009), pp. 35–50.

Finney, Brian, 'D. H. Lawrence's Progress to Maturity: From Holograph Manuscript to Final Publication of *The Prussian Officer and Other Stories*', *Studies in Bibliography*, 28 (1975): 321–32.

Ford, Ford Madox, *Portraits From Life* (London: Houghton Mifflin, 1938).

Fordham, Finn, 'Between Theological and Cultural Modernism: The Vatican's Oath against Modernism, September 1910', *Literature and History*, 22, no. 1 (2013): 8–24.

Fordham, Finn, *I Do I undo I Redo: The Textual Genesis of Modernist Selves in Hopkins, Yeats, Conrad, Forster, Joyce and Woolf* (Oxford: Oxford UP, 2010).

Fordham, Finn, 'Review of *Modern Manuscripts* by Dirk van Hulle', *Modernism/Modernity*, 22, no. 2 (2015): 412–15.

Forster, E. M., 'D. H. Lawrence', in *The Creator as Critic: And Other Writings by E. M. Forster*, ed. Jeffrey M. Heath (Toronto: Dundurn, 2008).

Froula, Christine, 'Modernity, Drafts, Genetic Criticism: On the Virtual Lives of James Joyce's Villanelle', *Yale French Studies*, 89 (1996): 113–29.

Froula, Christine, *To Write Paradise: Style and Error in Pound's Cantos* (London: Yale UP, 1984).

Gabler, Hans Walter, 'The Text as Process and the Problem of Intentionality', *Text*, 3 (1987): 107–16.

Gabler, Hans Walter, 'Unsought Encounters', in *Devils and Angels: Textual Editing and Literary Theory*, ed. Phillip Cohen (London: Virginia UP, 1991), pp. 152–66.

Gabler, Hans Walter, with Wolfhard Steppe and Claus Melchior (eds.), *'Ulysses': A Critical and Synoptic Edition*, with an Afterword by Hans Walter Gabler, 3 vols (New York and London: Garland, 1984 and rev. pbk. edn. 1986).

Galbraith, D., 'Writing as a Knowledge-constituting Process', in *Knowing What to Write: Conceptual Processes in Text Production*, ed. M. Torrance and D. Galbraith, (Amsterdam: Amsterdam UP, 1999), pp. 139–60.

Gilbert, Sandra M., *Acts of Attention: The Poems of D. H. Lawrence*, 2nd edition (Carbondale: Southern Illinois UP, 1990; 1st edition published by Cornell UP, 1972).

Gilbert, Sandra M., 'On the Road with D. H. Lawrence – or, Lawrence as Thought-Adventurer', *Partial Answers*, 5, no. 1 (2007): 1–15.

Goldie, David, *A Critical Difference: T. S. Eliot and John Middleton Murry in English Literary Criticism, 1919–2928* (Oxford: Clarendon Press, 1998).

Goodheart, Eugene, 'Censorship and Self-Censorship in D. H. Lawrence', in *Representing Modernist Texts: Editing as Interpretation*, ed. George Bornstein (Ann Arbor: Michigan UP, 1991), pp. 223–40.

Gouirand, Jacqueline, 'The Trespasser: Aspects Genetiques', *Etudes Lawrenciennes*, 1 (1986): 41–57.

Greetham, D. C., 'Editorial and Critical Theory: Modernism and Postmodernism', in *Palimpsest: Editorial Theory in the Humanities*, ed. George Bornstein and Ralph G. Williams (Ann Arbor: Michigan UP, 1993), pp. 9–28.

Greetham, D. C., 'Review of *Contemporary German Editorial Theory*', *Modern Philology*, 95, no. 2 (1997): 285–9.

Greetham, D. C., 'Textual and Literary Theory: Redrawing the Matrix', *Studies in Bibliography*, 42 (1989): 1–24.

Greetham, D. C., 'Textual Forensics', *PMLA*, 111, no. 1 (1996): 32–51.

Greg, W. W., 'The Rationale of Copy-Text', *Studies in Bibliography*, 3 (1950): 19–36.

Grésillon, Almuth, 'Slow: Work in Progress', *Word & Image*, 13, no. 2 (1997): 106–23.

Groden, Michael, 'Contemporary Textual and Literary Theory', in *Representing Modernist Texts: Editing as Interpretation*, ed. George Bornstein (Ann Arbor: Michigan UP, 1991), pp. 259–86.

Groden, Michael and Daniel Ferrer, 'Introduction: A Genesis of French Genetic Criticism', in *Genetic Criticism: Texts and Avant-Texts*, trans. Jed Deppman, ed. Jed Deppman, Daniel Ferrer and Michael Groden (Pennsylvania: Pennsylvania UP, 2004), pp. 1–17.

Harris, Janice H., 'D. H. Lawrence and Kate Millett', *The Massachusetts Review*, 15, no. 3 (1974): 522–29.

Harrison, Andrew, *D. H. Lawrence and Futurism* (Amsterdam: Rodopi, 2003).

Harrison, Andrew, 'Dust-jackets, Blurbs and Forewords: The Marketing of *Sons and Lovers*', in *New D. H. Lawrence*, ed. Howard J. Booth (Manchester: Manchester UP, 2009), pp. 17–33.

Hay, Louis, 'Does "Text" Exist?', *Studies in Bibliography*, 41 (1988): 64–76.

Hay, Louis, 'Genetic Criticism: Another Approach to Writing?', in *Research on Writing: Multiple Perspectives*, ed. Sylvie Plane et al. (Fort Collins: The WAC Clearinghouse and CREM, 2017), https://innovationtest2.colostate.edu/books/international/wrab2014/.

Hay, Louis, 'Genetic Criticism: Origins and Perspectives', in *Genetic Criticism: Texts and Avant-Texts*, trans. Jed Deppman, ed. Jed Deppman, Daniel Ferrer and Michael Groden (Pennsylvania: Pennsylvania UP, 2004), pp. 17–27.

Hay, Louis, 'Genetic Editing, Past and Future: A Few Reflections by a User', *Text*, 3 (1987): 117–34.

Hay, Louis, *La littérature des écrivains* (Paris: Conti, 2002).

Hewitt, Karen McLeod, 'Review of *The Composition of the "Rainbow" and "Women in Love": A History*', *The Review of English Studies*, 33, no. 131 (1982): 360–2.

Hopker-Herberg, Elisabeth, 'Reflections on the Synoptic Mode of Presenting Variants, with an Example from Klopstock's *Messias*', in *Contemporary German Editorial Theory*, ed. George Bornstein, Gillian Borland Pierce and Hans Walter Gabler (Ann Arbor: Michigan UP, 1991), pp. 79–93.

Hurlebusch, Klaus, 'Understanding the Author's Compositional Method: Prolegomenon to a Hermeneutics of Genetic Writing', *Text*, 13 (2000): 55–101.

Huxley, Aldous (ed.), *The Letters of D. H. Lawrence* (London: William Heinemann, 1932).

Hyde, Virginia, *The Risen Adam: D. H. Lawrence's Revisionist Typology* (Pennsylvania: Pennsylvania UP, 1992).

Ingersoll, Earl G., *D. H. Lawrence, Desire, and Narrative* (Gainesville: Florida UP, 2001).

Irigaray, Luce, 'The Sex Which Is Not One', in *The Sex Which Is Not One*, trans. Catherine Porter and Carolyn Burke (New York: Cornell UP, 1985), pp. 23–33.

Jackson, Dennis, '"At last, the real D. H. Lawrence"? – The Author and The Editors: A Reception History, 1975–93', in *Editing D. H. Lawrence: New Versions of a Modern Author, Ross*, ed. Charles L. Ross and Dennis Jackson (Ann Arbor: Michigan UP, 1995), pp. 211–39.

Jenny, Laurent, 'Genetic Criticism and Its Myths', *Yale French Studies*, 89, Drafts (1996): 9–25.

Kalnins, Mara, 'D. H. Lawrence's "Odour of Chrysanthemums": The Three Endings', *Studies in Short Fiction*, 13, no. 4 (1976): 471–9.

Kinkead-Weekes, Mark, *D. H. Lawrence: Triumph to Exile, 1912–1922* (Cambridge: Cambridge UP, 1996).

Kinkead-Weekes, Mark, 'The Marble and the Statue: The Exploratory Imagination of D. H. Lawrence', in *Imagined World: Essays On Some English Novels and Novelists in Honor of John Butt*, ed. Maynard Mack and Ian Gregor (London: Methuen, 1968), pp. 371–418.

Kochis, Mathew J. and Heather L. Lusty (eds.), *Modernists at Odds: Reconsidering Joyce and Lawrence* (Gainesville: Florida UP, 2015).

Kolocotroni, Vassiliki, Jane Goldman and Olga Taxidou (eds.), *Modernism: An Anthology of Sources and Documents* (Edinburgh: Edinburgh UP, 1998).

Larkin, Philip, *Selected Letters of Philip Larkin, 1940–1985*, ed. Andrew Thwaite (London: Faber & Faber, 1992).

Lawrence, D. H., *Apocalypse and the Writings on Revelation*, ed. Mara Kalnins (Cambridge: Cambridge University Press, 1980).

Lawrence, D. H., 'Corasmin and the Parrots', in *Mornings in Mexico and Other Essays*, ed. Virginia Crosswhite Hyde (Cambridge: Cambridge UP, 2009), pp. 9–18.

Lawrence, D. H., 'Democracy', in *The Death of a Porcupine and Other Essays*, ed. Michael Herbert (Cambridge: Cambridge UP, 1988), pp. 61–84.

Lawrence, D. H., 'German Books: Thomas Mann', *The Blue Review*, 1 (July 1913): 200–6.

Lawrence, D. H., *Introductions and Reviews*, ed. N. H. Reeve and John Worthen (Cambridge: Cambridge UP, 2005).

Lawrence, D. H., 'Introductory Note to *Collected Poems* (1928)', *The Complete Poems of D. H. Lawrence*, ed. David Ellis (Hertfordshire: Wordsworth, 2002), pp. 619–20.

Lawrence, D. H., *Lady Chatterley's Lover*, ed. Michael Squires (Cambridge: Cambridge UP, 2002).

Lawrence, D. H., 'Review of *Art Nonsense and Other Essays* (1929) by Eric Gill', in *Phoenix I*, ed. Edward D. McDonald (New York: Viking, 1974; rpt. 1936), pp. 394–6.
Lawrence, D. H., *Paul Morel*, ed. Helen Baron (Cambridge: Cambridge UP, 2003).
Lawrence, D. H., *Quetzalcoatl*, ed. N. H. Reeve (Cambridge: Cambridge UP, 2011).
Lawrence, D. H., *St Mawr and Other Stories*, ed. Brian Finney (Cambridge: Cambridge UP, 1983).
Lawrence, D. H., *Studies in Classic American Literature*, ed. Ezra Greenspan, Lindeth Vasey and John Worthen (Cambridge: Cambridge UP, 2003).
Lawrence, D. H., *The First and Second Lady Chatterley Novels*, ed. Dieter Mehl and Christa Jansohn (Cambridge: Cambridge UP, 1999).
Lawrence, D. H., *The First 'Women in Love'*, ed. John Worthen and Lindeth Vasey (Cambridge: Cambridge UP, 1998).
Lawrence, D. H., *The Letters of D. H. Lawrence Volume 1*, ed. James T. Boulton (Cambridge: Cambridge UP, 1979).
Lawrence, D. H., *The Letters of D. H. Lawrence Volume 2*, ed. George J. Zytaruk and James T. Boulton (Cambridge: Cambridge UP, 1981).
Lawrence, D. H., *The Letters of D. H. Lawrence Volume 3*, ed. James T. Boulton and Andrew Robertson (Cambridge: Cambridge UP, 1984).
Lawrence, D. H., *The Letters of D. H. Lawrence Volume 4*, ed. Warren Roberts, James T. Boulton and Elizabeth Mansfield (Cambridge: Cambridge UP, 1987).
Lawrence, D. H., *The Letters of D. H. Lawrence Volume 5*, ed. James T. Boulton and Lindeth Vasey (Cambridge: Cambridge UP, 1989).
Lawrence, D. H., *The Letters of D. H. Lawrence Volume 8*, ed. James T. Boulton (Cambridge: Cambridge UP, 2000).
Lawrence, D. H., *The Plumed Serpent*, ed. L. D. Clark (Cambridge: Cambridge UP, 1987).
Lawrence, D. H., *The Prussian Officer and Other Stories*, ed. John Worthen (Cambridge: Cambridge UP, 1983).
Lawrence, D. H., *The Rainbow*, ed. Mark Kinkead-Weekes (Cambridge: Cambridge UP, 1989).
Lawrence, D. H., *The Vicar's Garden and Other Stories*, ed. N. H. Reeve (Cambridge: Cambridge UP, 2009).
Lawrence, D. H., *Twilight in Italy and Other Stories*, ed. Paul Eggert (Cambridge: Cambridge UP, 1994).
Lawrence, D. H., *Women in Love*, ed. David Farmer, Lindeth Vasey and John Worthen (Cambridge: Cambridge UP, 1983).
Le Gall Sloan, Jacquelyn, 'Oppositional Structure and Design in D. H. Lawrence's Culture Critique: A Feminist Re-Reading', PhD Thesis, UMI, Ann Arbor (1998).
Leavis, F. R., *D. H. Lawrence: Novelist* (London: Chatto & Windus, 1955).
Lebrave, Jean-Louis, 'Rough Drafts: A Challenge to Uniformity in Editing', *Text*, 3 (1987): 135–42.
Lebrave, Jean-Louis and Denis Alamargot, 'The Study of Professional Writing: A Join Contribution from Cognitive Psychology and Genetic Criticism', *European Psychologist*, 15, no. 1 (2010): 12–22.

Lecompte, Francis, 'The Genetic Origins of Literary Works', *CNRS News*, 11 July 2018, https://news.cnrs.fr/articles/the-genetic-origins-of-literary-works.

Levinas, Emmanuel, *Totality and Infinity: An Essay on Exteriority*, trans. Alphonso Lingis (London: Kluwer, 1991).

Littlewood, J. C. F., *D. H. Lawrence I: 1885-1914* (London: Longman, 1976).

Littlewood, J. C. F., 'Lawrence's Early Tales', *The Cambridge Quarterly*, 1, no. 2 (1965): 107-24.

Littlewood, J. C. F., 'Son and Lover', *The Cambridge Quarterly*, 2, no. 4 (1969): 323-61.

Lodge, David, *After Bakhtin: Essays on Fiction and Criticism* (London: Routledge, 1990).

Lodge, David, 'Lawrence, Dostoevsky, Bakhtin: D. H. Lawrence and Dialogic Fiction', *Renaissance and Modern Studies*, 29, no. 1 (1985): 16-32.

Long, Jonathan, 'The Achievement of the Cambridge Edition of D. H. Lawrence: A First Study', *Journal of D. H. Lawrence Studies*, 3, no. 3 (2014): 129-51.

Martz, Louis, 'Introduction', in *Quetzalcoatl* (New York: Black Swan Books, 1995).

McDonald, Russell, 'Revision and Competing Voices in D. H. Lawrence's Collaborations with Women', *Textual Cultures*, 4, no. 1 (2009): 1-25.

McGann, Jerome J., *A Critique of Modern Textual Criticism* (Chicago: Chicago UP, 1983).

McGann, Jerome J., *Black Riders: The Visible Language of Modernism* (Princeton: Princeton UP, 1993).

McGann, Jerome J., *The Textual Condition* (Princeton: Princeton UP, 1991).

McGann, Jerome J., '*Ulysses* as a Postmodern Text: The Gabler Edition', *Criticism*, 27, no. 3 (1985): 283-305.

McKenzie, D. F., *Bibliography and the Sociology of Texts* (London: British Library, 1986; The Panizzi Lectures, 1985).

McLeod, Sheila, *D. H. Lawrence's Men and Women* (Bungay: The Chaucer Press, 1985).

Menary, Richard (ed.), *The Extended Mind* (Cambridge: MIT, 2010).

Moran, James, and contributors, *The Theatre of D. H. Lawrence: Dramatic Modernist and Theatrical Innovator* (London: Bloomsbury, 2015).

Morris, Nigel, 'Lawrence's Response to Film', in *D. H. Lawrence: A Reference Companion*, ed. Paul Poplawski (Westport: Greenwood, 1996), pp. 591-603.

Morsia, Elliott, 'A Genetic Study of "The Shades of Spring"', *Journal of D. H. Lawrence Studies*, 3, no. 3 (2014): 153-78.

Morsia, Elliott, 'Review of Luca Crispi's *Joyce's Creative Process and the Construction of Characters in 'Ulysses': Becoming the Blooms*', *Literature & History*, 25, no. 2 (2016): 244-6.

Morsia, Elliott, 'The Composition of "The Depressed Person"', *Textual Cultures*, 9, no. 2 (2015): 79-99.

Murry, John Middleton, *Son of Woman: The Story of D. H. Lawrence* (London: Jonathan Cape, 1931).

Nehls, Edward, *D. H. Lawrence: A Composite Biography, Vol. 1, 1885-1919* (Madison: Wisconsin UP, 1957).

Neilson, Brett, 'D. H. Lawrence's "Dark Page": Narrative Primitivism in *Women in Love* and *The Plumed Serpent*', *Twentieth Century Literature*, 43, no. 3 (1997): 310–25.

Nin, Anaïs, *D. H. Lawrence: An Unprofessional Study* (Paris: Edward W. Titus, 1932; rpt. London: Black Spring Press, 1985).

Parker, Hershel, *Flawed Texts and Verbal Icons: Literary Authority in American Fiction* (Evanston: Northwestern UP, 1984).

Parker, Hershel, 'The Text Itself'-Whatever That Is', *Text*, 16 (1987): 47–54.

Peckham, Morse, 'The Infinitude of Pluralism', *Critical Inquiry*, 3, no. 4 (1977): 803–16.

Pinkney, Tony, *D. H. Lawrence and Modernism* (Iowa City: Iowa UP, 1990).

Rapaport, Herman, *The Theory Mess: Deconstruction in Eclipse* (New York: Columbia UP, 2001).

Reeve, N. H. (ed.), 'Introduction', in *Quetzalcoatl* (Cambridge: Cambridge UP, 2011), pp. xvii–xliii.

Reeve, N. H., *Reading Late Lawrence* (New York: Palgrave MacMillan, 2003).

Reid, Susan, *D. H. Lawrence, Music and Modernism* (London: Palgrave, 2019).

Reid, Susan, '"The insidious mastery of song": D. H. Lawrence, Music and Modernism', *Journal of D. H. Lawrence Studies*, 2, no. 3 (2010): 109–30.

Rivers, Bryan, '"No Meaning for Anybody": D. H. Lawrence's Use of Hans Christian Andersen's *The Fir Tree* in the Original Version of *Odour of Chrysanthemums* (1910)', *Notes and Queries*, 61, no. 1 (2014): 114–16.

Roberts, Warren and Paul Poplawski, *A Bibliography of D. H. Lawrence*, 3rd edition (Cambridge: Cambridge UP, 2001).

Ross, Charles L., 'Revisions of the Second Generation in *The Rainbow*', *The Review of English Studies*, 27, no. 107 (1976): 277–95.

Ross, Charles L., *The Composition of The Rainbow and Women in Love: A History* (Charlottesville: Virginia UP, 1979).

Ross, Charles L. and Dennis Jackson (eds.), *Editing D. H. Lawrence: New Versions of a Modern Author* (Ann Arbor: Michigan UP, 1995).

Russell, Bertrand, *The Autobiography of Bertrand Russell, II* (1953; rpt. London: George Allen and Unwin, 1968).

Ryu, Doo-Sun, *D. H. Lawrence's The Rainbow and Women in Love: A Critical Study* (New York: Peter Laing, 2005).

Said, Edward, 'The Problem of Textuality: Two Paths', *Critical Inquiry*, 4, no. 4 (1978): 676–714.

Sagar, Keith, *The Art of D. H. Lawrence* (Cambridge: Cambridge UP, 1966; rpt. 1975).

Sagar, Keith, '"The Best I Have Known": D. H. Lawrence's "A Modern Lover" and "The Shades of Spring"', *Studies in Short Fiction*, 4 (1967): 143–51.

Sartre, Jean-Paul, *Being and Nothingness*, trans. Hazel E. Barnes (London: Routledge, 2003; First published as *L'Être et le néant* (Paris: Gallimard, 1943)).

Schulz, Victor, 'D. H. Lawrence's Early Masterpiece of Short Fiction: "Odour of Chrysanthemums"', *Studies in Short Fiction*, 28, no. 3 (1991): 363–71.

Shillingsburg, Peter, 'An Inquiry into the Social Status of Texts and Modes of Textual Criticism', *Studies in Bibliography*, 42 (1989): 55–79.

Shillingsburg, Peter, 'Interpretative Consequences of Textual Criticism', *Text*, 16 (2006): 63–5.

Shillingsburg, Peter, *Scholarly Editing in the Computer Age: Theory and Practice*, revised 3rd edition (Ann Arbor: Michigan UP, 1996).

Siegel, Carol, *Lawrence among the Women: Wavering Boundaries in Women's Literary Traditions* (Virginia: Virginia UP, 1991).

Simpson, Hilary, *D. H. Lawrence and Feminism* (DeKalb: Northern Illinois UP, 1982).

Smith, Jad, '*Völkisch* Organicism and the Use of Primitivism in Lawrence's *The Plumed Serpent*', *D. H. Lawrence Review*, 30, no. 3 (2002): 7–24.

Sotirova, Violeta, *D. H. Lawrence and Narrative Viewpoint* (London: Bloomsbury Academic, 2012).

Stelzig, Eugene, 'Romantic Reinventions in D. H. Lawrence's *Women in Love*', *Wordsworth Circle*, 44, no. 2–3 (2013): 93–7.

Stewart, Jack, *The Vital Art of D. H. Lawrence: Vision and Expression* (Carbondale: Southern Illinois UP, 1999).

Stewart, John, Olivier Gapenne and Ezequiel A. Di Paolo (eds.), *Enaction: Toward a New Paradigm for Cognitive Science* (Cambridge: MIT Press, 2011).

Sullivan, Hannah, *The Work of Revision* (London: Harvard UP, 2013).

Sullivan, Hannah, 'Review of *I do I undo I redo* by Finn Fordham', *Modernism/Modernity*, 21, no. 4 (2014): 1029–31.

Sultan, Stanley, 'Lawrence the Anti-Autobiographer', *Journal of Modern Literature*, 23, no. 2 (1999–2000): 225–48.

Tanselle, G. Thomas, 'Textual Criticism and Deconstruction', *Studies in Bibliography*, 43 (1990): 1–33.

Tanselle, G. Thomas, 'Textual Instability and Editorial Idealism', *Studies in Bibliography*, 49 (1996): 1–60.

Tanselle, G. Thomas, 'The Editorial Problem of Final Authorial Intention', *Studies in Bibliography*, 29 (1976): 167–211.

Tindall, William York, 'D. H. Lawrence and the Primitive', *The Sewanee Review*, 45, no. 2 (1937): 198–211.

Tindall, William York, 'Introduction', in *The Plumed Serpent* (New York: Knopf, 1952).

Torgovnick, Marianna, *Gone Primitive: Savage Intellects, Modern Lives* (Chicago: Chicago UP, 1990).

Van Hulle, Dirk, *Modern Manuscripts: The Extended Mind and Creative Undoing from Darwin to Beckett and Beyond* (London: Bloomsbury, 2013).

Van Hulle, Dirk, 'Modernism, Mind and Manuscripts', in *A Handbook to Modernist Studies*, ed. Jean-Michel Rabate (Sussex: Wiley-Blackwell, 2013), pp. 225–38.

Van Hulle, Dirk, *Textual Awareness: A Genetic Study of Late Manuscripts by Joyce, Proust, and Mann* (Ann Arbor: Michigan UP, 2004).

Van Hulle, Dirk, 'Undoing Dante: Samuel Beckett's Poetics from a Textual Perspective', *Text*, 16 (2006): 87–95.

Van Vliet, H. T. M., 'Compositional History as a Key to Textual Interpretation', *Text*, 16 (2006): 67–78.

Vogeler, Martha S., *Austin Harrison and the English Review* (Missouri: Missouri UP, 2008).
Von Uexküll, Jakob, *A Foray into the Worlds of Animals and Humans with A Theory of Meaning*, trans. Joseph D. O'Neill (Minneapolis: Minnesota UP, 2010).
Wallace, Brendan, Alastair Ross, John Davies and Tony Anderson (eds.), *The Mind, the Body and the World: Psychology after Cognitivism?* (Exeter/Charlottesville: Imprint Academic, 2007).
Wallace, David Foster, 'Greatly Exaggerated', in *A Supposedly Fun Thing I'll Never Do Again: Essays and Arguments* (London: Abacus, 1998), pp. 138–46.
Wallace, Jeff, *D. H. Lawrence, Science and the Posthuman* (New York: Palgrave Macmillan, 2005).
Wexler, Joyce, 'D. H. Lawrence through a Postmodernist Lens', *D. H. Lawrence Review*, 27, no. 1 (1997–98): 47–64.
Widdowson, Peter (ed.), *D. H. Lawrence* (London: Longman, 1992).
Williams, Linda Ruth, *Sex in the Head: Visions of Femininity and Film in D. H. Lawrence* (Detroit: Wayne State UP, 1993).
Wimsatt, W. K. Jr. and M. C. Beardsley, 'The Intentional Fallacy', *The Sewanee Review*, 54, no. 3 (1946): 468–88.
Woolf, Virginia, 'Craftsmanship', in *The Death of a Moth and Other Essays* (London: Hogarth Press, 1942), pp. 126–31.
Woolf, Virginia, 'Notes on D. H. Lawrence', in *The Moment and Other Essays* (London: Hogarth Press, 1941), pp. 93–8.
Worthen, John, *D. H. Lawrence: The Early Years, 1885–1912* (Cambridge: Cambridge UP, 1991).
Worthen, John, *D. H. Lawrence: The Life of an Outsider* (London: Penguin, 2005).
Worthen, John, 'Drama and Mimicry in Lawrence', in *D. H. Lawrence and Comedy*, ed. Paul Eggert and John Worthen (Cambridge: Cambridge UP, 1996), pp. 19–44.
Worthen, John, 'Introduction', in *The Prussian Officer and Other Stories*, by D. H. Lawrence, ed. John Worthen (Cambridge: Cambridge UP, 1983), pp. xix–li.
Worthen, John, 'Short Story and Autobiography: Kinds of Detachment in D. H. Lawrence's Early Fiction', *Renaissance and Modern Studies*, 29 (1985): 1–15.
Zeller, Hans, 'A New Approach to the Critical Constitution of Literary Texts', trans. Charity Meier-Ewert and Hans Walter Gabler, *Studies in Bibliography*, 28 (1975): 231–64.
Zeller, Hans, 'Record and Interpretation: Analysis and Documentation as Goal and Method of Editing', in *Contemporary German Editorial Theory*, ed. George Bornstein, Gillian Borland Pierce and Hans Walter Gabler (Ann Arbor: Michigan UP, 1991), pp. 17–58.
Zeller, Hans, 'Structure and Genesis in Editing: On German and Anglo-American Textual Criticism', in *Contemporary German Editorial Theory*, ed. George Bornstein, Gillian Borland Pierce and Hans Walter Gabler (Ann Arbor: Michigan UP, 1991), pp. 95–124.

Index

aristocracy (nobility) 198, 205–6
avant-texte 27–8, 31, 127

Bakhtin, Mikhail, dialogism 36, 127, 148, 162
Barrie, J. M, Peter Pan 200
Barthes, Roland, 'The Death of the Author' 19, 26
Beckett, Samuel, *Murphy* 140
Beer, John 208, 210
being, *see* ontology
Bell, Michael, *D. H. Lawrence: Language and Being* 4, 9, 82, 162, 185, 194, 210
Bell, Vanessa 77
Black, Michael 39, 66–7, 81
Booth, Howard J. 4, 46
Boulton, James T. 45
Brecht, Bertolt, *The Threepenny Opera* 147
Brexit 219
bullfighting 172–5
Bushell, Sally 14, 18, 27–30, 211, 214–15
Byatt, A. S. 3

Carswell, Catherine 77
Chambers, Jessie and David 219–20
Chaudhuri, Amit 4, 34–5
Clark, L. D. 48, 165–8, 179
cognition 30–2, 193, *see also* memory
constructivism 32–4, 125, 169, 211–13
craftsmanship 33, 125, 169, 214–15, *see also* constructivism
creativity 6, 22, 27–8, 57, 64–6, 88, 107, 143, 154, 196–7, 213
Cushman, Keith 25, 44–6, 57–9

death 45, 56–8, 125, 135–6, 138–9, 160–1, 176
depression 174–7, 180–1, 206–7
Derrida, Jacques 5, 19, 34, 159

Don Quixote 201, 204
Dyer, Geoff 4–5, 82

Eagleton, Terry 3–4
earnings 2, 9, 70, 81
education 95–100
Eggert, Paul 21, 82
Eliot, T. S. 16, 18, 108
Ellis, David 167, 179
The English Review 43, 52, 55
evil 153–4, 209
existentialism 55–8, 93–5, 101, 130–4, 196–7, *see also* Heidegger; Nietzscheanism; ontology
expressionism 93, 157–9

fascism 4, 33, 36
feminism 3, 9, 36, 144–6, 158–9
Ferrer, Daniel 35, 38, 169
The First World War 3, 34, 70–3, 89–91, 95, 98, 131, 160–1, 213, 219
Flaubert, Gustave 14, 32–3, 39, 64, 98, 125–6, 212–14, 218
Ford, Ford Maddox (né Ford Hermann Hueffer) 43–4, 55, 88, 218
Fordham, Finn 14, 28–9, 38, 88, 211, 214
Forster, E. M. 3, 168
Foucault, Michel 19, 27

Gabler, Hans Walter 17–18, 21, 125, 211
Garnett, Edward 68–71, 73, 77, 80–1, 88, 90, 98
genetic criticism 5, 13–14, 26, 88, 169, 211–12, 214, *see also Genetic Criticism: Texts and Avant-Textes* and writing methods
  criticism of 14, 27–8, 32–4
  recent developments 30–2
Genetic Criticism: Texts and Avant-Textes (eds. Deppman, Ferrer and Groden) 15, 17–18, 23, 26, 211–12

genetic dialogism   34, 64, 127, 139, 142, 146, 148–9, 155, 171, 215
God   8, 53, 153, 158–9, 176–7, 196–200, 213
Goodheart, Eugene   20
Greetham, D. C.   16–17, 37, 211
Grésillon, Almuth   21, 26, 32, 34

Harris, Janice   4, 9
Harrison, Andrew   38, 81
Harrison, Austin   43, 47, 52–3, 55
Hay, Louis   13–15, 32
Heidegger, Martin *Being and Time*   5, 9, 29
homosexuality   101, 103–4, 151–2, 160–1
Hurlebusch, Klaus   32
Huxley, Aldous   3, 38, 77

ideology   3, 33, 80, 168
industrialization   48–9, 146

Joyce, James   2, 8–9, 17–18, 31, 32, 64, 140, 159, 192, 212–13, 220

Kinkead-Weekes, Mark   18, 23–5, 29, 31, 65, 80–2, 87, 158

Larkin, Philip   3
Lawrence, Arthur John (1846–1924)   2–3
Lawrence, D. H.
    the archive of   15
    The Cambridge Edition of   5, 16–17, 21–3, 48, 63, 66, 87, 125–6, 141, 218
    'Democracy'   220
    Lady Chatterley's Lover   3, 5, 9, 36, 48, 167, 185, 208, 219
    the life of   1–2, 31, 43, 58–9, 63, 69–71, 74, 77–8, 80–1, 97, 165–6, 186, 219
    The Lost Girl ('The Insurrection of Miss Houghton')   65, 67–8, 74, 80–1
    'The Man Who Loved Islands'   219
    'Moony'   7, 131, 135, 157–9, 161
    Mornings in Mexico   213
    Movements in European History   4
    'Odour of Chrysanthemums'   1, 6, 7, 43–59, 71, 215–16
    the plays of   5, 80

The Plumed Serpent   7, 8, 48, 120–3, 134, 164–210, 216–17
The Prussian Officer and Other Stories   71
Quetzalcoatl (see *The Plumed Serpent*)
The Rainbow   2–3, 22–5, 44–6, 63, 65, 69–70, 73–4, 82, 94–5, 103, 111, 130, 162, 216
'The Sisters'   62–70, 74–9, 84–94, 100–7, 109–10, 112, 161
Sons and Lovers ('Paul Morel')   1, 22, 25, 37–8, 64–5, 68, 70–1, 88, 127, 218
Studies in Classic American Literature   169
'Study of Thomas Hardy'   71, 97
The Trespasser   37, 107, 127, 140
'The Wedding Ring'   62, 69–73, 78–9, 84, 94–100, 111, 123, 130, 133, 174
The White Peacock   7, 25, 140, 184
'With the Guns'   72–3
Women in Love   6–7, 8, 22–5, 56–7, 62–162, 171, 173, 176–7, 188, 216–17
Writing methods   22, 56, 64–7, 86–8, 100–1, 123–6, 167, 169–70 179, 184, 215
Lawrence, Frieda   2, 46, 219
Lawrence, Lydia Beardsall (1851–1910)   2–3
Leavis, F. R.   2–4, 10, 44
Levinas, Emmanuel, *Totality and Infinity*   131
Littlewood, J. C. F.   25, 44–5

McDonald, Russell   36
McGann, Jerome J.   19, 211
Mann, Thomas   33, 64, 213
memory   30, 131–3, 148–9, 193, *see also* cognition
Millett, Kate, *Sexual Politics*   3, 9, 168
modernism   2, 5, 8, 15, 29–33, 38, 77, 88, 91, 98, 108, 125, 127, 135, 144, 146, 157, 162, 168–9, 211–14

New Bibliography   16
New Criticism   16, 18, 27, 29
Nietzsche, Freidrich (Nietzscheanism; Nietzscheism)   5, 102, 133, 196
Nin, Anaïs   6

ontology   9, 29, 72, 88–9, 98, 101, 103, 133, 154–5, 194, 196–7, 199, 215
organicism   3–4, 34, 67, 86–7, 133–4, 142–3, 168, 177–8, 198–9, 215

phenomenology   28–30, 149
Pinkney, Tony, *D. H. Lawrence and Modernism*   162, 168
Poe, Edgar Allan   15, 33, 211–13
Pound, Ezra   32, 88
primitivism   35, 168, 200, 210

Reeve, N. H.   10, 35–6, 38, 46–7
Ross, Charles L.   22–3, 83
Russell, Bertrand   33, 38, 82

Said, Edward   19
selfhood   20, 29–31, 88–90, 95, 99–100, 131–2, 136, 143, 154–5, 189, 201–9
Shillingsburg, Peter   17–19, 211
Sotirova, Violeta, *D. H. Lawrence and Narrative Viewpoint*   36–7, 127
soul   53, 103, 126–7, 136, 150–1, 154, 159, 171, 175–6, 188–9, 205

the sublime   129–30, 134–6, 157
Sullivan, Hannah   14, 28, 108, 127, 211
Synge, J. M., *Riders to the Sea*   57

teleology   25, 28, 32, 45, 89, 124, 138–9, 143
Tindall, William York   168, 197
trauma   72–3, 91–2, 99, 136, 172–4, 192

Vadé, Jean-Joseph   208
Van Hulle, Dirk   14, 17–18, 27–8, 31, 140, 211–12

Wallace, David Foster   26, 211
Wallace, Jeff   4, 9–10
Wilde, Oscar   104, 153
Williams, Linda Ruth, *Sex in the Head*   4
Woolf, Virginia   8, 77, 169, 185, 214
working-class   1, 5, 8, 34, 50, 175–6
Worthen, John   25, 31, 46, 64
Writing methods   31–2, 187, *see also* Lawrence, D. H.; Writing methods

Zeller, Hans   16–17, 21, 211

www.ingramcontent.com/pod-product-compliance
Lightning Source LLC
Chambersburg PA
CBHW050514020526
44111CB00052B/1962